INCARNATE WORD, INSCRIBED FLESH

The Bible in the Modern World, 6

Series Editors
J. Cheryl Exum, Jorunn Økland, Stephen D. Moore

Editorial Board
Alison Jasper, Tat-siong Benny Liew, Hugh Pyper, Yvonne Sherwood,
Caroline Vander Stichele

INCARNATE WORD, INSCRIBED FLESH

JOHN'S PROLOGUE AND THE POSTMODERN

Ela Nutu

SHEFFIELD PHOENIX PRESS

2007

Copyright © 2007 Sheffield Phoenix Press

Published by Sheffield Phoenix Press
Department of Biblical Studies, University of Sheffield
Sheffield S10 2TN

www.sheffieldphoenix.com

A CIP catalogue record for this book
is available from the British Library

Typeset by Forthcoming Publications
Printed by Lightning Source

Hardback ISBN 1-905048-25-4
Hardback ISBN 978-1-905048-25-0

ISSN 1747-9630

CONTENTS

Acknowledgments   ix
Abbreviations   xi
Permissions   xii

Chapter 1
POSTMODERNISM, TEXTS AND SELVES   1

Chapter 2
READING THE PROLOGUE THROUGH
THE POSTMODERN LENS   7
    The Chicken, the Egg and the Basket Case:
    Glitter and Graffiti on the Johannine Prologue   7
        Act One   8
            Scene One   8
            Scene Two: We Follow Derrida   12
        Act Two   17
            Scene One   17
            Scene Two   21
    Derrida and Deconstruction   21
      Signs   22
      Mimēsis   26
      Seeing with our 'I's   28

Chapter 3
THE INCARNATION OF THE WORD AND THE INSCRIPTION
OF THE FLESH: JOHN'S PROLOGUE AND *THE PILLOW BOOK*   32
    John 1.1, 14, *The Pillow Book*, and Poststructuralism   32
      The *Jeu* and *Jouissance* of Text and
        Textual Interpretation   33
      The Pillow Book, or The Inscription of the Flesh   35
    John's Prologue, or The Incarnation of the Word   44
      The Desire of God   50

The 'I' in Lacanian Psychoanalysis   52
   The Freudian Ego   53
   The Lacanian 'I'   55
   The 'I' and Desire   58
   The Mirror Stage   59
   The Imaginary, the Symbolic and the Real   61
   Lacan and Cinema   63
   The Name of the Father and the Phallus   73

Chapter 4
THE 'I'S OF THE FEMININE AND THE VEILED WORD   77
   Post-Lacanian Continental Feminisms   77
      Julia Kristeva   78
      Luce Irigaray   82
   A Veil of One's Own? Feminine Identity,
   John's Prologue and *The Pillow Book*   87
      Veils and Sails   87
      The Pillow Book, or Exhibiting Veils 91
      John's Prologue, or the Veiled Word 104

Chapter 5
OPENING MOUTHS AND LEGS, OR WOMEN'S TALK:
GENDER, JOHN'S PROLOGUE AND *THE FIFTH ELEMENT*   121
   In Brief on Body and Self   121
   The Female Saviour and The Fifth Element:
   Can One Hear the Mother of Christ in John's Gospel
   and Leeloo in Luc Besson's *The Fifth Element*?   127
      Opening Legs, or the Discourse of the Mother 127
      Opening Mouths, or the Discourse of the
      Woman Saviour   138
      'One' or 'I'?   143
      A New Script?   144

Chapter 6
AUTOBIOGRAPHY? THE SOCIO-POLITICAL LOCATION
OF THE SELF AND *THE MATRIX*   146
   The Self in Context and Criticism   146
      Autobiography?   151
   Red Herrings in Bullet-Time:
   The Matrix, the Bible, and the Postcommunist I   156
      Recalling Fiction   158

Neo, a New Messiah?   159
Myth and *The Matrix*   165
The Matrix of *The Matrix*   170
Through the 'I's   172
Playing the Game   177

Chaper 7
NOT QUITE A CONCLUSION   180

Bibliography   184
Index of References   194
Index of Authors   196
Index of Subjects   198

ACKNOWLEDGMENTS

I wish to thank Stephen Moore and Barry Matlock, without whom this work would never have existed. In his unparalleled style, Stephen inspired me to brave the unsettled seas of postmodernism. Barry's kind support ensured both my safe sailing and the freedom to choose my own course.

My thanks also go to Cheryl Exum, whose encouraging remarks on my work I never deserved yet received most gratefully, and whose guidance has always been stimulating.

This work is a tribute to my family and friends: my husband, Christopher Hall, whose love and challenging observations heartened me to see it through; my sisters, Gabi, Georgia and Crista, whose love and unwavering faith in me always kept me going in the darkest of times; my friends Pat and Andrew Scaife and Marion and Jack Jones, whose support played an enormous role in making my journey possible.

ABBREVIATIONS

AAR	American Academy of Religion
AV	Authorised Version
BibInt	*Biblical Interpretation*
BZ	*Biblische Zeitschrift*
CBQ	*Catholic Biblical Quarterly*
FemTh	*Feminist Theology*
JAC	*Jahrbuch für Antike und Christentum*
JR	*Journal of Religion*
JSNT	*Journal for the Study of the New Testament*
JSNTSup	JSNT Supplement Series
LivB	Living Bible
NEB	New English Bible
NLH	*New Literary History*
NovT	*Novum Testamentum*
NRSV	New Revised Standard Version
NTS	*New Testament Studies*
SBL	Society of Biblical Literature
WBC	Word Biblical Commentary

PERMISSIONS

Fragments from 'The Incarnation of the Word and the Inscription of the Flesh: John's Prologue and *The Pillow Book*' were published as 'The Seduction of Word(s) and Flesh and the Desire of God: John's Prologue, *The Pillow Book*, and Poststructuralism', in *Biblical Interpretation* 11 (2003), pp. 79-97 (reprinted by permission).

An earlier version of 'Red Herrings in Bullet Time: *The Matrix*, the Bible and the Postcommunist I' was published in Fiona C. Black (ed.), *The Recycled Bible: Autobiography, Culture, and the Space Between* (Semeia Studies, 51; Atlanta: Society of Biblical Literature, 2006), pp. 69-85 (reprinted by permission).

1

POSTMODERNISM, TEXTS AND SELVES

Becoming what one is is a creative act comparable with creating a work of art.

—*Anthony Storr*[1]

It might be that we are all tattooed savages since Sophocles. But there is more to Art than the straightness of lines and the perfection of surfaces. Plasticity of style is not as large as the entire idea... We have too many things and not enough forms.

—*Gustave Flaubert*[2]

Although old hat within literary and cultural studies, deconstructive criticism and poststructuralism in general are still rather microscopic a presence within biblical studies. The suggestion that interpretation could move on from fundamentals and principles (like Truth, Transcendence, Word, Consciousness, God, Being, Humanity, etc.) is still viewed with much scepticism. Yet, pursuing literary and cultural approaches to biblical interpretation is inevitable. Biblical texts do exist outside of Theology and Biblical Studies university departments, and indeed outside the Church. Any truly interested student would want to go along their dissemination route.

Since medieval times, Christianity has used image to communicate scripture; the visual arts have been used to illustrate almost every aspect of theology, mediating the written word to the community of believers. Understanding and explaining the nature of the relationship between visual and textual meanings has been a persistent problem for a number of related disciplines, which include art-history, aesthetics, linguistics, philosophy, and psychology. With the growing secularization of imagery from the period of the Renaissance, the relationship between the written

---

1. Anthony Storr, *Music and the Mind* (London: Harper Collins, 1992), p. 153.
2. Gustave Flaubert, *Préface à la vie d'écrivain* (Paris: Seuil, 1963). See Jacques Derrida, 'Force and Signification', in *idem, Writing and Difference* (London: Routledge & Kegan Paul, 1978), pp. 3-30 (3).

word and the visual arts has changed. Reading artistic theory from the fifteenth through to the eighteenth centuries can lead one to realize that the aesthetic discourses of the time found no place for the appreciation of visual values that we now try to articulate. European theories of painting from the Renaissance to the eighteenth century elevated the genre of 'history of painting' to the highest rank of the visual arts. This theory valued creations that contained literary narratives relating grand religious or political themes. The more inarticulate, purely visual genres such as landscapes, still lives and portraits were demoted exactly because they were more 'painterly'. Allegorical signification was, therefore, one of the main conventions whereby visual forms were translated into discursive, literary meaning; conversely, within writing lay also the convention that the figurative meanings in language were translated into non-representational codes. Thus, allegory was perceived as transmuting immediate, visual sense into elaborated, discursive value.

With the invention of the *camera obscura* and the magic lantern in the fifteenth century and the publication of Kircher's *Ars Magna* in the seventeenth century, a new concept was introduced: that of pictures in motion. In true artistic tradition, this was first attempted by Kircher through the use of eight slides of the life, death, burial, and resurrection of Christ. Lumière's invention of the *Cinématographe* in the late nineteenth century only meant that the relationship between the written and the visual, between narrative discourse and allegory, developed even further, to the point that the new visual art was a combination of both image and script: the mute film of the early twentieth century. Further still, the transition from the mute to the sound film witnessed the vanishing of the written in favour of the spoken script, yet it also marked an increase not only in cinematic production but also in cinematic symbolism. Grand productions like *Ben Hur*, *The Ten Commandments*, and *Gone with the Wind* inscribed themselves in the consciousness of thousands of viewers as mediators of biblical, historical, and political themes once again.

At the dawn of a new millennium, films continue to play an important role in the cultural development of society; even moving away from the self-confessed biblical films, new productions like *Contact*, *The Pillow Book*, *The Fifth Element* and *The Matrix* mediate elements of biblical narrative, theology, allegory, ethics and identity, and for many it is difficult to decide where the text finishes and the image begins, and vice versa.

In the domain of Christian theology and exegesis, the literal and the figurative meanings of biblical texts have conjointly informed the process of reading: historical, literal narrative also conjured typological truths. Rather than a case of patching additional strata of meaning to the 'divine' text, reading and interpretation have been considered at one time or another as means of discerning the truths and prophecies that had been divinely yet somewhat obscurely inscribed within the biblical texts. Although common to many religious traditions, this hermeneutic was indispensable for the Christian Church, because the sense of the Old Testament, the Hebrew Bible, was to be 'revised' and understood through the prism of the New Testament. The two simply had to fit together. Yet, the same dichotomy may have been the principal contributor to the development of valuable Christian hermeneutics encompassing the idea of difference (quite unique when compared, for instance, to the Islamic attitudes to interpretation, derived from the supposed unity of the Qur'an).

The concept of a plurality of meanings was commonplace for medieval and Renaissance allegory, for writing and interpretative ingenuity was expected. Yet, as new ideas about nature and taxonomies of knowledge developed in the seventeenth and eighteenth centuries, allegory lost its supreme position. Empirical knowledge displaced the traditional, theological assumptions. Within biblical studies, this led to a demand for authority, for power given by scriptural knowledge, and thus to a censored, confined, often maladroit hermeneutic.

More recently, however, postmodern theory has allowed for a revival of allegory, because it can expose the merely conventional nature of the derivation of meaning, while insisting on the interpretative distance between the literal presence of a visual figure and the attributed, abstract sense. Met initially with considerable animosity, the new wave has also influenced the domain of biblical studies; thus, over the past decade, cultural and literary critical methods of interpretation have been allowed to penetrate slightly the tight insulation around biblical hermeneutics, in a much-needed development. Commenting on some of the shortcomings of biblical interpretation as he knew it, C.S. Lewis lamented the lack of literary judgement in biblical critics and their inability to read not only between the lines but even the lines themselves.

In the late 1960s, literary studies witnessed the arrival of poststructuralism as a rigorous critique of structuralism, its possibilities, implications and shortcomings. Poststructuralism tends to expose the fact that the meaning of any text is unstable, that signification itself is unstable. The heart of this instability appears to be Saussure's fundamental distinction between signifier and signified; this very distinction is seen as revealing not coherence between signs (as intended by Saussure), but an inherent incoherence. Poststructuralism takes the Saussurean idea that there are 'only differences without positive terms' further by showing that the signifier and the signified are not only oppositional but plural, influencing each other and thus creating numerous deferments of meaning, apparently endless criss-crossing paradigms and sequences of meaning: 'disseminations'. This concept of the indeterminacies of text is essential for deconstruction, the principal aspect of poststructuralist theory used in literary practice, introduced by Jacques Derrida. His theory of *différance* concerns the principle of the continuous deferral of meaning through difference.

Since Derrida claims that *'il n'y a pas de hors-texte'*,[3] it follows—and this is to put it very simply—that, within the postmodern, everything is text. Even human beings (see the work of the artist Tom Phillips, for example). The aspect of this corollary that I find most fascinating is that of individual identity. The concept of identity seems to find itself stuck between essentialist and non-essentialist claims; thus, between claims that identity *per se* is fixed and unchanging and claims that identity is fluid and marked by difference. The former are informed by assumptions linked to nature; for instance, elements like 'race' and 'sex' are roped into the process of interpreting an identity as 'fixed', 'centred', 'objective' truth, part of the larger categories that are seen as forming human experience and society. The latter are informed by poststructuralist sensibilities, in as much as the concept of objective, transcendental Truth is rejected in favour of subjective, individual 'truths', and structure is replaced by continuous deferral of meaning. Thus, identity is seen as a matter of 'taking up' a subject position that is created through a relational rapport to others, its symbolic markings never fixed but under continuous change. Identities are never unified. The eternal 'Who am I?' and 'Where do I come from?' questions take on postmodernist hues and, entangled in a new discourse—the discourse of identity—become 'Who do I wish/ choose to be?' and 'Where am I now?'

The pivotal elements within the process of subject positioning are those of *representation* and *identification*. As a cultural process, representation helps create and promote individual and collective identities through the employment of symbolic systems and the media. The semiotics of TV and cinema, for example, can construct subject positions to be aspired to by the audience. Identification is the process by which this is achieved. Central to psychoanalytical studies, identification is concerned with the process by which the individual 'identifies' with others usually through a misplaced sense of 'unity' (perceived similarities) with others.

---

3. 'There is no outside-text'.

The study of representation and identification plays an important role in film theory, as it seeks to interpret the emergence of unconscious wishes and desires into conscious experience through relations to images of other people; in other words, the influence film has on its audience in terms of subject formation and positioning. Jacqueline Rose has argued that the question of identity, namely the means by which it is constituted and maintained, is the central issue through which psychoanalysis converges with the political field. She insists that *identity formation*—and identification in particular—is 'one reason why Lacanian psychoanalysis came into English intellectual life, via Althusser's concept of ideology, through the two paths of feminism and the analysis of film (a fact often used to discredit all three)'.[4] Feminism because analysis of the psychic processes underlying assuming a sexual identity and thus a prescribed gender role will focus on similar forms of inequality and subordination that form feminism's agenda for change. Film because its power as an 'ideological apparatus' is predicated upon the means of identification and sexual fantasy that, according to Rose, 'we all seem to participate in, but which—outside cinema—are for the most part only ever admitted on the couch'.[5]

Attempting to re-assess the relationship(s) between image/text and the reader—more precisely between biblical texts as literature and motion pictures as new myths or allegorical representations—and personal identity, my work will concentrate on, and develop through, poststructuralist theory and practice. Thus, deconstructive criticism, semiotics, gender and psychoanalytical studies will inform my interpretation of John's Prologue and selected films.

As Erich Auerbach in his 1953 monograph, *Mimesis: The Representation of Reality in Literature*, has convincingly argued, the Bible is indeed the narrative text upon which the self-definition of Western culture and its perception of the world are built.[6] I have chosen the prologue to John's Gospel because it harbours what has been perceived as the pre-existent, transcendent Logos/Word, commonly identified with Christ. Postmodernism sees a move away from the idea that there is such a thing as the transcendent Logos, or the 'centre' to all science and humanities, and my work produces new readings of John's Prologue that accommodate such postmodern impulses. Furthermore, John's Prologue addresses the idea of

---

4. Jacqueline Rose, *Sexuality in the Field of Vision* (London: Verso, 1986), p. 5.
5. Rose, *Sexuality in the Field of Vision*, p. 5.
6. Erich Auerbach, *Mimesis: The Representation of Reality in Literature* (trans. Willard Trask; Princeton, NJ: Princeton University Press, 1953).

'identity', namely that of the 'children of God', as acquired through the interaction with the visible Word-become-flesh.

The scope of this book is to explore the contours of identity as a decentred, fragmented work of the subject through identification with elements of visual, legible texts. Since it is the 'subject-of-language' that interests me, I investigate the theory that identities are constructs of the reiterative power of discourse to create that which it also names and 'orders'; that identities are determined in and through difference and thus inherently dislocated—dependent upon an 'outside' that both denies them and provides the premise of their prospect; and that subjects are 'inter-pellated' by, or 'sutured' to, the subject positions made available in discourse through the function of the unconscious.[7] As the Bible continues its influence on society and the formation of subject positions, biblical texts are re-interpreted, recycled within many discourses. I follow the fragmented afterlives of John's Prologue and their different discursive effects on subject formation (with a particular focus on feminine 'I's) through postmodern film, aided by contemporary theoretical currents.

---

7. The term 'subject-of-language' was coined by Paul du Gay, Jessica Evans and Peter Redman, in their edited volume, *Identity: A Reader* (London: Sage Publications, 2000), p. 2.

2

READING THE PROLOGUE THROUGH
THE POSTMODERN LENS

The Chicken, the Egg and the Basket Case:
Glitter and Graffiti on the Johannine Prologue

A Play

A play. Does that mean time for 'playing'? My inspiration for this chapter
came with reading Terry Johnson's 'Hysteria'. His characters include Sigmund Freud and Salvador Dali, and I truly enjoyed reading it. Johnson is
a master of the ridiculous. At the time I was still battling with the implications of deconstruction, swimming in a sea of ideas with no island in
sight. I thought, 'Why don't I allow my thoughts to play out?', and so I
began to write this play.

Who are my characters? As you probably guessed from the title, my
interests revolve around Jacques Derrida and the Johannine Prologue. So,
Derrida simply had to be one of my playing partners. Then, I had to think
of somebody else, somebody who would readily lock swords with Derrida
I chose Raymond Brown; his work on John is representative of the traditional interpretation(s) of the Prologue. Anybody else? Well, yes. You'll
see.

What is it that I am producing? I'm trying to provide a deconstructive
reading of the Prologue while making sure that the background of traditional criticism is showing.

But why don't you start reading it?

Setting
Sometime before the postdeconstructive movement.

Madonna's temple; her boudoir; or perhaps just her drawing room. A large yet small-
feeling room, giving an air of red brown. The furniture is richly layered in three-
dimensional art.

French windows and a red carpet lead to a clean, blue pool.

There is a large sofa vis-à-vis an armchair, but neither is better than the other; size does not matter.

The walls are full of graphemes and the air full of phonemes. Signifiers.

Note: This is *my* setting. You—yes, *you*—make your own.

Characters

Madonna	Like a virgin in a ray of light
Jacques Derrida	The enigmatic Deconstructor (with a pipe and a woollen jumper, but without a French moustache)
Raymond E. Brown	The traditional defender of transcendence and metanarrative (with an ironic smile and something which is almost a halo)
The Other	A string of question marks
Figments	God, Logos, Speech/Writing, Life/Death, Presence/Absence, Writer/Reader, Light/Darkness, Knowledge/Ignorance, Irony and *Différance*

The style of the playing varies as Derrida's reason, speech and tissue.

Act One
Scene One

[*Afternoon. Three people have just woken up and are now having tea and cake. One of them would much rather have coffee and croissant, another some yoga, and the other some jam.*]

Madonna: I've had a dream. I am to write children's books. Oh, and there was something else there, which I didn't understand. I've asked my guru to interpret it for me, but he couldn't. It was all in Greek, and he only knows Sanskrit.

Brown [*with a lost gaze and his ironic smile*]: Children, you say. That's very interesting. How do you know it was Greek?

Madonna [*in a slightly spoilt manner*]: I knew it then, and I know it now. People *know* things in dreams. Anyway, it said, 'In the beginning …' Hold on, I've got it all written down. [*She takes out a piece of paper.*] Here.'

Derrida [*knowingly*]: Your dream *said*? 'Il n'y a pas de hors-texte'. Again, our Western *metaphysics of presence*: she's got a text that *says*. The vocalization of words appears to emanate life. *Orality* has long enough been considered the metaphor of truth and authenticity, a source of self-present, living speech as opposed to the lifeless emanations of writing. The presence of the *creator*—the speaking one—weighs the weight of meaning as the progeny of an intimate connection between sound and *sense*; the naked new-born equals naked and pure understanding. [*He takes a sip of his tea.*]

Madonna [*to Brown*]: I've had it translated. 'In the beginning ...'

Derrida: Hmmm. [*He shakes his head.*] Translated!

Madonna [*not paying attention to Derrida*]: 'In the beginning there was the word'.

Brown [*surprised*]: Oh! [*He draws closer.*]

Derrida [*before Brown can continue*]: How did you dream it? Did you hear a voice reciting (or declaring) it, or did you see it written? Or was it written on you, like a *pillow book*?[1]

Madonna: What *difference* [*in French accent, but not knowing of différance*] does it make?

Derrida: Does Edmond Jabès say anything to you?

Madonna: From my *La Isla Bonita* video? We're no longer on speaking terms.

Brown [*smiles and opens mouth to say something*]

Derrida: Mais non. He's a Jewish poet. He wrote—how do you say in English? [*He looks at Brown.*] 'Le Livre ...'?

Brown: The Book of Questions.

Derrida: Yes-yes-yes. 'The Question of the Book'. The question of the orphan. Jabès is 'he who writes and is written'. The poet (the man of speech and writing) finds himself—in the very experience of his freedom—both bound to language and delivered from it by speech, whose

---

1. The reference is to Peter Greenaway's film *The Pillow Book* (Kasander & Wigman Productions IBV/Alpha s.a.r. Woodine Films Ltd, Film Four Distributors, 1995).

master he himself is. He says that words choose a poet. In question is a labour, a deliverance, a slow gestation of the poet by the poem whose father he is. 'In the beginning there was the word'. 'The creator poet is indeed the subject of the book, its substance and its master, its servant and its theme; and the book is indeed the subject of the poet, the speaking and knowing being, who *in* the book writes *on* the book'.[2]

Madonna: Excuse me. Who came first, the chicken or the egg? Clearly, speech came before writing; it was there—maybe not from the beginning, but ...

Derrida: Oh, the at once trivial and philosophical question of the logical, chronological, or ontological priority or superiority of cause over effect.[3] But isn't the effect the cause of discovering the cause, which thus becomes an effect? Allow me to be disagree*able*. I wish to say, 'In the beginning was the text'. Writing is the *precondition* of language and, therefore, prior to speech. Writing is not merely the graphic or inscriptional representation of language. It is the *play* of undecidability within every communication system: the perpetual game of *différance*; the game that escapes the self-consciousness of speech and its deceived impression of the jurisdiction of concept over language, of signifieds over signifiers.

Madonna: [*a bit puzzled*]: I've always found speech more playful than writing. Can you laugh in writing??? [*She laughs.*]

Brown [*smiles*]

Derrida: Again, to you speech is *alive*, because you lend it your personality; your roots are showing: Saussure's *natural bond* between sound and soul. Your words are *alive* because they seem not to leave you; not to fall outside you, outside your breath, at a visible distance; not to cease to belong to you. Writing to you—as for Plato—must be only the auxiliary *aide-mémoire* to the living memory: the supplement, the 'clothing'. The blind prejudice of classical linguists!

Madonna [*with a serious face*]: What I know is that language—whether spoken or written—is a medium. Ultimately, thought comes before

---

2.   Jacques Derrida, 'Edmond Jabès and the Question of the Book', in *idem*, *Writing and Difference*, pp. 64-78 (64).
3.   Jacques Derrida, *Dissemination* (trans. Barbara Johnson; London: Athlone Press, 1993), p. 88.

language. Language communicates thought. We use language as a tool, to get what we want; and we use it differently for different things: one type of language to get food, another to get sex, yet another to understand the meaning of life and the origin of the universe.

Brown [quickly but softly]: Nominalist. [*He then speaks louder.*] The late view that our understanding of the world is constructed by language— and not vice versa—plays a crucial role in the de-centring of Western philosophy, alas, because language is no longer perceived as a result of our experience, but rather as the conceptual framework that creates our experience.

Madonna: Ha! First we see an enormous hole in the ground; then we call it the Grand Canyon.[4]

Brown [to Madonna, with a slight frown]: Don't worry, there is nothing new under the sun. One can always make an old language-game look bad by thinking up a better one; replace an old tool with a new one by using an old word in a new way, or by replacing it with a new word. Yet, this need for replacement is *ours*, not the concept's. The concept does not go to pieces; rather, we set it aside and replace it with something else.[5]

Derrida [shaking his head]: As if there was a foundation to meaning! Thought, Truth, Reason, Logic, and the Word are erroneously conceived as existing in itself, transcendent, fundamentals. All Western philosophy is—alas—orientated towards, and rooted in, this logocentrism of meta-physics. DECONSTRUCT Plato, Rousseau, Hegel, Saussure, and Husserl, I write and write and write.

Brown [whispering to the Other]: In all philosophy we seem to be looking for something solid, something which would be the supreme arbiter for all truth, the foundation of all there is, that something beyond which we don't need to go. For theologians—I guess our pursuit is similar, but not identical, to that of philosophers—this ultimate is God. Our text here makes clear reference to God, and his indeed transcendent Word, or Logos, as the creative element. The parallels to the Genesis—namely the Creation account …

    4.   This exclamation belongs to Lois Tyson, *Critical Theory Today: A User-Friendly Guide* (New York: Garland, 1999), p. 250.
    5.   Richard Rorty, 'Is Derrida a Transcendental Philosopher?', in David Wood (ed.), *Derrida: A Critical Reader* (Oxford: Basil Blackwell, 1992), p. 241.

Madonna [*interrupting*]: Is that the 'Adam and Eve' story?

Brown: Well, yes, I suppose. Anyway, God …

Derrida [*interrupting*]: All names related to fundamentals, to principles, or to the *centre* have always designated the constant of a presence.[6] God, Being, Essence, Existence, Substance, Subject, Object, Consciousness. But, in order to function, presence needs the qualities of absence. Excuse me. [*He leaves the room.*]

Scene Two:
We follow Derrida.

[*The interior of a richly supplied bathroom. Over the toilet and completely ignoring the golden-tapped bidet, a man with a woollen jumper and without a pipe is lost in thought and inspiration, watching the trajectory of his own urine.*]

Derrida's thought bubble reads: Hmmm. I wonder whether Zeno truly contemplated the flight of an arrow when demonstrating the paradox, or impossibility, of motion. What that demonstrates more easily are the difficulties of a system based on the idea of *presence*. If reality is what is present at any given instant, my stream creates a paradox. At any given moment it is in a particular point in time and space; each of its particles are always in a particular point in time and space and hence never in motion. Yet, the stream *is* in motion at every moment from the beginning to the end of its trajectory; its motion is never present at any instant of presence. Therefore, the presence of motion is credible only if every moment is already marked with the traces of the past and the future. Motion is present only if the present moment is not something given but a product of the relationship between past and future. Something can be happening at a given moment only if the moment is already divided within itself, inhabited by the non-present. Presence must already be marked by *différance*, so difference and deferral.[7] There. Done.
[*Then Derrida looks up again.*]

[*We do not stay long enough to see whether he washes his hands.*]

6. Derrida, 'Structure, Sign and Play', in *idem*, *Writing and Difference*, pp. 278-93 (279).

7. Jacques Derrida, *Of Grammatology* (trans. Gayatri Chakrovorty Spivak; Baltimore: The Johns Hopkins University Press, corr. edn, 1997), p. 166.

[*In Derrida's absence, the Conversation is still going. Brown, Madonna and the Other are present and alive, but not in motion.*]

Brown [*to the Other, whose confusion is beyond disguising*]: Jacques likes deconstructing the opposition between things: speech and writing, presence and absence. [*He smiles.*] I think he's asking you, for instance, 'What if the illegal alien, the parasite, were already within? What if speech were already the host of writing? What if the immediacy of speech, the sensation of presence it produces, were but a mirage?'⁸ If you ask me …

[*Enter Derrida, with the woollen jumper and the pipe.*]

Derrida: 'The crack between speech and writing is nothing. The crack is what one must occupy'.⁹ Writing is the incessant displacement of meaning which both rules *lingua* and places it perennially beyond the reach of a constant, self-authenticating knowledge.

Madonna [*singing and clicking her fingers*]: There is no place to hide. To have and not to hold.¹⁰

Derrida: You were talking about me, as if I were dead. My talking about *me* makes me half dead, outside myself.

[*Someone plays Ray of Light at a distance. Figments are dancing.*]

Madonna [*opens mouth, then changes her mind and closes it; then changes her mind again and speaks*]: What of recorded speech?

Derrida: A recording only demonstrates that speech is, just like writing, a sequence of signifiers, open to interpretation. Speech does not deliver a direct presence of a thought; however expeditiously and ethereally it dissolves, the spoken word is still a material structure which, just like the written word, works through its differences from other structures. Although speech and writing may create different types of tissue of signification, there are no grounds for claiming that voice delivers thoughts

8. Stephen D. Moore, *Poststructuralism and the New Testament: Derrida and Foucault at the Foot of the Cross* (Minneapolis: Fortress Press, 1994), p. 31.

9. Jacques Derrida, *Glas* (trans. J.P. Leavey, Jr and R. Rand; Lincoln: University of Nebraska Press, 1986), p. 207.

10. Madonna, 'The Power of Good-bye', in *Ray of Light* (Maverick Recording, Warner Bros., 1998).

directly, as may seem to be the case when one hears oneself speak at the instant of speaking. So, a recording of one's speech would only prove that speech, too, works by the differential play of signifiers, though it is precisely this work of difference that the privileging of speech attempts to suppress. [*He takes a breath, then carries on.*] 'Through suppression of *différance* is our auto-affection, the speech and consciousness of speech (or simply consciousness as self-presence) is experienced. The very origin of what we call *presence* is this presumed suppression of *différance*, this *phenomenon*, this lived reduction of the opacity of the signifier.'[11]

Madonna [*reading and hearing herself speak*]: Hmmm. Right. 'In the beginning there was the word, and the word was with God, and the word was God. He was with God in the beginning.'

Brown: The λόγος, and the θεός, in the beginning. *Theos* speaks and thus creates the beginning.

Derrida [*with a mouth full of cake*]: Theuth created writing: the *grammata*.

Madonna [*reading still, with rounded mouth movements*]: Through him all things were made; without him nothing was made that has been made.

Derrida: Calculation, geometry and astronomy, not to speak of draughts and dice.

Brown: The universe, light, all the vegetation, all the fauna. Humankind!

Derrida: Why is the/a beginning better than the/an end?

Madonna: Ah. The beginning can be an end, and an end can be a beginning. The beginning can only exist if there is an end, and the end can only exist if there is a beginning. There are traces of an end in every beginning and traces of a beginning in every end. Neither is better than the other.

Brown [*pensively*]: Hmmm. This is not—as in Genesis—the beginning of creation, I don't think. It is my opinion that 'beginning' here refers to the period prior to creation, and is a designation—more qualitative than temporal—of the sphere of God.[12]

---

11. Derrida, *Of Grammatology*, p. 166. Emphasis in the original.
12. Raymond E. Brown, *The Gospel according to John* (Anchor Bible 29, 29A; New York: Doubleday, 1966), p. 4.

Madonna: 'Who is the *he* here? Who was *with* God? Is the word a *he?*'

Derrida: ὁ λόγος is masculine, but *la parole* is feminine. Translations. Ha!

Brown: The *word/speech/reason/logos* is here a metaphor for Jesus Christ, and that's why a 'he'. The entire passage is an apologetic to the transcendence and divinity of Christ, a description of the *Heilsgeschichte*—[to *Madonna*] salvation, history of salvation, that is. The emphasis is principally on God's relation to humans, rather than on God in Himself. The very title 'Word' evokes a revelation. Creation is an act of revelation.[13]

Madonna: Like my dream?

Brown [*not answering*]: As I said, revelation—not so much a divine idea, but a divine communication.

Madonna [*interrupting*]: Enlightenment!

Brown: All creation bears the stamp of God's Word, hence the insistence that God is recognisable through his creatures.[14] Moreover, the Word's role in creation suggests that Jesus has a claim on all. The expression 'all' (πάντα) is a quasi-liturgical formula that captures the fullness of God's creation.[15]

Derrida [*interrupting*]: Is *la parole* God, or is God *la parole*? Or perhaps it is true that 'God becomes God when creation *says* God'. [*He then sounds tired.*] Because God no longer speaks to us; he has interrupted himself. 'The garden is speech, the desert writing. Writing is displaced on the broken line between lost and promised speech. The difference between speech and writing is sin, the anger of God emerging from itself, lost immediacy, work outside the garden.'[16]

Brown: Perhaps work *in* and *on* the garden. Hmmm. [*He paces and talks more to himself.*] Jeremias has suggested that the revelation of God in the Word, or through Christ, was formulated against a background of God's previous silence. In Jewish estimation, before Christ's ministry, no

---

13. Brown, *John*, p. 25.
14. A reference to Wis. 13.1; Rom. 1.19-20.
15. Brown, *John*, p. 25. Reference is made to Rom. 11.36; 1 Cor. 8.6; Col. 1.16.
16. Derrida, 'Edmond Jabès and the Question of the Book', p. 65.

prophet had spoken in the land for centuries.[17] In the rabbinic exegesis of Gen. 1.1-3 it was maintained that before God spoke there was silence. Is the Prologue presenting God's Word as once more coming forth from the divine silence? Surely, such a picture would appeal to the Hellenistic world, where, as we know from the magical papyri and from the hymns to silence, silence was a mark of the *Deus absconditus*.[18] Ignatius of Antioch, too—he seems to offer an early echo of Johannine thought—speaks of God as one 'who manifested Himself through Jesus Christ His Son, who is His Word proceeding *from silence*'.[19] An attractive hypothesis, but one without adequate proof.[20] [*He looks up.*] No. The *word/reason/logos* is a metaphor for Jesus Christ. Christ has always existed in the sphere of God, had a relationship with God, and was ultimately God; it is all very brief, and I don't think we should engage in metaphysical speculation. The Word simply was. There is no need to know how he came to be. What is important here is not the origin of the Word, but the actions of the Word.[21] If one looks at the Semitic background, the Hebrew equivalent for the *logos* is *dabar*, meaning more than the spoken word; it also means 'thing', 'affair', 'event', 'action'. Therefore, because it covered both word and deed, in Hebrew outlook *dabar*—translated as *logos* in the LXX—had a certain dynamic energy and power of its own; once spoken, a word had a quasi-substantial existence of its own. There are a number of passages in the Old Testament in which the word of God exercises independent functions that are almost personal. Isaiah 55.11, for instance, depicts the word on a mission to 'accomplish what [God] wants and prosper in the things for which [God] had sent it'.

Derrida: It all becomes esoteric then. For you, the reader needs special knowledge, special *gnosis*, in order to understand the text. You posit this knowledge on superior grounds. What makes you think, what gives you the right to place yourselves above the text, look down on it, and pretend to know what it means?

Brown: 'We make no pretence to facile answers; all that we pretend to do is to give a working hypothesis for the study of the text, a hypothesis that

---

17. Ps. 74.9: 'there is no longer any prophet'. Passages like 1 Macc. 4.41-50; 14.41 and the *T. Benj.* 9.2 show a nostalgic longing for a new prophet.
18. Brown, *John*, p. 524.
19. *Magn.* 8.2.
20. Brown, *John*, p. 524.
21. Brown, *John*, p. 4.

combines the best details of various theories and data'.[22] We endeavour to understand. The more we study, the more we realize that we know very little; it's true. Nonetheless, one needs to create the most *plausible* context, the *legitimate* environment, in which interpretation can be born. Obviously, one cannot truly know the exact intentions of the writer, but one can endeavour to understand the text through the prism of socio-historical and linguistic considerations, the prism of the elements that shaped the text. Interpretation cannot indulge extensive regard for a hybrid that never existed before it emerged as the brainchild of the critic.[23] Yet, even if errors are committed, 'scholarship cannot return to pre-critical days, nor should it ever be embarrassed by the fact that it learns through mistakes. Indeed, it is the admirable honesty of biblical criticism and its ability to criticize itself that has led to a more conservative estimation of the historical value of the Fourth Gospel', for instance.[24]

Derrida: What makes the environment legitimate? A *légitime mariage*, before you? It is then quite clear: in your opinion, a *bâtard(e)* can only be the parent of a *bâtard(e)*, and so on. You will never be able to legitimize the birth of text—be it creative or critical, if you make that distinction—unless you recognize its equal rights. You require the existence of both its parent (creator) and its familial archives; their absence will always pronounce the text not the orphan but the illegitimate child in your estimation.[25] If you cannot interpret a text as it stands, independently of the mind, Being, *Sein* of its author, you have already judged.

Madonna [*in a surprisingly domestic voice*]: Coffee, anybody?

Act Two
Scene One

[*Brown and Madonna are having a tête-à-tête. Derrida is not in sight.*]

Brown: You see, it was at Ephesus—the traditional site of John's Gospel—that Heraclitus first introduced *logos* into Greek philosophical thought—in the sixth century BCE. Striving to explain the continuity in the midst of

22. Brown, *John*, p. xxxix.
23. Brown, *John*, p. xxvii.
24. Brown, *John*, p. xxii.
25. Derrida, *Dissemination*, p. 148.

all the flux that is visible in the universe, Heraclitus resorted to *logos* as the eternal principle of order in the universe. In other words, the *logos* is what makes the world a *kosmos*. [*He makes round hand movements.*] For the Stoics, the *logos* was the mind of God—a rather pantheistic God, who penetrated all things—guiding, controlling, and directing all things. Philo used the *logos* theme—over 1200 times in his works—in his attempt to bring together the Greek and Hebrew worlds of thought. For Philo, the *logos*, created by God, was the intermediary between God and his creatures; God's logos was what gave meaning and purpose to the universe. It was almost a second god, the instrument of God in creation, and the pattern of human soul. [*He then turns to himself.*] However, neither the personality nor the pre-existence of the *logos* were clear in Philo, and the Philonian *logos* was not connected to life. [*He turns back to Madonna and speaks louder.*] 'In the later Hermetic literature, the *logos* was the expression of the mind of God, helping to create and order the world. In the Mandaean liturgies we hear of 'the word of life', 'the light of life', etc. These may be distant echoes of appropriations from Christian thought. As for the more general field of Gnosticism, 'the Word' does occur in the newly discovered Gospel of Truth: 'The Word who is called the Saviour'.[26] It is possible that this Valentinian Gnostic use was influenced by John, since the Gospel of Truth is dated considerably later than John.[27] It is, however, my opinion that the Prologue's description of the Word is far closer to biblical and Jewish strains of thought than it is to anything purely Hellenistic. In the mind of the theologian of the Prologue, the creative word of God, the word of the Lord that came to the prophets, has become personal in Jesus, who is the embodiment of divine revelation. Jesus is the divine Wisdom, pre-existent, but now comes among humans to teach them and give them life. He is the presence of God among humans. And yet … [*Brown's face is red and his eyes bright.*] Even though all these strands are woven into the Johannine concept of the Word, this concept remains a unique contribution of Christianity. It is beyond all that has gone before, even as Jesus is beyond all who have gone before.[28]

[*Enter Derrida, without the jumper but with damp hair.*]

Derrida [*to Brown*]: Are you creating disciples? Where is the freedom?

26. *The Gospel of Truth* 16.34-37
27. Brown, *John*, p. 520.
28. Brown, *John*, p. 524.

Brown: In informed choices.

Derrida [*sits down*]: Having lent his house and his language, the Greek cannot be absent while the Jew and the Christian meet in his home. Greece is not a neutral, provisional territory, beyond borders. The history in which the Greek *logos* is produced cannot be a happy accident providing grounds for understanding to those who understand eschatological prophecy, and to those who do not understand at all. It cannot be *outside* and *accidental* for any thought. The Greek miracle is not this or that, such and such astonishing success; it is the impossibility of any thought to treat its sages as 'sages of the outside'. In having recognized from its second word (for example, in the *Sophist*) that alterity has to circulate at the origin of meaning, in welcoming alterity in general into the heart of the *logos*, the Greek thought of Being forever has protected itself against every absolutely *surprising* convocation. Are we Jews? Are we Greeks? We live in the difference between the Jew and the Greek, which is perhaps the unity of what is called history. We live in and of difference, that is, in *hypocrisy*, about which Levinas so profoundly says that it is 'not only a base contingent defect of man, but the underlying rending of a world attached to both the philosophers and the prophets'.[29]

Madonna: I'm glad you came. Did you enjoy the swim?

Derrida: I always do. It's play.

Madonna: Shall we carry on? [*She goes to read on, then stops.*] How is the Word God, again?

Derrida: The Word is *a* god, more precisely.

Madonna [*knowingly*]: Ah.

Brown: This has been the subject of much discussion; it is a crucial text pertaining to the divinity of Christ. θεός here has no definitive article, which would indeed make it 'a god' rather than 'the God'.

Derrida: Ha!

---

29.   Emmanuel Levinas, *Totality and Infinity* (trans. A. Lingis; Pittsburgh: Duquesne University Press 1969), p. 24. Cited in Derrida, 'Violence and Metaphysics', in *idem*, *Writing and Difference*, p. 153. For this argument see Derrida, 'Violence and Metaphysics', pp. 152-53.

Brown [unfazed]: Some explain it with the simple grammatical rule that the predicative nouns are anarthrous, although such rule does not necessarily hold for a statement of identity, as for instance the 'I am' formulae.[30] To preserve the different nuance of *theos* without the article, some English translations have it as 'the Word was divine'.[31] But this seems too weak; and, after all, there is in Greek the adjective 'divine' (*theios*), which the author did not choose to use. The NEB paraphrases the line: 'What God was, the Word was', and this is certainly better than 'divine'. For a modern Christian reader whose trinitarian background supports *God* as a larger concept than 'God the Father', the translation 'the Word was God' is quite correct. One must remember that for the Jews, however, *God* meant the unique Yahweh, the heavenly Father, and until a wider understanding of the term was reached, it could not be readily applied to Jesus.[32]

Madonna [reading further]: 'In him was *life* and …'

Brown: See, the Word creates life. It is not the Demiurge—at a distance thus from Gnostic thought.[33]

Madonna [continuing]: 'That *life* was the light of humans. The *light* shines in the darkness, but the darkness has not understood/overcome it.' I like this. 'Nothing takes the past away like the future; nothing makes the darkness go like the light'.[34]

Derrida: Again, you perceive these elements hierarchically, with the light as the superior factor in its seemingly antagonistic position to darkness. Yet, the darkness makes the light what it is. One could say that the darkness creates the light, in as much as light cannot be (through difference) without darkness. This very need dethrones Light as the central, superior *combatant*.

Madonna: Light is better than darkness. I've always been afraid of the dark. Light makes everything better, clearer, brighter, happier. [*She gesticulates*.] Plus, aren't we all looking for some en*light*enment? For some answers?

30. Jn 11.25; 14.6; in both places with the article.
31. Moffatt.
32. Brown, *John*, pp. 5, 24.
33. Brown, *John*, p. 26.
34. Madonna, 'Nothing Really Matters', in *Ray of Light*.

Brown: One could say, *wisdom*. 'I saw that wisdom is more profitable than folly, even as light is more profitable than darkness' (Eccl. 2.13).[35] 'He who finds me, finds life', Wisdom says in Prov. 8.35.[36] Like the Word, Wisdom is perceived as being light and life for humans and as an active agent in creation—Prov. 8.27-30.[37] The Torah also is perceived as *light*.

Derrida: The striking issue here is that of the two readings—καταλαμ-βάνω as 'to understand, to comprehend' and 'to overtake, to overcome'. They display two different scores. In the latter, darkness is the stronger, more muscular element; the light is the trembling candle flame, cornered, assaulted, sabotaged by the hounding lightlessness, the all-consuming black hole. The former, on the other hand, is flavoured with irony. The inferior ignorance, the thick denseness cannot understand what is staring it brightly in the (de)face(d). The light is caught in the defensive/offensive/defensive/offensive motion.

Brown: Irony is indeed one of the strongly distinguishable elements of Johannine style.

Scene Two

[*Darkness is slightly taking over. Electric bulbs are lit up to defuse some knowledge.*]

To be continued …

Derrida and Deconstruction

The *Play* was not meant to reinforce the misconception that, within postmodernism, 'everything goes', but rather to show that, with the removal of established (read 'prescribed') structures, postmodern approaches to textual interpretation are decentred, playful, tentative and creative and no longer centred and authoritative, as the historical-critical method would have it. The *Play* aimed to illustrate the complex yet unique relationship that I had with John's Prologue at the moment of writing. It meant to show that the biblical text is never found in a vacuum; that reading is always an individual process, informed by the subject's own

35. See also Prov. 4.18-19.
36. See also Bar. 4.1.
37. Brown, *John*, p. 522.

contours; cumulative patches of knowledge and experience come together for a chosen purpose. Reading is discoursing. Reading is writing one's echoes. As Roland Barthes would have it, '[T]he text is not a line of words releasing a single, "theological" meaning (the "message" of an Author-God) but a multi-dimensional space in which a variety of writings, none of them original, blend and clash. The text is the tissue of quotations drawn from the innumerable centres of culture.'[38]

Another aspect of reading that comes forth from the *Play* is that of the imagination. Anyone reading it would find him- or herself in the position of imagining the scenes, conjuring familiar images (or signs) to accompany the written text. (Did you?) As Joseph Marty would say, 'There is no human life or faith without images, because they are a fundamental reality of all language and culture'.[39]

In this section, I shall expound on the playful character of interpretation and return to the role of images at a later point.

Signs

> A science that studies the life of signs within society is conceivable; it would be a part of social psychology and consequently of general psychology; I shall call it *semiology* (from Greek *sēmeîon*, 'sign'). Semiology would show what constitutes signs, what laws govern them (Ferdinand de Saussure).[40]

Deconstruction and Derrida's rejection of *logocentrism* find their roots in Saussurean linguistics, the science of signs,[41] which Vincent Leitch calls 'a modern Adamic enterprise', or 'the groundwork for intellectual crisis in our time';[42] *la sémiologie*, or semiotics, as it is now better known.[43]

38.   Roland Barthes, *Image, Music, Text* (trans. Stephen Heath; London: Fontana Press, 1987), p. 146.
39.   Joseph Marty, 'Toward a Theological Interpretation and Reading Film: Incarnation of the Word of God—Relation, Image, Word', in John R. May (ed.), *New Images of Religious Film* (trans. Robert G. Robinson; Communication, Culture and Theology; Kansas City: Sheed & Ward, 1997), pp. 131-50 (132).
40.   Ferdinand de Saussure, *Course in General Linguistics* (trans. Wade Baskin; New York: Philosophical Library, 1959), p. 16.
41.   The linguistic theories of Ferdinand de Saussure (1857–1913) developed in parallel to the work of Charles Sanders Peirce (1829–1914), on the other side of the Atlantic. As my work focuses principally on continental philosophy, I remain with Saussure. For further information on Peirce, see Charles Sanders Peirce, *The Writings of Charles Sanders Peirce. II. Collected Papers* (ed. C. Hartshorne, P. Weiss and A.W. Burks; Cambridge, MA: Harvard University Press, 1931–58) and Douglas Greenlee, *Peirce's Concept of Sign* (The Hague: Mouton, 1973), among others.
42.   Vincent B. Leitch, *Deconstructive Criticism: An Advanced Introduction* (London: Hutchinson, 1983), p. 7.

The theory of Ferdinand de Saussure builds on the idea that language is a system of elements and concepts that are defined by and through their differences from, and relations to, one another within the system. Language, therefore, is perceived as a differential network of meaning. Between signifier (the word, spoken or written) and signified (the concept the word evokes) there is no self-evident connection. On the surface of things, they mark meaning through the interplay of the differences of sound and appearance. At a very basic level, 'lot' and 'pot' mean different things because the first consonant in each is different. The same applies to 'cat' and 'cut', where the middle vowel is different. In this sense, language is also diacritical, in other words dependent on a relatively reduced resource of linguistic elements (like the alphabet) to signify a large spectrum of meanings. Signification, therefore, was predicated on nothing else except noncoincidence. Or 'a sign is what all others are not'.[44]

Structuralism was born and developed from Saussure's idea that all cultural systems (of which language is one) could be studied *synchronically* (as opposed to the *diachronic* approaches to linguistics and literature of the nineteenth century, concerned with the historical study of language—through such methods as philology). Thus, the aim was to identify and study the relationships of signification within a code, or discourse. Structuralism understood codes as arbitrary (all signs are arbitrary), without which we could not apprehend reality. Within literary criticism, structuralism challenged the long-standing belief that a work of literature (or any kind of literary text) reflected a given reality. Instead, structuralism purported that any literary text was, rather, constituted of other conventions and texts. As language (Saussure's *langue*, or the communicative system, as different from *parole* as 'word'/'speech', one fragment of many forming the *langue*) offers the very possibility of sign, there is no before or outside of language.

If one is to consider the origins of language, however, the spoken word seems to take priority, as the element preceding the written word. Yet, even if one were to go as far back as the primitive communication system

---

43.   I use the term 'semiotics' rather than 'semiology' for the simple reason that the former is more frequently encountered these days. 'Semiotics' predates 'semiology', for it was coined by the seventeenth-century English philosopher John Locke, although it was the twentieth-century linguist Saussure who developed the 'science of signs'. See John Locke, *An Essay Concerning Human Understanding* (London: J.M. Dent & Sons, 1947), IV, ch. xxi, sections 2–4, p. 354, where '*Semeiotike*, the doctrine of signs' is introduced, next to *Physike*, or natural philosophy, and *Praktike*, ethics.

44.   Leitch, *Deconstructive Criticism*, p. 8.

used by cave people (as Jonathan Culler does)[45] and consider the first grunt with signification ('food', 'fight', or something else), one is faced with the fact that even with the most primitive of signifiers one must presuppose an organizational background from which meaning springs forth. In other words, for one grunt to mean 'food' there must be other grunts that mean anything else but 'food' in order for the new grunt to be distinguished.[46] It is on this, the concept of structure and organization of language, that Derrida comments arduously in his early works:

> We can extend to the system of signs in general what Saussure says about language: 'The linguistic system (*langue*) is necessary for speech events (*parole*) to be intelligible and produce their effects, but the latter are necessary for the system to establish itself'. There is a circle here, for if one distinguishes rigorously *langue* and *parole*, code and message, schema and usage, etc., and if one is to do justice to the two principles here enunciated, one does not know where to begin and how something can in general begin, be it *langue* or *parole*. One must therefore recognize, prior to any dissociation of *langue* and *parole*, code and message, and what goes with it, a systematic production of differences, the *production* of a system of differences—a *différance* among whose effects one might later, by abstraction and for specific reasons, distinguish a linguistics of *langue* from a linguistics of *parole*.[47]

This *différance*, a neologism that Derrida coins here, means to incorporate within it the undecidable oscillation between structure and event, between difference and deferral. Thus, from the verb *différer* which represents both actions, 'to differ' and 'to defer', Derrida constructs *différance* to mean metonymically 'difference-differing-deferring', representing therefore both the passive difference that already exists within the system of language and the active act of deferring meaning (because of the play of difference). Derrida explains,

> *Différance* is a structure and a movement that cannot be conceived on the basis of the opposition presence/absence. *Différance* is the systematic play of differences, of traces of differences, of the spacing by which elements relate to one another. This spacing is the production, simultaneously active and passive (the *a* of *différance* indicates the indecision as regards activity and passivity,

---

45. Jonathan Culler, *On Deconstruction: Theory and Criticism after Structuralism* (London: Routledge, 1983), p. 96.

46. Even if the grunt meaning 'food' is the first signifier, the inception of language, and is accompanied thus by a gesture or piece of food or both, its meaning within *language* is created on the basis of subsequent differences. No other grunt from then on can represent 'food'.

47. Jacques Derrida, *Positions* (Paris: Minuit, 1972); ET: *Positions* (Chicago: University of Chicago Press, 1981), p. 28.

that which cannot yet be governed and organized by that opposition), of intervals without which the 'full' terms could not signify, could not function.[48]

Yet Saussure insists that language is a system of differences, namely the difference between langue and parole, that sound itself cannot be a part of the system of differences, of *langue*, since it only facilitates the expression of fragments of it through acts of speech, *parole*. Saussure goes as far as declaring that 'in the linguistic system there are only differences, without positive terms'.[49] Thus, while the common understanding is that language is comprised of words, positive elements that are organized in an inter-relational system, Saussure claims that, contrary to this view, *signs* are the product of the differential system, not positive but effects of difference.

If language comprises of only differences, however, meaning cannot be *present* at any given moment. If 'lot' means 'lot' because of its difference from 'pot', its meaning may be impossible to catch if the identity of 'pot' is not yet established (because its meaning itself depends on its difference from 'pod', for example', and 'pod' from 'top' and 'top' to 'bottom', etc.), the meaning of 'lot' can never be fixed, never present. Derrida observes,

> The play of differences involves syntheses and referrals that prevent there from being at any moment or in any way a simple element that is present in and of itself and refers only to itself. Whether in written or in spoken discourse, no element can function as a sign without relating to another element which itself is not simply present. This linkage means that each 'element'—phoneme or grapheme—is constituted with reference to the trace in it of the other elements of the sequence of system. This linkage, this weaving, is the *text*, which is produced only through the transformation of another text. Nothing, either in the elements or in the system, is anywhere simply present or absent. There are only, everywhere, differences and traces of traces.[50]

There we have a structure without exact schemata, of infinite referral in which there are only traces of presence and absence.

While Saussure's theory of language without positive terms could be seen as a critique of *logocentrism* (the concept that Derrida attacks, also), or the system of meaning and signification predicated on presence, Saussure moves away from it by seemingly endorsing the logocentric condition when declaring later that 'the object of linguistic analysis is not defined by the combination of the written word and the spoken word: the spoken

48.   Derrida, *Positions*, p. 27.
49.   Ferdinand de Saussure, *Course in General Linguistics* (London: Peter Owen, 1960), p. 120.
50.   Derrida, *Positions*, p. 26.

word alone constitutes the object'.[51] Speech is again considered superior
to writing.

Perceiving in this a problem larger than merely the speech/writing
opposition, Derrida sets out to show that the entire Western metaphysics
exists on the basis of a hierarchical system of binary oppositions: speech/
writing, mind/body, presence/absence, above/below, knowledge/igno-
rance, culture/nature, etc., in which one element in these dualities is
perceived as superior to the other. By starting with the speech/writing
opposition, Derrida offers the first deconstructive critical analysis. Deconstruction enters the field of philosophical enquiry—and more importantly
that of literary or textual criticism—as the act by which hierarchical
systems in language and signification are discredited and eventually dismissed by the very texts that propose them. Furthermore, deconstruction
sees the dawn of poststructuralism, the movement that upholds the idea
that structures are illusory. There is a lot to be said about deconstruction
and poststructuralism, and I will return to these notions later.

Mimēsis

One of the concepts affected by deconstruction is *mimēsis,* the process
of reproduction, or 'producing a thing's double'. Due to its hierarchical
oppositions between original and imitation, object and representation, it
became one of Derrida's topics of analysis. *Mimēsis* can be approached
from different angles; it can be attacked for the substitution of originals
with copies, commended for reproducing the original faithfully, or considered neutral, where the value of the representation depends on the
value of the original.[52] In 'Economimesis' Derrida follows a certain aesthetic tradition by which he allows even imitations to be superior to the
objects represented provided the artist imitates 'the creative nature of
God' in his or her creativity. Derrida argues that in such cases, 'the
absolute discernability of the imitated and the imitation' is sustained.

In 'The Double Session', Derrida comments on Plato's *Philebus* (38e-
39e) when he connects *mimēsis* and *mnēmē,* memory, because memory is
seen as a type of *mimēsis,* or representation. Derrida argues,

> If Socrates is able to *compare* the silent relation between the soul and itself, in
> the 'mute soliloquy' ... to a book, it is because the book imitates the soul or
> the soul imitates the book, because each is the image or *likeness* of the other
> ('image' has the same root as 'imitari' [to imitate]). Both of these likenesses,
> even before resembling each other, were in themselves already reproductive,

51. Saussure, *Course in General Linguistics,* pp. 23-24.
52. Jacques Derrida, 'The Double Session', in *idem, Dissemination,* pp. 172-286
(183-87).

imitative, and pictorial (in the representative sense of the word) in essence. *Logos* must indeed be shaped according to the model of the *eidos*; the book then reproduces the *logos*, and the whole is organized by this relation of repetition, resemblance (*homoiosis*), doubling, duplication, this sort of specular process and play of reflections where things (*onta*), speech, and writing come to repeat and mirror each other.[53]

Because Plato insists that painting and writing, in their literal sense, are 'incapable of any intuition of the thing itself',[54] because they deal only in copies and in copies of copies, there exists within *mimēsis* an internal division, a self-duplication of repetition itself, and *ad infinitum* (because the movement fuels its own promotion). The *logos* functions for Plato as the pure indicator of the essence of thought (or discourse) conceived as image, representation, repetition. Thus *mimēsis* is perceived as predicated upon the concept of *truth*, or *logos* as the faithful image of the *eidos*.

As Derrida notes, however, 'truth' has always meant two different things, 'the history of the essence of truth—the truth of truth—being only the gap and the articulation between the two interpretations or processes'.[55] Echoing Heidegger, Derrida explains that 'truth' can be: (i) *alētheia*, or the unveiling, the *present*-ing of what is hidden (concealed in oblivion); and (ii) *homōiosis*, *adaequatio*, or 'a relation of resemblance or equality between a re-presentation and a thing (unveiled, present), even in the eventuality of a statement of judgement'.[56] Since *mimēsis* is always commanded by the process of truth, it either (i) signifies the presentation of the thing itself, the unveiling/presenting of nature (*phusis*), thus on a par with memory, *mnēmē*, since memory too is an unveiling/unforgetting (so bringing into the present), *alētheia*; or (ii) sets up a relation of *homoiosis* or *adaequatio* between two entities, coming closer to 'imitation' therefore. Yet, a 'good imitation will be one that is true, faithful, like or likely, adequate, in conformity with the *phusis* (essence of life) of what is imitated; it effaces itself of its own accord in the process of restoring freely, and hence in a living manner, the freedom of true presence'.[57]

If acquiring an identity is indeed 'a creative act comparable with creating a work of art',[58] then our visible identity is a work of *mimēsis*, either as an unveiling of a certain natural essence or a relation of equivalence, a negotiated imitation of those elements that constitute our identities.

---

53. Derrida, 'The Double Session', pp. 187-88.
54. Derrida, 'The Double Session', p. 190.
55. Derrida, 'The Double Session', p. 192.
56. Derrida, 'The Double Session', p. 193.
57. Derrida, 'The Double Session', p. 193.
58. Storr, *Music and the Mind*, p. 153.

Seeing with our 'I's

> The image *supervenes* upon reality, the representation upon the present in
> presentation, the imitation upon the thing, the imitator upon the imitated ...
> One should constantly bear in mind, henceforth, the clinical paradigm of
> *mimēsis*, the order of the three beds in the Republic X (596a ff): the painter's,
> the carpenter's, and God's.

—*Derrida*[59]

> My *hypothesis*: The subject as multiplicity

—*Nietzsche*[60]

Derrida's legacy within cultural studies has been most apparent in studies
focusing on postmodern identity and visual culture (TV and cinema, in
particular). From deconstructed text one travels towards deconstructed
self in a move that seems the most natural progression. Thus, postmodern
identity is perceived as decentred and fluid, a state of the disintegration
of the subject into a 'flux of euphoric intensities, fragmented and disconnected',[61] which is no longer the locus of anxiety (one of the
characteristics of modern, existentialist identity), for it lacks the depth,
substantiality and coherency (other modern ideals) for it.[62] Poststruc-
turalists claim that subjective identity is merely a construct of language
and society, an overcharged illusion that human beings are truly substantial subjects, with a fixed identity.[63] Thus identity in a postmodern age is
viewed as highly unstable and shifty:

> The TV self is the electronic individual *par excellence* who gets everything
> there is to get from the simulacrum of the media: a market identity as a
> consumer in the society of the spectacle; a galaxy of hyperfibrillated moods ...
> traumatized serial being.[64]

59. Derrida, 'The Double Session', p. 192.
60. Friedrich Nietzsche, *The Will to Power* (trans. Walter Kaufmann; New York:
Vintage Books, 1968), p. 270.
61. Douglas Kellner, *Media Culture: Cultural Studies, Identity and Politics between the
Modern and the Postmodern* (London: Routledge, 1995), p. 233.
62. Jean Baudrillard, 'The Ecstasy of Communication', in Hal Foster (ed.), *The Anti-
Aesthetic: Essays on Post-Modern Culture* (Seattle: Bay Press, 1983), pp. 126-34; Fredric
Jameson, *Postmodernism, or the Cultural Logic of Late Capitalism* (Durham: Duke Univer-
sity Press, 1991).
63. Rosalind Coward and John Ellis, *Language and Materialism* (London: Routledge
& Kegan Paul, 1977); Fredric Jameson, 'Postmodernism and Consumer Society', in
Foster (ed.), *The Anti-Aesthetic*, pp. 111-25.
64. Arthur Kroker and David Cook, *The Postmodern Scene* (New York: Saint
Martin's Press, 1986), p. 274.

Many postmodern theories of self-formation do privilege media culture as the 'site for the implosion of identity and fragmentation of the subject', the postmodern scene as the 'society of the spectacle'—the 'proliferation and dissemination of images without depth; glitzy, high-tech produced intensities; pastiche and implosion of forms; quotation and repetition of past images and forms'[65]—all responsible for the loss of substance in the individual. Fredric Jameson notes that postmodernism can be equated to 'the emergence of a new kind of flatness or depthlessness, a new kind of superficiality in the most literal sense—perhaps the supreme formal feature of all postmodernisms'.[66]

Although I recognize the role that media/visual culture plays within subject formation (and I will return to that later), I would like to argue that postmodern identities are not superficial, flat and one-dimensional, without substance and meaning, 'lost in the vacuities of the moment'. Instead, I argue that subjectivity within the postmodern milieu is no longer singular and fixed; that change and depth can coexist (even though not as an essentialist claim). The very concept of *a* postmodern identity is problematized already, as a construct of modernity. Instead, I should like to propose postmodern identi*ties*, or identity as multiplicity (echoing the Derridian vision of multiplicity of meaning).

I consider visual culture to offer the means by which identity formations follow certain patterns of structuring selves (even polymorphously) according to new myths in society. Images and cinematic narratives feed the viewing subjects with new myths and subject positions, pleasures, discourses, images and narratives available for appropriation. However, I believe that there exists a certain relationship—that is collaboration, resistance, or very often hybrids of the two, through negotiations—between the powerful forces in society that claim or summon the individual to certain subject positions and the conscious and unconscious drives of the individual that may or may not desire these positions. This *relationship* betrays elements presumed dead within the postmodern scene, namely depth and substance. I argue for lived selves and lived bodies.

I also argue that it is perhaps the lack of close studies of identity formation and visual culture in the postmodern milieu that may have produced their dismissal as flat. It may be, as Douglas Kellner suggests,

65. Kellner, *Media Culture*, p. 234. Kellner also laments the fact that there are not many studies exploring postmodern processes of identity-formation.

66. Fredric Jameson, 'Postmodernism, or the Cultural Logic of Late Capitalism', *New Left Review* 146 (1984), pp. 53-93 (60).

preferable to analyse both form and content, image and narrative, and
postmodern surface and the deeper ideological problems within the context of
specific exercises which explicate the polysemic nature of images and texts,
and which endorse the possibility of multiple encodings and decodings.[67]

That is why I wish to explore the relationships between self/selves and
biblical texts as disseminated within the visual culture of postmodernism.
I choose films that are not self-confessed religious films but which nevertheless accommodate the afterlives of biblical texts and themes. Thus, I
consider films as social texts—multidimensional, coded, polysemic—that
mediate and facilitate the formation of identities; texts that, in turn,
function as *intertexts*, texts to be read within con-texts (be they fluid), in
the light of other postmodern developments; texts that find negotiated
meanings on the site of the encounter with the viewing subjects.

Joseph Marty has suggested that '[c]inema is at the crossroads of photography, theatre, opera, and painting; it inscribes itself in the vast universe
of art'.[68] As such and like all arts, it attracts to itself elements of anthro-
pology, the history or religions, of civilizations and of art, 'notably in the
aspect of representation, doubles, *mise en scène*, liturgy, celebration,
magic, mystery, and the sacred'.[69] Thus, the cinema is one of the privileged loci that unveil the functioning of human psychology through the
imaginary and arouse, through the awakening of the symbolic and the
sacred, the *homo religiosus*. Marty observes that the cinema

> enlivens human dimensions that are somewhat underdeveloped in our scien-
> tific, technological and, to a bitter end, rationalised cultures: the symbolic and
> the poetic, sensibility and emotion. It strengthens weakened possibilities that
> have to do in part with the religious. It brings back to life the sense of mystery
> by making us love what is not immediately perceivable, what is beyond
> appearance and evidence. It suggests the invisible.[70]

Even if postmodern selves were to enjoy surfaces *only* (as Jameson would
argue), the encounter with cinematic narrative still appeals to a sense of
the invisible, the *beyond*—beyond the screen, beyond the page, beyond
today, beyond me, beyond here, beyond this or that. Criticism that offers
flatness as its contention betrays a modern, essentialist view that there
must be more to something than its surface, there must exist a solid
essence to everything, essence that can be categorized and thus regulated.
I argue that substance does exist, but in a fluid and polymorphous state,

---

67. Kellner, *Media Culture*, p. 238.
68. Marty, 'Incarnation of the Word of God', p. 134.
69. Marty, 'Toward a Theological Interpretation and Reading of Film', p. 134.
70. Marty, 'Toward a Theological Interpretation and Reading of Film', p. 135.

always flowing and thus existing in a dimension that escapes strict categorizations and obvious control.

I do not know whether the *homo religiosus* that Marty invokes (which is the same that Mircea Eliade defined) should be perceived as *inherent* in all human beings, as Marty believes. My own inclinations lead me to a concept of the *homo religiosus* as itself a subject position constituted through the discursive powers of language and culture, an aspect of identity to which we become, one way or another, *sutured* for a time (however long, however coloured). It is, however, an extremely complex state of being, as it can accommodate many and difficult concepts and emotions as religious experiences including, as Marty suggests, 'birth, love, work, hope, fidelity, joy, death, or their inseparable opposites treachery, lies, jealousy, hate'. The cinema binds us to these 'even through subjects that are profane, scientific or areligious', it seems.[71]

Let us turn now to an intertextual and poststructuralist reading of biblical and cinematic texts, mediated through the 'I's.

---

71. Marty, 'Toward a Theological Interpretation and Reading of Film', p. 136.

3

THE INCARNATION OF THE WORD
AND THE INSCRIPTION OF THE FLESH:
JOHN'S PROLOGUE AND *THE PILLOW BOOK*

John 1.1, 14, The Pillow Book, and Poststructuralism

If speech could be purely present, unveiled, naked, offered up in person in its truth, without the detours of a signifier foreign to it, if at the limit an undeferred logos were possible, it would not seduce anyone.[1]

There is the 'system' and there is the text, and in the text there are fissures or resources that cannot be dominated by the systematic discourse. At a certain moment, the latter can no longer answer for itself; it initiates its own decon-struction. Whence the necessity of an interminable, active interpretation that is engaged in a micrology of the scalpel, both violent and faithful

—*Jacques Derrida*[2]

In this chapter I examine Peter Greenaway's film *The Pillow Book* and John's Prologue (particularly Jn 1.1-2, 14) with the intention of reading afresh the Incarnation of the Word in the latter and the Inscription of the Flesh in the former, while focusing on the seduction of word(s) and flesh, the dynamics of speech and writing, and the desire of God, through poststructuralist theory. It investigates the relationship between text and image, and text, image, and reader, and it exposes the *ocular-erotic* char-acter of reading. Connected to one of the most valuable collections of writings in Japanese literature, namely *The Pillow Book of Sei Shonagon*, Greenaway's film treats the 'delights of the flesh' and the 'delights of literature' as indistinguishable from each other. My reading defends the idea that the Incarnation exposes the *reciprocity* of desire of God: God desires our flesh as much as we desire his Word; and it identifies the

1. Jacques Derrida, 'Plato's Pharmacy', in *idem, Dissemination*, pp. 61-172 (71).
2. Jacques Derrida, 'The Almost Nothing of the Unpresentable', in *Points … Interviews, 1974–1994* (ed. Elisabeth Weber; trans. Peggy Kamuf *et al.*; Stanford: Stanford University Press, 1995), pp. 78-88 (82).

Incarnation as the *hymen* which both unites and separates the human and the divine, the immanent and the transcendent, the flesh and the word, the audience and the book, this world and the other, foreplay and orgasm.

The Jeu *and* Jouissance *of Text and Textual Interpretation*

Since Plato, it seems that all Western thought has been centred around the concept of Truth as the supreme arbiter for all knowledge, the foundation of all there is. Throughout his work, Jacques Derrida laments this keen desire for the metaphysics of presence, the presence of all fundamentals and principles (like Truth, Transcendence, Word, Consciousness, God, Being, Humanity, etc.), which he calls the *logocentric* condition. The poststructuralist suggestion that we could disregard fundamentals has been met with at least two very different reactions in the world of those who make thinking their business. There is the camp of those who imagine and embrace even all too quickly a world of decentred humanity and decentred text, who send out invitations for orgies of immanence and freeplay, and there is the other camp, of those who either lock their doors, cancel the milk for fear of contamination, and pretend that Derrida has not nailed his theses to the door, or indeed go out protesting against those enamoured with Derrida's unnameable progeny.[3]

A common mistake, which the man himself has often tried to put right, is the idea that Derrida severs interpretation from the metaphysical, from the transcendent. In fact, Derrida admitted to Julia Kristeva as early as June 1968 that *Il n'y a aucun sens à se passer des concepts de la metaphysique*.[4] Even in his 1989 interview with Derek Attridge, Derrida insisted on the fact that the metaphysical and the transcendent are indeed inescapable: 'A text cannot ... avoid lending itself to a "transcendent" reading. A literature which forbade that transcendence would annul itself', Derrida commented.[5]

Furthermore, Derrida's *jeu* was not meant to promote *freeplay* but simply *play* (as in play on words, play in tennis, play at cards, which can,

---

3. This progeny proclaims *itself* 'under the species of the nonspecies, in the formless, mute, infant, and terrifying form of monstrosity'. See Jacques Derrida, 'Structure, Sign, and Play in the Discourse of the Human Sciences', in *idem*, *Writing and Difference*, pp. 278-93 (293).

4. 'It makes no sense to do without the concepts of metaphysics. / There is no way one can escape metaphysics.' See Jacques Derrida, 'Semiology and Grammatology: Interview with Julia Kristeva', in *Positions* (first published in *Information sur les sciences sociales* 7, 3 June 1968; trans. Alan Bass; London: Athlone Press, 1972), pp. 15-36.

5. As cited in Valentine Cunningham, *In the Reading Gaol: Postmodernity, Texts, and History* (Oxford: Basil Blackwell, 1994), p. 58.

therefore, follow rules). When Derrida introduced *déconstruction* in one of his first lectures in the USA, 'The Two Interpretations of Interpretation',[6] in 1966, his thesis was translated into English very quickly. Alas, the French *jeu* was erroneously translated as 'freeplay'[7] (although all the subsequent translations chose 'play' as the correct rendering), and thus Derrida was seen as giving away free indulgences to all forms of interpretation. Perhaps Valentine Cunningham is right when sighing, 'Freeplay: how many crimes have been committed in your name!'[8]

Since I am quite strongly set on keeping my hands blood-free, and seeing that I much rather prefer *fore*play to *free*play, I would like to approach John's Prologue (particularly Jn 1.1-2, 14) and Peter Greenaway's film *The Pillow Book* playfully, in order to *look* again at the Incarnation of the Word in the former and the Inscription of the Flesh in the latter, focusing on the relationship between text and image, and text, image, and reader, and to expose the *ocular-erotic* character of reading. I shall start with the film, but not before saying a few words about another lover of pleasure, the pleasure of the text no less, Roland Barthes.

Barthes is enamoured with text, and a little possessive of it, too, in the sense that he allows little if any room for the presence of the author. Barthes has been hailed as being the one and only critic to have produced an 'erotics of reading',[9] hence my interest. Moving on slightly from semiotics, Barthes reaches in his late works a stage akin to Derrida's own work, by allowing the text to run freely, to be metonymic rather than comprehensive, to be irreducibly plural and thus respond not to 'an interpretation, even a liberal one, but to an explosion, a dissemination'. He allows the text to play, and the reader to play

> twice over, playing the Text as one plays a game, looking for a practice that reproduces it, but, in order that that practice not be reduced to a passive, inner *mimesis* (the Text is precisely that which resists such a reduction), also playing the Text in the musical sense of the term.[10]

6.   Now published with the title 'Structure, Sign, and Play in the Discourse of the Human Sciences', in *Writing and Difference*. The French *jeu* is indeed translated there as 'play' and not 'freeplay'.

7.   J. Derrida, 'Structure, Sign, and Play in the Discourse of the Humanities', in R. Macksey and E. Donato (eds.), *The Languages of Criticism and the Sciences of Man: The Structuralist Controversy* (Baltimore: The Johns Hopkins University Press, 1970), pp. 247-65.

8.   Cunningham, *In the Reading Gaol*, p. 57.

9.   Richard Howard, 'Note on the Text', in Roland Barthes, *The Pleasure of the Text* (trans. Richard Miller; Thetford: Lowe & Brydone, 1976), p. viii. Italics in original.

10.   Roland Barthes, *Image, Music, Text* (trans. Stephen Heath; London: Fontana Press, 1987), pp. 155-64. Italics in original.

Barthes understands reading as 'consuming', where the text 'asks of the reader a practical collaboration'[11]—a partaking in the *jouissance*, or *bliss*, of the process of reading. I am particularly interested in this collaboration, in this communion between text and reader, between image and audience, in the Prologue and *The Pillow Book*.

Barthes also distinguishes between *figuration* and *representation*. For him, figuration is 'the way in which the erotic body appears (to whatever degree and in whatever form that may be) in the profile of the text', and thus attests to a figure of the text, *sine qua non* to the bliss of reading. In the light of this, Barthes sees film as that which will always be figurative, even if it represents nothing.[12] However, representation is, for Barthes, '*embarrassed figuration*, encumbered with other meanings than that of desire: a space of alibis (reality, morality, likelihood, readability, truth, etc.)'. When desire is *represented*, Barthes insists that such desire 'never leaves the frame, the picture; it circulates among the characters'.[13] He calls this the *semiotics of representation* as any semiotics that holds desire within the context of those upon whom it has an effect, in other words, when 'nothing leaps out of the frame: of the picture, the book, the screen'.[14] Will anything leap out at me?, I wonder.

The Pillow Book, *or The Inscription of the Flesh*

Peter Greenaway's film bears his traditional signature: intriguing visual elements coupled with overwhelming sensuality. Connected to *The Pillow Book of Sei Shonagon*, this is a film about calligraphy on human parchment, both *vivant* and *mort*. When the circle of life and death is complete, death appears to be the natural context for the written word. Is that so, however?

The film starts with a father writing on his daughter's face. He writes her name in slow yet firm brush strokes, beautifully. He speaks, 'When God created the first clay model of a human being, he painted in the eyes, the lips, and the sex'. God *wrote*, therefore, his creation into being.[15] 'Then he painted in the name of each person, lest its owner should forget it. If God approved of his creation, he signed his own name.' The girl

11. Barthes, *Image, Music, Text*, pp. 162-63.
12. Barthes, *The Pleasure of the Text*, pp. 55-56.
13. Barthes, *The Pleasure of the Text*, pp. 56-57.
14. Barthes, *The Pleasure of the Text*, p. 57.
15. To be noted here is the pictorial character of oriental writing. For many viewers, the writing will not be understood (even when subtitles are provided). It is more likely that it plays purely a visual role; an invitation to look upon the bodies which though naked appear veiled by the writing.

turns, and the father signs on the back of her neck: a seal of approval. Graphemes and phonemes are thus engaged equally in the genesis of text, almost a *writing aloud* (of which Barthes is so fond).

The girl is Nagiko, and she shares this, her first name, with one of the greatest writers of Japanese prose: Sei Shonagon. Written approximately a thousand years ago, *The Pillow Book of Sei Shonagon* is still considered one of the most beautiful and informative collections of writings in Japanese culture,[16] and it betrays a strong passion for literature. 'Writing is an ordinary enough occupation, yet how precious it is', Sei Shonagon ponders. 'If there were no writing, one dreads to think of the depression' (Section 154).[17]

Greenaway's Nagiko becomes a woman of letters through a complicated formative process. She begins to look forward to her birthdays, the writing her father would perform on her skin and the readings from Sei Shonagon's *Pillow Book*, in which her aunt would submerge her. She quickly develops a sense of pleasure associated with writing. On her eleventh birthday she starts to write her own pillow book, supposed to become filled with 'all manner of observations' and even accounts of all her lovers. When Nagiko is later married to a man who is incapable of either good communication or beautiful calligraphy, she is immensely disappointed. She confides in her pillow book increasingly, and, unlike those of Sei Shonagon, her lists are all negative. Among the 'Things that Irritate', Nagiko writes of 'prejudice against literature'. Misunderstood, she eventually runs away. Alone in Hong Kong, Nagiko tries to recreate her father's blessing by typing her own name and gluing the paper onto her chest (Fig. 1). Dissatisfied with the artificiality of the exercise, she begins to crave writing and thus an identity. Her skin becomes the paper for a string of calligraphers (Fig. 2), until one of them challenges her to become the brush. Nagiko then begins to write on human parchment. Her work numbers thirteen books, for which publication proves to be difficult. The cost of the enterprise is an unimaginable one: death. Not the death of the author, but the death of the word bearer, her lover.

16. Sei Shonagon served as a lady-in-waiting to Empress Sadako during the last decade of the tenth century ('Shonagon' means 'Minor Counsellor'). A pillow book was probably a generic term used to describe a collection of casual writings which men and women would compose when they retired to their rooms at night—somewhat like a diary—and which would be kept in the drawers of their wooden pillows.

17. While an English translation of the Japanese book exists, it seems that Greenaway took the artistic liberty to imply that the texts presented in the film are direct quotations from *The Pillow Book of Sei Shonagon*, which they are not. See Ivan Morris (ed.), *The Pillow Book of Sei Shonagon* (trans. Ivan Morris; Harmondsworth: Penguin Books, 1967). I use Greenaway's style of pseudo-quoting.

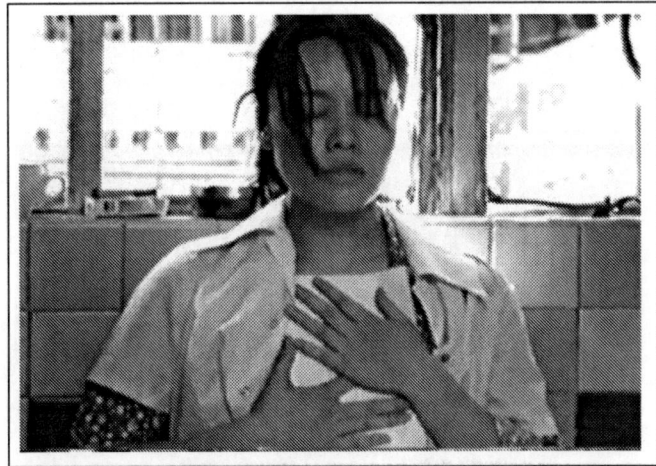

Figure 1. *Nagiko (Vivian Wu), trying to recreate her father's blessing.*

Figure 2. *Nagiko's skin becomes paper for many calligrapher lovers.*

Nagiko meets Jerome in a café. 'I need writing. Don't ask me why. Just take out your pen and write on me', she demands of him. Intrigued by the bizarre request and enchanted by the beauty of the one behind it, Jerome obeys, only to find himself pronounced 'a scribbler'; his work, 'not writing but distasteful scribbling'. Nagiko's cutting remarks lead Jerome to challenge her to write. 'Use my body like the pages of a book; your book', the Englishman throws at her (Fig. 3). Yet Nagiko hesitates: 'I cannot get pleasure out of writing on you. You have to write on me.'[18] She runs away but succumbs to the haunting challenge only hours later. She begins to

18. Nagiko's desire to be written upon (as well as the entire text of the film) does lend itself to a psychoanalytical reading, which is the topic of the following chapter.

experiment on foreigners who would be quite ignorant of oriental calligraphy yet have a taste for oriental women. Nagiko's trade seems fair, however, to her unique sense of value.

Figure 3. *Jerome (Ewan McGregor) challenges Nagiko,*
'Use my body like the pages of your book'.

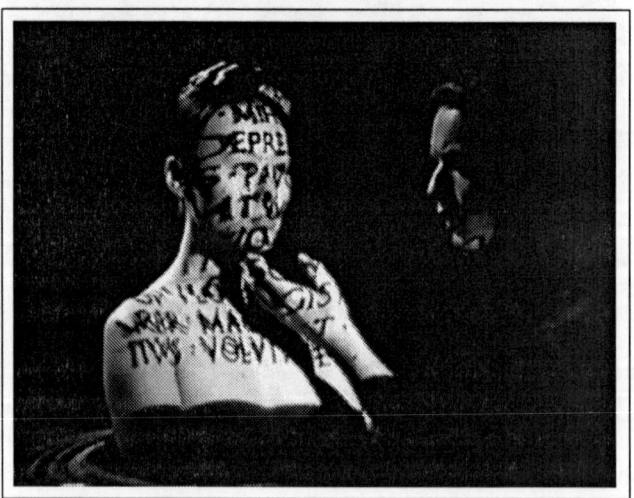

Figure 4. *Nagiko wears a 'hat with a veil in Italian'.*

She writes random thoughts on random bodies and photographs them. The pictures make the book, which she sends to her chosen publisher. This is, however, the same man who had sexually abused Nagiko's father for years in exchange for the publication of his books. The same man now rejects the works of the daughter; his ruling is that her book 'is not worth the paper it is printed on'. Not knowing any new tricks, yet quite determined to succeed, Nagiko the writer decides to persuade the publisher by seducing his lover, who is, surprisingly, Jerome.

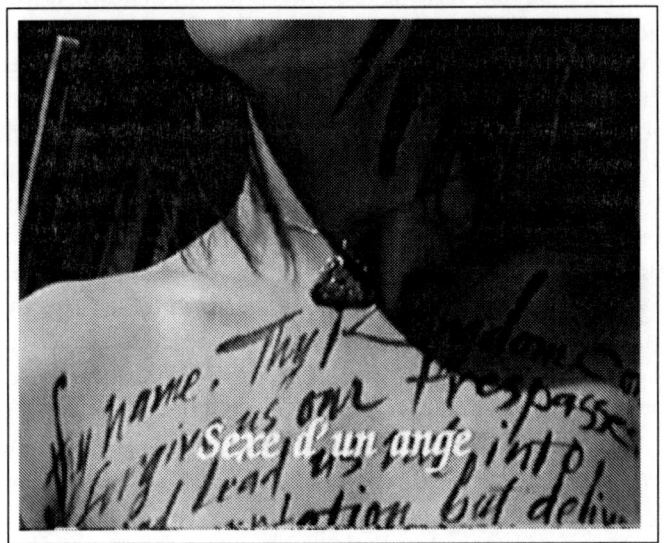

Figure 5. *Nagiko bears the Lord's Prayer*
on her skin, as written by Jerome.

The affair takes both writer and translator by surprise, however. They fall in love, and love befalls them; a melting pot of words and flesh: *d'un parfait mélange*,[19] as the subtitles accompanying the soundtrack of the film suggest. Jerome writes on Nagiko's skin in all the languages he knows, and thus she wears imaginary shoes in German, stockings in French, gloves in Hebrew, and a hat with a veil in Italian (Fig. 4). Nagiko becomes, in the words of Greenaway, 'a signpost, pointing East, West, North and South', like the beginning of an adventure, the beginning of knowledge. She is a book on a shelf, connecting with others. She is a scroll bearing the Lord's Prayer (written in English and Latin), arms stretched sideways evoking the Crucifixion (Fig. 5). Then she is canvas; she is the primal woman, Eve, in a Botticelli pose, one hand covering her pubic area. The passing of time is reversed to the initial innocence of Eden. The subtitles and the music (graphemes and phonemes together) suggest purity, through *sexe d'un ange*. It looks as if the text of the Lord's prayer acquired her forgiveness. There is certainly no utterance. Writing is thus associated with first

19. 'A perfect mixture'.

creation, first life, first love. The garden here is not speech, as for the
poet Edmond Jabès (on whose works Derrida comments arduously), but
writing. In the beginning was the text. Jerome Adam *knew* Nagiko Eve
through writing first and then sex. Then through writing again. And
through sex yet again. Writing. Sex. Each as intoxicating as the other.

The pleasures of calligraphy, which Sei Shonagon praises in her *Pillow
Book*, are indistinguishable from the pleasures of the flesh in Greenaway's
film. The elements of writing become symbolic. The ink reminds Sei
Shonagon of lacquered hair, and the scent of fresh paper recalls the scent
of a new lover's skin. She associates the writing brush[20] with the penis, or
'that instrument of pleasure whose purpose is never in doubt, but whose
surprising efficiency one always, always forgets' (Section 167). In a less
romantic fashion, loveless Nagiko had already disagreed with the lady-in-
waiting and compared the penis to 'a sea slug or a pickled cucumber, not
an instrument of writing at all'. However, in the throws of love, Nagiko
remembers and subscribes to the wisdom of Sei Shonagon: 'there are two
things which are dependable in life: the delights of the flesh and the
delights of literature' (Section 172). Mirroring the good fortune of the
Heian writer, Greenaway's lovers appear to 'enjoy them both equally'.
Writing is ~~part of~~ sex. Sex is ~~part of~~ writing.

When Nagiko takes the brush, she declares her intention of honouring
her father by becoming a writer. Jerome becomes her paper, and *The First
Book of Thirteen* is written (Fig. 6). Her book goes out alone, for, as
Derrida declares, 'to write is to draw back. Not to retire to one's tent, in
order to write, but to draw back from one's writing itself. To be grounded
far from one's language, to emancipate it or lose one's hold on it, to let it
make its way alone and unarmed.'[21] One looks at Jerome's written body
incapable of discerning the superior beauty: that of flesh, or that of calligraphy. Perhaps they are meant to be indistinguishable. The word-bearer
lends writing his beauty in as much as the word lends its bearer its own.
Perhaps carrying such delights is not saying farewell to arms altogether.

The publisher is, quite unsurprisingly, dazzled by this *beau idéal*. He
immediately desires it, wants to take possession of it, and his first gestures
betray both weakness and strength—the vulnerability of passion—the
sensuality of reading. The man of letters licks the writing and tastes the
flesh bearing it (Fig. 7). Deciphering the text is also discovering its tex-
ture: word and skin in one. Thus, word becomes flesh, and flesh becomes
word.

20. This is, misguidedly in my opinion, translated as 'quill' in the film.
21. Derrida, 'Edmond Jabès and the Question of the Book', p. 70.

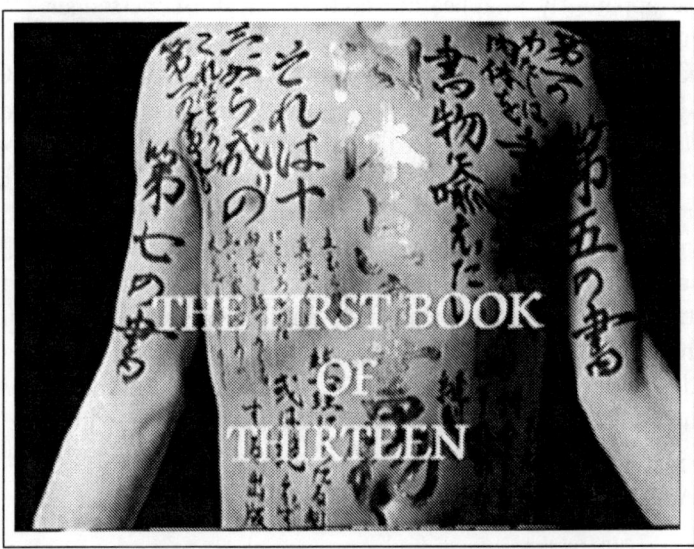

Figure 6. *Jerome's written body, as Nagiko's 'first book'.*

Figure 7. *The publisher (Yoshi Oida) takes the book and the body.*

Greenaway does, however, present a progression of distinction between the word and flesh, in which the written word (here) becomes superior. When presented with the Fifth Book (*The Book of the Exhibitionist*), the publisher ignores his Adonis-like yet momentarily writing-less lover, Jerome (who had left Nagiko and moved back in with the publisher by now), to pay attention to the extraordinary beauty of the words inscribed

on the apparently unappealing body of the fifth messenger.[22] When
Jerome realizes his loss, it is alas all too late. As a result of her own pain,
Nagiko rejects him, too, and the film takes a turn worthy of a Greek
tragedy. Not far from it, Greenaway introduces *Romeo and Juliet* and
Othello with one stroke. Nagiko's jealous friend advises Jerome towards
the dramatic. Desperate, the Englishman swallows the pills with ink.
Separated from writer and writing, the paper tries to write itself. Indeed,
it seems that liquid is the medium of writing, as Derrida remarks in 'Plato's
Pharmacy': 'Sperm, water, ink, paint, perfumed dye: the *pharmakon* always
penetrates like a liquid; it is absorbed, drunk, introduced into the inside,
which it first marks with the hardness of the type, soon to invade it and
inundate it with its medicine, its brew, its drink, its potion, its poison'.[23]
Jerome's *adieu* note reads of his dissemination into 'every library':

> Nagiko, I'm waiting for you. Meet me at the Library ...
> Any Library ... Every Library.
>
> Yours, Jerome

His elegy becomes Nagiko's sixth volume, *The Book of The Lover*. Her
beautiful calligraphy covers Jerome's dead body, a letter of introduction
for the passage into the other world. It looks as if the ink he drank re-
surfaced to expose him to all; his essence is legible: he is Text, and he is
the Lover.

Jerome's fate is not sealed, however. Greenaway treats his audience to
a violent resurrection. In love with the textandflesh that Jerome was, and
incapable of separating the word from the man, the publisher has Jerome's
body exhumed and skinned; his skin scraped of all bloody flesh and treated
until it becomes parchment; and the parchment bound until it becomes a
book in three volumes: the Pillow Biblia. The flesh becomes word; the
sarx becomes *logos*. The human *tissue* becomes the *timpan* that separates
and unites life and Hades, word and flesh, pleasure and pain, literature
and sex. The publisher takes it out regularly, reads it, reveres it, kisses it
(Fig. 8). He clothes himself with it in a gesture betraying both passion and
devotion, *committing* a metaphor known so well in Christian circles (Fig.
9). The literal expression of this metaphor is presented by Greenaway as
sin, however, and attracts both judgement and punishment, delivered by
the final, thirteenth book: *The Book of the Dead*. The publisher is killed
by the messenger of this final book, and Evil is thus *excommunicated*.

22. It is certainly not my intention, however, to offend those for whom 'large is
beautiful'.
23. Derrida, 'Plato's Pharmacy', p. 152.

Figure 8. *The publisher reveres the pillow book made of Jerome written skin.*

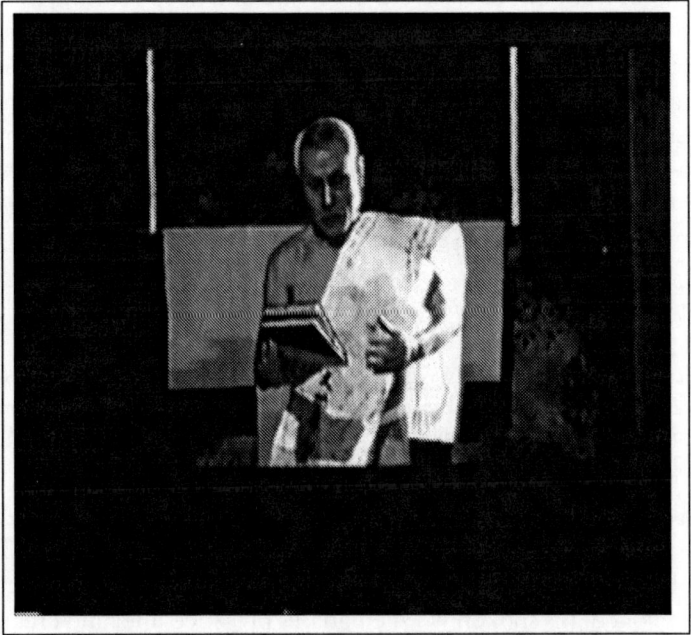

Figure 9. *The publisher clothes himself with the pillow book made of Jerome's written skin.*

The film finishes with the promise of new life and new text. Nagiko is heavy with child; as for Jabès, *the book multiplies the book.*[24] The re-covered Text of Jerome is committed back to earth. He finds peace under the roots of the bonsai tree that watches (over) as Nagiko writes the blessing on the face of her newborn baby-girl. A new book. The circle is complete.

Greenaway does not answer all questions, however; his is not a perfect picture. Nagiko's seventh book reads without answers:

> Where is a book before it is born?
> Who are a book's parents?
> Does a book have two parents—a mother and a father?
> Can a book be born inside of another book?
> Where is the parent of the book of books?
> How old does a book have to be before it can give birth?

Perhaps quite aptly, the seventh book is called *The Book of the Seducer*. Its echoes seem to wear primordial colours. Perhaps, like Jabès, Greenaway desires to expose the seduction of beginnings, the seduction of origins, that of the questions surrounding all geneses. We may never know the Truth, but we will always ask questions about the Truth. We are all victims of logocentrism. The concept of wisdom (perfect knowledge coupled with ultimate reason) is our tantalising, bright-orange carrot dangling in front of our noses. We salivate and keep running in circles, which feels like moving forward although we very rarely can tell the difference. The promise of Truth seduces, but we read that Truth itself is a liberator. Do we keep running because we are fated for liberation, or do we desire liberation because we are fated to keep running? We may not have a perfect picture, but we definitely seem to have a *perpetuum mobile*.

For me, the perfect book of births and beginnings, of the Logos and the Text, is the Prologue of John's Gospel.

John's Prologue, or The Incarnation of the Word

> In the beginning was the Word, and the Word was with God and the Word was God ... And the Word became flesh and dwelt among us full of grace and truth; we have beheld his glory, glory as of the only Son from the Father (Jn 1.1, 14).

When one reads Jn 1.1, the spoken, creative word of God that occupies centre stage in the book of Genesis is the strongest echo. It shuffles the pages. Knees tremble, and jaws open. The very presence of the Almighty is thus evoked; his spoken word emanates presence, life, and creation *ex*

---

24. Derrida, 'Edmond Jabès and the Question of the Book', p. 76.

nihilo. In Eden God speaks. On Sinai God writes. *The garden is speech, the desert writing.*[25] Thus, it is not the written word, 'the dead and rigid knowledge shut up in biblia, piles of histories, nomenclatures, recipes and formulae', as Derrida volunteers,[26] but rather the spoken word, the Logos, the reason, the wisdom, that comes forth and through the veil of written paper. And it is precisely the dynamics of these relationships, that between speech and writing and that between text and reader that preoccupy me here and which entice me to a good chase. I'm game.

What is clear to me is that all genesis seduces; the 'once upon a time' formula grips us with the promise of a good story. Everyday language is indeed far from innocent or neutral. It is the language of Western metaphysics, and, as Derrida believes, it carries with it not only a considerable number of presuppositions of all types, but also presuppositions inseparable from metaphysics, which, 'although little attended to, are knotted in a system'.[27] *Being* present *with* God *in, at, through,* even *after* the *Beginning* enthrones the word, the Logos, as the ruler supreme even before one knows anything else. Within the first verse, John employs (and is employed by) three fundamentals: God, Logos, and Beginning, all in a cemented alliance through *presence*. Thus, in the pro-logue of John's Gospel, the Logos is πρὸς τὸν θεόν, with God, towards God, in the presence of God in the beginning.

In his analysis of the work of the Jewish poet Edmond Jabès, namely *Le livre des questions*,[28] Derrida pursues his deconstructive impulses by exposing the associations of the spoken word with life and of the written word with death. Choosing to consider the work inversely as 'The Question of the Book' (the question of the orphan), Derrida salutes its author with, 'he who writes and is written'. For Jabès, the difficulty of being a Jew is correlated to the difficulty of writing; 'Judaism and Writing are but the same waiting, the same hope, the same depletion', he laments. 'The garden is speech, the desert writing. A race is born of the book', Jabès writes.[29] On this, Derrida postulates writing as being 'displaced on the broken line between lost and promised speech'. 'The difference between speech and writing is sin', Derrida continues, 'the anger of God emerging from itself, lost immediacy, work outside the garden'.[30] And yet there seems to be in writing a passion for the garden, for a return to the

25. Derrida, 'Edmond Jabès and the Question of the Book', p. 65.
26. Derrida, 'Plato's Pharmacy', p. 73.
27. Derrida, 'Semiology and Grammatology', p. 19.
28. Edmond Jabès, *Livre de questions* (Paris: Gallimard, 1936).
29. Derrida, 'Edmond Jabès and the Question of the Book', p. 65.
30. Derrida, 'Edmond Jabès and the Question of the Book', p. 68.

imagined free, direct questions and answers. Understandably, 'to write is to have the passion of the origin'.[31]

At the heart of the book of Jabès there is absence: of God, of location, and of the writer (who is like God). The creator = the writer *leaves* creation = writing. To *leave* writing means, for Derrida, to be there only in order to provide a passageway for it, to be 'its diaphanous element of its going forth: everything and nothing'.[32] Being written is not sufficient in order to have a name, however; one must write. So, letters write themselves while missing the writer. Creation creates itself in the absence of God. 'My name is a question', Jabès cries. 'Without my texts, I am more anonymous than a bedsheet in the wind'.[33] One could say that, without his creation, God would be more anonymous than *all*. On that, Derrida recalls Meister Eckhart's dictum, 'God becomes God when creation *says* God'. I volunteer: God becomes God when text *shows* God; or (here), God becomes God when the human body accepts his word and his glory.

Derrida sees the poet as finding himself both bound to language and delivered from it by a poem, a speech, whose master he himself is. The creator poet is indeed the subject of the book, its substance and its master, its servant and its theme; and the book is indeed the subject of the poet, the speaking and knowing being, who *in* the book writes *on* the book.[34] Thus, God, as the poet, is *the child of his name*.

'The word was God', John pronounces (Jn 1.1b), and I ask: If God is the Creator and the word his instrument, how can they be one and the same? Is there just the illusion of speech not leaving its parent, not falling outside the parent's breath, of being alive because of a very alive parent? Is the *Word* God, or is God the *Word*?

Why should the Logos be reduced to *speech*, however? God is the parent of both speech and writing; both the garden and the desert. There are traces of each in the other; genealogy and etymology are interwoven. Yes, the one considered first born, speech, may be perceived not only as alive (because it has 'a living father, who is present, standing near it, behind it, within it, sustaining it with his rectitude, attending it in person in his own name'[35]), but also almighty, because it has an Almighty parent. By contrast, writing appears as the half-dead orphan; the parent is absent, the intimacy broken. The power of writing, its own

31. Jacques Derrida, 'Ellipsis', in *idem, Writing and Difference*, pp. 294-300.
32. Derrida, 'Ellipsis', p. 70.
33. As quoted by Derrida in 'Edmond Jabès and the Question of the Book', pp. 70-71.
34. Derrida, 'Edmond Jabès and the Question of the Book', p. 65.
35. Derrida, 'Edmond Jabès and the Question of the Book', p. 77.

dunamis—mere resilience fed by silence, sand, and misery—is perceived as suspicious. Like Plato's *pharmakon*, writing is either *medicine*, while loyal to its parent, its genetic structure, and its moral law, or *poison*, if allowing for a metamorphosis of violence, even patricide.

Speech can also be perceived as inferior to writing, however. The *living* speech does indeed need the *half-dead* writing to record wisdom and history. Since need always produces vulnerability, and since the increase of knowledge is directly proportional to this need, no one would truly be surprised should birthrights change ownership; should writing, or the *aide-mémoire* supplement, bear not only the father's print, but his signet ring, too. Perhaps without writing, speech cannot impress; it cannot function. As Derrida put it, 'If speech could be purely present, unveiled, naked, offered up in person in its truth, without the detours of a signifier foreign to it, if at the limit an undeferred *logos* were possible, it would not seduce anyone'.[36] Like Greenaway's publisher, we too need the word to become flesh before it can seduce us.

On that, Barthes dreams of *writing aloud* as an aesthetic of textual pleasure; its aim is seen not as 'the clarity of message, the theatre of emotions'; rather, this *writing aloud* 'searches for (in a perspective of bliss) the pulsional incidents, the language lined with flesh, a text where we can hear the grain of the throat, the patina of consonants, the voluptuousness of vowels, a whole carnal stereophony: the articulation of the body, of the tongue, not that of meaning, of language'.[37]

> And the Word became flesh and dwelt among us full of grace and truth; we beheld his glory, glory as of the only Son from the Father (Jn 1.14).

While Sei Shonagon was taken with cherry blossoms and indigo paper, far away, in a different (con)text, Athanasius—who comes to mind because of some unfinished business and my taste for pastiche—was consumed with thoughts on the incarnation of the word of God: 'The word of God himself became Man that we might be made God. He manifested himself by means of a body that we might perceive the Mind of the unseen Father', he wrote (*De incarnatione Verbi Dei*, 8.54).

Presented in Alexandrine framework, Athanasius's theology is mainly built around the deity of Christ. His is a word-flesh, or high Christology, in which the word is the governing principle within the paradox of the Incarnation. Thus, Athanasius presented 'God, the word and the wisdom of the true God' (3.16) descending on earth and assuming a human body

36. Derrida, 'Plato's Pharmacy', p. 71.
37. Barthes, *The Pleasure of the Text*, pp. 66-67.

'as a temple for himself as an instrument, through which he was known and in which he dwelt' (2.8). It is thus Christ's deity rather than his humanity that preoccupied the writer of *De incarnatione*.

Thus, *the word and the wisdom* assume a material body as an instrument of communication. Could not one read, therefore, 'logos assumes graphein'; 'the sound clothes itself with the inscription'? The λόγος becomes σάρξ, the word becomes flesh; speech becomes writing. As for Jabès, the difference between speech and writing here is that between the garden and the desert: sin. Thus, the garden and the desert come together in the incarnation; they *are* one, but *not yet*. Thus, speech becomes writing as *différance*. The *logos* that holds everything together shows itself as *text*, the outside of which does not exist.

Could one also say that the Word 'came into being'? I am reminded of Roland Barthes' *The Pleasure of the Text* and Richard Howard's *hors texte*, namely his comments on the translation of Barthes's *jouissance* into *bliss* in Richard Miller's rendering:

> But of course he cannot come up with 'coming', which precisely translates what the original text can afford. The Bible they translated calls it 'knowing' while the Stuarts called it 'dying', the Victorians called it 'spending', and we call it 'coming'; a hard look at the horizon of our literary culture suggests that it will not be long before we come to a new word for orgasm proper—we shall call it 'being'.[38]

The 'coming into being' of the Word as the 'coming' or the 'being' of God? 'Begotten, not made', after all. Yet, while other gods can shamelessly take credit for creation as a product of sexual activity (even masturbation), Judaeo-Christian anthropomorphism does not easily lend itself to such notions. The biblical Logos is usually presented as having parents, a mother and a father (although John banishes the mother from his unique birth narrative—the topic of a different chapter).

In the Johannine text, God is the Father of the Logos, and the Logos is God; the pro-geny (who is, indeed, pre- and pro-genesis) is the arch-Logos who is indeed *archē*-less: supreme, yet without beginning. Beginning is that which starts, but only in reference to a stopping and an end. In its moment of inception, Beginning is the end of that which has been or not been before. The End itself is not an end, it does not begin to be an end until Beginning begins to be a beginning. The arch-Logos cannot be arch-, or supreme, for it is *archē*-less; how could anything that lacks something be arch-anything? The progeny cannot be that without some genesis, beginning, birth. How can one without birth and outside genesis

---

38. Barthes, *The Pleasure of the Text*, pp. v-vi.

be a progeny? How can the Logos be God if God is the father of the Logos? Can the Logos be his own Father? Is 'God', θεός, simply the family name, the *sur*(super)name? And how can God be a Father without a process of creating a son who is himself? Can the Father be his own son? Is this paradox? duplicity? both? neither? something else?

Scholars of the Bible have struggled with these questions for centuries. Discussing the different actions of Christ in the light of what he and many others understood as the *paradox* of the Incarnation,[39] Athanasius wrote in a letter:

> These are not events occurring without any connection, distinguished accord-
> ing to their quality, so that one class may be ascribed to the body, apart from
> the divinity, and the other to the divinity, apart from the body. They all
> occurred in such a way that they were joined together.[40]

This *joining* reminds me of the Derridian *crack, margin, veil, hymen, timpan.* Through the incarnation, the two elements are united and separated simultaneously. Divine–human, transcendent–immanent, present–absent, full–empty, now–not yet, infinite–finite, life–death, forgiveness–sin, speech–writing.

When Derrida introduced his 'Two Interpretations of Interpretation', Barthes took the same opportunity to ask the audience to recognize that 'cultural facts are always double', while drawing attention to Benveniste's remark that 'the discovery of the *duplicity* of language gives Saussure's reflection all its value'. Indeed, as Cunningham noted recently, 'the true Saussurean, the true Derridian, the *linguistic* case is that meaning arises at that duplicitous, slippery place where apparent opposites apparently con-join, so that both of the connecting, opposed sides of that border must inevitably get taken and be read and interpreted conjointly. This is the betweenness of writing.'[41]

In view of this duplicity of language (and text, therefore), it seems that texts which appear to foreground certain binary oppositions (central in recent criticism) like presence/absence, speech/writing, fullness/empti-ness, metonymy/metaphor, ideology/scripture will perhaps, as Cunning-ham would have it, 'not allow any dominance by either side of the binary

---

39. Explaining the unity between the full deity ('homoousios' rather than 'homoiousios' with the Father—*contra* Arius) and full humanity of Christ (who is indeed the Son of God, yet not in a subordinate position—*contra* Origen) was one of the principal concerns of Athanasius.

40. Athanasius, 'Epistulae ad Serapionem', IV.14, in J.P. Migne, *Patrologia Graeca*, 26.656 C-657B.

41. Quoted by Cunningham, *In the Reading Gaol*, p. 60.

coin, even if criticism and critical theory might wish or attempt to priori-
tize one or the other'. Indeed, the texts in question will 'present meaning
as arising precisely in the busy overlap, interaction, clash, between the
two ... the real enactments of what Saussure perceived as language's
dualité oppositive and actualizations of what is really arresting Derrida in
the marginality of textuality'.[42]

Thus, since nothing can be either truly present or truly absent; either
simply spoken or simply written, I propose that *in the beginning was the
text*, or the collaboration of difference and deferral. Identities fail without
difference and referents. All is encompassed by the play of *différance*, and
indeed there is nothing outside of it. 'And, to infinity', to quote Derrida.

The Desire of God

Whose will be done, however? So, creation is written, and then the word
creates himself; the word writes himself into flesh. Is this the result of our
desire for God's word, or God's desire for our flesh? Whose was the gift?
Was there a gift? Perhaps we should entertain the thought that there
should not be a question of either one or the other, as John D. Caputo
would be eager to interject, 'but of inhabiting the distance between the
two with as much grace and ambience and hospitality as possible'.[43] It is
all about seduction, after all.

When writing on the desire of God, or Derrida's 'God as the other
name of desire',[44] Richard Kearney puts forward the theory that there are
two ways of desiring God: *onto-theological* and *eschatological*. The *onto-
theological* 'construes desire as *lack* ... as the drive to be and know absolutely',[45] or that which has been deemed as '*the evil drive* (yezer hara) to
be God by refashioning Yahweh in our own image'.[46] Kearney sees this as
the same impulse about which 1 John warned its readers, namely 'the lust
of the eyes' for what shines and seduces. In an inspired gesture, he quotes
Augustine's critique of the *concupiscentia oculorum*, or the 'ocular erotic

---

42. I am indeed indebted to Valentine Cunningham for his clear thesis on this. See
his 'Word and World', in *idem*, *In the Reading Gaol*, pp. 4-61.

43. John D. Caputo, *The Prayers and Tears of Jacques Derrida: Religion without Religion* (Bloomington: Indiana University Press, 1997), p. 173.

44. Jacques Derrida, *On the Name* (ed. Thomas Dutoit; Stanford: Stanford
University Press, 1995), p. 10.

45. Richard Kearney, 'Desire of God', in John D. Caputo and Michael J. Scanlon
(eds.), *God, the Gift, and Postmodernism* (Bloomington: Indiana University Press, 1999),
pp. 112-45 (112).

46. Richard Kearney, *The Wake of Imagination* (London: Routledge, 1994),
pp. 37-53.

drive to appropriate the ephemera of the visible universe, the obsessive epistemological *curiositas* with regard to absolute knowledge'.[47] Indeed, as Greenaway's Nagiko is admonished at one point, 'Some cultures permit no images; perhaps some cultures ought to permit no visible text'.

Augustine's *insight* became a preface to the work of many other theologians and found climax (as Heidegger pointed out) in the work of Martin Luther, who spoke strongly against the 'fornication of the spirit', the *fornicatio spiritus*, which seems to endeavour to possess God through metaphysical vision, or *visio dei*.[48] Luther argued that the attempts to objectify the *deus adventurus* is only a 'desire to dominate and master' (echoed later by Hegel's 'Master–Slave' dialectic, predicated on desire). Instead, Christians were encouraged by Luther to entertain a Pauline desire for the kingdom of God as 'hope for what we do not see'.

Yet, as Kearney argues, this Judaeo-Christian criticism of onto-theological desire is not the clear equivalent of the rejection of it:

> The Nietzschean verdict that 'Christianity gave Eros poison to drink' is not quite as self-evident as it seems. On the contrary, the destruction of onto-theological desire might be more properly conceived as a spur to transcend our captivation by all that is (*ta onta*) for another kind of desire—a desire for something that eye has never seen nor ear heard. That is to say, *eschatological* desire.[49]

To his aid, Kearney invokes Augustine again, by quoting erotico-ecstatic passages from his *Confessions*, his descriptions of the erotic restlessness of the soul in search of God, the *inquiteum cor nostrum*: 'You shed your fragrance about me; I drew breath and now I gasp for your sweet odour. I tasted you and now I hunger and thirst for you. You touched me and I am inflamed with love' (*Confessions*, VI).[50]

This desire seems to have been initiated by God himself, however. It was he who *shed* [his] *fragrance* and *touched* Augustine first. Almost like the double Genitive, the desire of God plays between its subjective and objective domains and embodies them both in *reciprocity*. Somehow, I am reminded of Athanasius's understanding of the Incarnation: 'The word of God himself became Human that we might be made God. He manifested himself by means of a body that we might perceive the Mind of the unseen Father', he wrote (*De incarnatione*, 8.54).

---

47. Augustine, *Confessions* (trans. R. Pine-Coffin; New York: Penguin, 1961), pp. 174-80, 245-47. Cited by Kearney, 'Desire of God', p. 113.

48. John van Buren, *The Young Heidegger: Rumor of the Hidden King* (Bloomington: Indiana University Press, 1994), pp. 189-210. Cited by Kearney, 'Desire of God', p. 113.

49. Kearney, 'Desire of God', p. 113.

50. Cited by Kearney, 'Desire of God', p. 113.

It seems to me that, in the Incarnation, God desires our flesh as much as we desire his word. Both parties express ocular-erotic inclinations, in which the onto-theological and the eschatological modes of desire couple. Reciprocity is the ground of fecundity. Thus, in order to be—and be known as—God, the Word desires our flesh as an inscription of himself, whose *glorious* radiance can—and is meant to—be *beheld* (Jn 1.14b). Becoming text is the means of seduction. Now, we read about the word becoming flesh, and we feast our eyes on the inscribed letters in front of us while our hearts are racing with the hope for a reality beyond the page. The *now but not yet* of our being with the Word—visible in print and invisible in concept—makes us gasp with desire. Ours is the *foreplay*, and the promise of a *glorious* climax is *guaranteed* by God's applying his seal of ownership on us, by inscribing it onto our hearts, our souls (2 Cor. 1.22), while it is anticipated actively by us through our devotional, controlled orgies. We read the word, eat his flesh, drink his blood, and celebrate our communion with him.

Derrida is right when calling God 'the other name of desire'. Perhaps we should indeed subscribe to the wisdom of Sei Shonagon, who declared that 'there are two things dependable in life: the delights of the flesh and the delights of literature' (Section 172). I will not agree this time with Cunningham and his idea that textuality rhymes all too conveniently with sexuality.[51] What seems rather clear is that Christians, the self-declared seduced, do inhabit the territory of reciprocity, which is but a *hymen* uniting and separating the human and the divine, the immanent and the transcendent, flesh and word, this world and the other, the audience and the book, desire and its fulfilment. The subject and object of our desire is the Word, who in the Biblia writes on the Biblia. With the hope of orgasmic heaven, we clothe ourselves with our own Pillow Book, allow our flesh to be inscribed through fugitive foreplay, and dream of becoming one with the Word while we read of the Word becoming one with us.

The 'I' in Lacanian Psychoanalysis

> The first being of which we are aware is that of our own being ... In loving God it is ourselves we love, and by first loving ourselves—a convenient charity, as they say—we render to God the appropriate homage.
>
> *Jacques Lacan*[52]

---

51. Cunningham, *In the Reading Gaol*, p. 56.
52. Jacques Lacan, 'God and the Jouissance of Woman', in Jacqueline Rose and Juliet Mitchell (eds.), *Feminine Sexuality: Jacques Lacan and the École Freudienne* (London: Macmillan, 1982), p. 142.

The Freudian Ego

Essential to the discourse of psychoanalysis is the concept of the unconscious, which first explained what Sigmund Freud called the 'uncanny' (*unheimlich*) feelings of doubleness in human beings, the sense that something unfamiliar co-exists with the recognized, comfortable, homely (*heimlich*) part of self.[53] As that dimension of the human psyche which is a repository of repressed feelings, desires, memories and illicit drives (to do mostly with sexuality and violence), the unconscious is only partially accessible to the conscious dimension of the human mind, through dreams and neurotic symptoms. As repression of instinctual, animal inclinations is 'essential to civilization', it follows that the unconscious part of self is a considerable part of human life, what Julie Rivkin and Michael Ryan call 'a stranger within'.[54]

This stranger Freud introduced as the id, destined to be forever in conflict with the conscious self, or the ego. The ego is accompanied in its role of regulating the instinctual drives located within the id—ἔρως and θάνατος, or love and death, sexuality and violence—by the superego, or one's conscience, the punitive voice within, mostly constructed by one's cultural context.

When there is a breakdown in the balance between the id, the ego and the superego, and the repressed id manifests itself in the realm of conscious experience (and not through dreams, the safe domain for that expression), it does so through psychotic symptoms. Says Freud,

> The ego's relation to the id might be compared with that of a rider to his horse. The horse supplies the locomotive energy, while the rider has the privilege of deciding on the goal and of guiding the powerful animal's movement. But only too often there arises between the ego and the id the not precisely ideal situation of the rider being obliged to guide the horse along the path by which it itself wants to go.[55]

Therefore, Freud understood psychoanalysis as a science meant 'to strengthen the ego', 'to widen its field of perception and enlarge its organization so that it can appropriate fresh portions of the id'.[56] In other words, and much as on an archaeological site, the ego must become able to exercise increasingly more control over the id through systematic

53. Sigmund Freud, 'The Uncanny', in Julie Rivkin and Michael Ryan (eds.), *Literary Theory: An Anthology* (Oxford: Basil Blackwell, 1998), pp. 154-67 (154-57).

54. Julie Rivkin and Michael Ryan, 'Strangers to Ourselves: Psychoanalysis', in Julie Rivkin and Michael Ryan (eds.), *Literary Theory*, pp. 119-27 (119).

55. Sigmund Freud, *New Introductory Lectures on Psycho-Analysis* (London: Penguin, 1973), pp. 77.

56. Freud, *New Introductory Lectures on Psycho-Analysis*, p. 80.

digging, or by unearthing and interpreting forgotten memories, images or feelings related to them. Thus, the reality principle masters the pleasure principle.

At the centre of Freud's work is his theory on human sexuality. According to Freud, human sexuality is evident from early childhood until death. The well-known Oedipus Complex represents an experience that all children go through, a rite of passage from infancy and a poly-morphous, perverse sexuality into maturity and centred sexuality. Need-less to say, Freud's primary concerns focus on the development of the male child and his healthy adjustment to a heterosexual identity (seen as the norm). The theory is that all male children experience a strong desire towards the mother, a powerful attachment that is sexual in nature. At this point the father must intervene and forbid the development of this relationship, thus preventing incest. The authority of the father is established through the perceived fear of castration. As a result, the male child learns to relinquish his pre-Oedipal desire for the mother and emu-late, or identify with, the father, seeking other women than the mother on whom to focus his desire. Thus the male child avoids the fate of Sophocles' King Oedipus, who kills his father, Laius, and marries his mother, Jocasta, with tragic consequences.

Freud's theory on the development of the female child is less convinc-ing. The female child is said to experience an early attachment to the father and, as a result, wants to be and replace her mother as the father's sexual object. Again, the father intervenes and the female child learns to renounce her desire for the father, to identify with the mother and desire other men, outside the family. The reason why this theory is not con-vincing is that it is built on an improbable foundation. The premise that the female child's first attachment is to the father is questionable, since all children—be they male or female—develop a desire for the mother first and foremost (due primarily to their physical bond and the fulfilment of the child's needs—like feeding, for instance). It follows that the devel-opment of the female child takes a route by which the girl can identify more easily not with the mother, but with the father. (Hence Hélène Cixous' theory of woman's bisexuality, more of which will be said later.)

Freud circumvents this problem by insisting that the key to the girl's development is penis envy. She perceives her lack of a penis as a failure on the part of the mother, which attracts the girl's resentment towards the mother and a shift of focus in her desire, where the father replaces the mother. The girl's determination to have or get a penis is perceived as her wish to bear her father a child. This explanation has been contested by many female scholars, from Simone de Beauvoir to contemporary feminists, and the theory offered in its place is that 'penis envy' should read 'power envy'. As the father represents absolute authority, the penis is associated with his position of power. It is, after all, the premise on which the male child obeys the Father's Law and learns to identify with the father; he hopes that one day he will also be that powerful. It is poor logic to say that the girl would deliberately wish to identify with the powerless parent. Then again, Freud died without finding successful theories for the female psyche and confessed that he must leave unanswered the question that still poses many problems today: 'What do women want?'

Freud's theories have been the topic of much scholarly work, and that is why I will not expand further on them here. His work on the Oedipus Complex is significant, as it represents the moment when human beings encounter the law and all ethics and morality within their cultural context. It is the moment where the child's superego is born, and the interplay of id, ego and superego furnish the preface to the human subject. One of Freud's most notable merits is his insight into the link between sexuality and identity-formation. While for other psychoanalysts sexuality was a matter of biological pressure discharged in the act of sexual intercourse, Freud insisted that sexuality is part of human identity, and it thus relates to our capacity to experience pleasure in ways that are not generally perceived as sexual. Building on Freud's theories, psychoanalysis today sees a close connection between sexuality and identity, placing the origin of the sexual being in the nature of the affirmation or disruption of the self that occurs in childhood. Thus, sexuality is seen to represent not biological drive-discharge mechanisms but rather meanings.

The Lacanian 'I'

> You can be Lacanians; as for me, I'm a Freudian.

> —*Jacques Lacan*[57]

The one to develop Freud's theory further was Jacques Lacan (1901–1981), whose work is often labelled as 'neo-Freudian' and lends itself to a strong school of literary criticism. Based on Saussurean linguistics, Lacan's take on psychoanalysis is that the unconscious is structured like, and by, language. In fact, in his 1977 works Lacan declares that psychoanalysis is not a science, but rather like rhetoric. Considering language and its workings, Lacan understands text as an unending interplay of signifiers,

---

57. Jacques Lacan, 'Opening Address to the Caracas Conference, July 1980', in *L'Ane* 1 (1980), pp. 30-31.

differential and semiotic, and not a fixed entity to be studied empirically. The text is a matrix of signifiers and not a constant and united substance, thus allowing for gaps and inconsistencies. Furthermore, the Lacanian signifier has priority in relation to the signified. In other words, meaning is preceded and constructed through the signifying process and not vice versa. Lacan reverses Saussure's algorithm, according to which there is symmetry and equilibrium between the signifier and the signified within the sign. He insists instead on a new algorithm, S/s, where the signified slips beneath the signifier and thus successfully resists attempts to be located and defined. It is the signifier that has the active power, the power to colonize and anticipate the signified. Thus, the relation between the signifier and the signified is arbitrary—an idea that Lacan borrows from structuralism. This arbitrariness indicates that the transition from signifier to signified, from language to meaning, from human behaviour to its psychological significance, cannot be natural, or self-evident. Lacan's S/s (read 'signifier *over* the signified'[58]) introduces a barrier between signifier and signified, a fraction line, a bar that represents resistance to signification.

Lacan insists that 'the unconscious means that man is inhabited by the signifier',[59] that, in Barbara Johnson's words, the 'I' is always 'knotted up, entangled in semiotic relations'.[60] Due to his emphasis on language, Lacan claims that the unconscious does not reside inside of us, in a private and isolated region of self. Instead, the unconscious exists between us and around us. It weaves itself through us, like language; never entirely within our control. Like language, the unconscious is not pre-existent or pre-given. The unconscious, indeed the human subject, is constructed, by and through language, which is external. Lacan claims,

> Meaning is the fact that the human being isn't master of … language. He has been thrown into it … Here man isn't master in his own house. There is something into which he integrates himself, which through its combinations already governs … Man is engaged with all his being in the procession of numbers, in a primitive symbolization which is distinct from imaginary representations. It is in the middle of that that something of man has to gain recognition.[61]

58.   Jacques Lacan, 'The Instance of the Letter in the Unconscious or Reason since Freud', in Rivkin and Ryan (eds.), *Literary Theory*, pp. 190-205 (191).

59.   Lacan, *Ecrits*, p. 257.

60.   Barbara Johnson, 'The Frame of Reference', *Yale French Studies* 55–56 (1977), pp. 457-505 (461).

61.   Jacques Lacan, *The Seminar. Book II: The Ego in Freud's Theory and in the Technique of Psychoanalysis* (trans. Sylvana Tomaselli; Cambridge: Cambridge University Press, 1988), p. 307.

In short, 'the human animal is born into language and it is within the terms of language that the human subject is constructed'.[62] If language had before been conceived as the means of communication between subjects who mastered it fully and consciously, Lacan's theory is that language is performed with a lack of mastery on the part of the speaking subject. This is what explains, Lacan insists, the Freudian slips of the tongue and spontaneous puns and jokes. Echoing Freud, Lacan describes the human subject as caught in, and tortured by, language.[63]

Therefore, the ego/I, in Lacanian thought is not the master of the unconscious—the role that the ego had in Freudian analysis, as the homogenous, centred and unified, *heimlich* part of self—but a mere mirage of unity, always lacking and never fully able to know and control the unconscious. Lacan's writings of the 1950s borrow Hegelian undertones, particularly Hegel's Master–Slave dialectic, when discussing the relation between the 'I' and Desire, or the Subject–Other dynamics.[64] Hegel's *Phenomenology of Spirit* laid the foundations for man as self-consciousness, where any human being becomes conscious of their own unique existence when saying 'I'. When contemplating his or her surroundings, the subject is absorbed by the object of their contemplation. The only element to achieve the subject's return, the subject's being brought back to himself, is Desire (like the desire for sustenance, for example). The result of desire is action, which disquiets the subject's passive pensiveness. However, all action is negation, since it destructs, or assimilates, transforms, internalizes, the desired object by fulfilling desire. Thus, generally speaking, the 'I of Desire' is 'an emptiness that receives a real positive content only by negating action that satisfies Desire in destroying, transforming and "assimilating" the desired non-I'.[65] Moreover, human desire is that, namely human, only when desire goes beyond the body, when it is Desire of the Other, and essentially desire for recognition—as human. This battle for recognition constructs the Master–Slave relationship for Hegel, as it can only allow for one party to win the battle, the master, and thus assimilate the other, the slave. The fate of the master is a tragic one, however, as recognition must come from one whom the master recognizes worthy of the task. Being recognized by someone the master does not recognize defeats the entire purpose of the battle and its victory.

62. Madan Sarup, *Jacques Lacan* (London: Harvester Wheatsheaf, 1992), p. 15.

63. Jacques Lacan, cited in Jean-Jacques Lecercle, *Philosophy through the Looking Glass: Language, Nonsense, Desire* (London: Hutchinson, 1985), p. 133.

64. See particularly Jacques Lacan, 'The Subversion of the Subject and the Dialectic of Desire in the Freudian Unconscious', in *idem*, *Ecrits*, pp. 294-324.

65. Sarup, *Jacques Lacan*, p. 32,

As the master only subscribes to these rules, the master's identity is rigid, unable to change, go beyond itself. By contrast, the slave does not consider his identity as fixed; by becoming master of nature and not other humans, the slave becomes free. 'The future and history hence belong not to the warlike Master, who either dies or preserves himself indefinitely in identity to himself, but to the working Slave'.[66]

The 'I' and Desire

Lacan, it is said, combined Hegel's theory of recognition with Freud's take on the libido and constructed his own theory on desire. Of principal importance for Lacan is the role of the Other as vital in the expression of human desire. Worth mentioning is that Lacan's Other is polysemantic, depending on the context in which it is used (like other Lacanian concepts). Thus the Other can refer to the Subject–Other (as in Hegelian dialectics), the Father or the Mother, Patient and Analyst, and even the Unconscious. As Madan Sarup observes, in saying that 'the unconscious is the discourse of the Other', Lacan is weaving together a number of assumptions: the human subject is divided; the unconscious has a linguistic structure; the subject is inhabited by the Other; psychoanalysis is a variety of speech. In Sarup's opinion 'there is a hint too that there is a kinship between the structure of language and the structure of the subject; both are articulations of difference; neither has a centre; both involve endless displacement; neither has a point of plenitude or stasis'.[67]

Thus, because desire is built on the loss of the object (the mother), it follows that desire does not assure the subject in his or her identity. On the contrary, desire throws a large question mark over this perceived identity. Desiring the Other only exposes a lack, a division within the subject. Lacan thus dethrones the ego as the pivot, the centre of human psychical life. The unified self is exposed as a mere illusion. Instead, the narcissistic ego is fluid and mobile, formed through a 'series of identifications, internalizations of images/perceptions'.[68] Thus, while other psychoanalysts would want to focus on the patient's behaviour and speech, Lacan insists that the location of the patient within language/speech is more important. Moving away from Descartes's *cogito ergo sum*, Lacan proposes, 'I think where I am not, therefore I am where I do not think'.[69]

According to Lacan, the ego is pieced together through imaginary concepts and narcissistic fantasies, while continuing to be blind to its

---

66. Sarup, *Jacques Lacan*, p. 33.
67. Sarup, *Jacques Lacan*, p. 77.
68. Sarup, *Jacques Lacan*, p. 40.
69. Lacan, *Ecrits*, pp. 128-29, 299-300.

own impulses, drives, the unconscious, and its location and determination by language, or the Symbolic Order. As Rivkin and Ryan explain, 'before language assigns us an "I", we possess no sense of self. It is language that gives us identity (while simultaneously taking it away in the sense of something pre-given or internal).'[70] The infant starts as a set of fragmented drives, impressions and desires, which come together in an imaginary unified identity. The symbiosis between the infant and the mother produces a mistaken and narcissistic sense of unity. Thus, the infant assumes that the (m)Other is him- or herself, and the desire for her is in fact the desire for her desire of him or her. The realization of this desire as well as desire itself are perceived to be immediate, but the fulfilment of a homogenous self and the satisfaction of desire (*jouissance*)— what Lacan calls the Real, or the area beyond expression—is impossible. The mother does not give the child the wholeness he or she desires; instead she is nothing more than a collection of part objects (*l'objet petit a*[*utre*]—representing the lacking, lost object) that give only fragmentary pleasures (such as those connected to feeding and the breast, or the face with the gaze and the voice; also 'the lips, the enclosure formed by the teeth, the rim of the anus, the tip of the penis, the vagina, the slit formed by the eyelids',[71] elements to do with an edge or a cut). The illusion of a unified identity is nothing more than self-deception as means of negating the existence of separation, or *béance*, that primal fissure between infant and mother. The 'I' is not formed within the realm of the mythic identity of the ego, therefore, but on what Lacan calls our *manque-à-être*, our initial lack-of-being; the experience of rupture from the imaginary fullness of being, from the mother, from the object of desire. The identity that we take on is given to us from outside, produced by the 'Symbolic Order of our culture, the social languages that identify us and lend us identities, all of which exceed consciousness and never assume the form of knowable or conscious identity (which, for Lacan, is always phantasmatic). Our identity is given to us from outside, and we are constitutively alienated.'[72]

The Mirror Stage

It is at the mirror stage that the infant[73] enters this social world, the Symbolic Order. Thus, between the ages of six and eighteen months, the dyadic relationship with the mother, the symbiotic bond between them,

---

70. Rivkin and Ryan, 'Strangers to Ourselves', p. 123.
71. Jacques Lacan, 'The Signification of the Phallus', in *idem*, *Ecrits*, p. 315.
72. Rivkin and Ryan, *Literary Theory*, p. 124.
73. Lacan prefers the term *infans*, representing the child before language, so 'speechless'.

must be relinquished. Before being able to speak and have control over his/her motor skills, the infant learns to recognize him/herself in the mirror. The act of recognition is rather complex, as the infant has to realize that the image is not him/herself, but only a reflection of him/herself. The process is aided by the father's 'no', namely the incest taboo. The child learns that he or she is different, separate from the mother and accepts his or her place within the Symbolic Order. This inception of subjectivity, of the 'I', comes through seeing a reflection of the embodied self that has boundaries, which becomes the model for all future identifications; the subject acquires an identity by virtue of that 'I' being reflected *by* the other and from the *location* of the other, back to the subject. As Lacan has it, 'this development is lived like a temporal dialectic that decisively projects the formation of the individual in history'.[74] Jane Gallop sees this as the crux of the 'high tragedy' that she considers the mirror-stage to be. She associates it with the story of Genesis and the expelling of Adam and Eve from paradise. Thus just as the first man and woman cannot enter the human condition before they are expelled from Eden, so with the child, who, already born, cannot become an individual self until experiencing the mirror stage. Both developments are like dual birth processes: once born into nature, and the second time into history. While Adam and Eve anticipate mastery when eating the forbidden fruit, only to acquire sight of their nakedness, the child anticipates a totalised, mastered body, only to recognize his or her inadequacy.[75]

Lacan associates the dawn of individuality in the infant with the acquisition of language. Rather than a Cartesian *res cogitans*, or thinking being, Lacan's subject is a speaking subject, the subject of speech, *parle-être*, not only in the sense that the subject speaks but also in the sense that the subject is 'spoken through by language'. It is language that makes the subject, meaning that when one learns to say the name of an object one has to accept separation from it; the object is sacrificed, because the presence of the sign/word represents the absence of the signified thing itself. The entrance into the Symbolic and the breaking of the Imaginary thus consists of the 'installation of a combined linguistic/psychological separation of the child both from its initial object, the mother, and from the undifferentiated matter of natural existence'.[76] The body of the mother is forbidden, and the desire for it slips under the bar of the signifier,

74.   Lacan, *Ecrits*, p. 97.

75.   Jane Gallop, *Reading Lacan* (Ithaca, NY: Cornell University Press, 1985), pp. 82-85.

76.   Rivkin and Ryan, *Literary Theory*, p. 124.

entering thus the unconscious. From that moment on, the mother becomes the Other, symbolic of all forbidden desires and lost objects, the absence of which will leave a gap that we try to fill but never succeed in filling. Lacan suggests that throughout life, we try to come to terms with this separation, the gaps in our existence, our *manque-à-être*. Thus, we slide along a chain of signifiers, a play of metonymy, parts rather than a whole.

Therefore, according to Lacan, we are forever split within/from ourselves and can never attain a unified self (against object-relation theory and ego-psychology). In the words of Lacan, 'the "*ce suis-je*" of the time of Villon has become reversed in the "*c'est moi*" of the modern man. The *moi*, the ego, of modern man ... has taken on its form in the dialectical impasse of the *belle âme* who does not recognize his very *raison d'être* in the disorder that he denounces in the world.'[77] The illusion of the unified ego is only the delusion of the ego. The point for Lacan is to accept the lack that defines our being. We cannot be one with ourselves. The 'I' is never quite 'One'.

The Imaginary, the Symbolic and the Real
Thirteen years after he first presented his theory of the mirror stage, Lacan developed this concept by addressing the three 'orders' or 'registers' that are present in his theories: the Imaginary, the Symbolic and the Real. The Real, as Lacan describes it, is that which is 'in its place', 'the impossible to symbolize'. It is outside of the Symbolic and the Imaginary, not connected with reality, and it echoes Freud's concept of the id. As I mentioned earlier, the Real represents that which never takes place but is always desired, the dyadic unity with the mother, unity within self, that which finds sudden, unpredictable and unsettling expressions. Lacan maintains that the Real predates the birth of the subject, as the Symbolic Order does.

The Imaginary emerges during the mirror stage (with the infant's specular ego) and develops throughout life, playing an important role in the subject's adult experience of others and the world in general. Lacan sees the Imaginary as a veil, an item of clothing, functioning as armour. Lacan says,

> We have only to understand the mirror stage *as an identification*, in the full sense that analysis gives to the term: namely, the transformation that takes place in the subject when he assumes an image—whose predestination to this

77. Lacan, 'The Symbolic Order', in Rivkin and Ryan (eds.), *Literary Theory*, pp. 184-89 (188).

phase-effect is sufficiently indicated by the use, in analytic theory, of the
ancient term *imago*.[78]

Thus, the Imaginary performs the function of misrecognition (*méconnaissance*) in opposition to knowledge (*connaissance*). Like the mirror, the
Imaginary plays on the interdependence between image, identity and
identification. Lacan confesses,

> I am led ... to regard the function of the mirror-stage as a particular case of
> the function of the *imago*, which is to establish a relation between the organism and its reality—or, as they say, between the *Innenwelt* and the *Umwelt*.[79]

The process of establishing this relation between the inner world and the
outer world is a complex one, and it can attract different reactions from
the subject. Sarup observes the paradox of the situation in which the
child finds him/herself, of both narcissistic and aggressive nuances. 'The
subject finds or recognizes itself through an image which simultaneously
alienates it, and hence potentially confronts it ... There are ... first, the
factors of aggression, rivalry, the image as alienating, and second, the
fundamental misrecognition which is the foundation of subjectivity.'[80]

In explaining the process of assuming an image and coming to terms
with external reality, Lacan finds his inspiration in Freud's 1914 paper
entitled 'On Narcissism: An Introduction', in which Freud comments on
Ovid's Narcissus and his moment of apparent 'mirrored reciprocity'.
Freud's thesis is that the subject has four choices of narcissistic images: (i)
what he himself is, (ii) what he himself was, (iii) what he himself would
like to be, and (iv) someone who was once part of himself.[81] The most
important distinction for Lacan seems to be that between the Ideal-I and
the I-Ideal. The ideal ego is generally constructed on narcissistic, infantile
models of omnipotence, while the I-Ideal is an agency of the personality
fashioned by narcissism, or the idealization of the ego, and identification
with parents or their substitutes. As Sarup notes, there is a recognisable
association between the ideal ego and what 'he himself was', and between
the I-Ideal and what 'he himself would like to be'. Related to the mirror

---

78. Jacques Lacan, 'The Mirror Stage as Formative of the Function of the I as
Revealed in Psychoanalytic Experience', Paper delivered at the Sixteenth International
Congress of Psychoanalysis, Zürich, 17 July 1949, in Robert Con Davis and Ronald
Schleifer (eds.), *Contemporary Literary Criticism: Literary and Cultural Studies* (trans.
Alan Sheridan; New York: Longman, 3rd edn, 1994), pp. 382-86 (382).

79. Lacan, 'The Mirror Stage', p. 384.

80. Sarup, *Jacques Lacan*, p. 102.

81. Sigmund Freud, *On Metapsychology: The Theory of Psychoanalysis* (London:
Penguin Books, 1984), p. 84.

stage, the Ideal-I is the projected image with which the subject identifies, while the I-Ideal would be a secondary introjection.[82] Lacan insists that the Ideal-I belongs to the Imaginary and is above all a narcissistic construct, which finds its inception at the mirror stage.

What is the difference, however, between Imaginary identification and Symbolic identification? Sarup argues convincingly that the imaginary identification, or the formation of the ideal ego, sees the subject linked to an image that she or he likes, in which the subject appears the way she or he would like to be, while the symbolic identification, or the formation of the ego ideal, sees the subject linked to the location from which the subject looks at him- or herself, to the subject's gaze, at the end of which the likeable 'I' resides:

> Imaginary identification is always identification on behalf of a certain gaze in the Other. We should always ask: for whom is the subject enacting this role? This gap between the way I see myself and the point from which I am being observed to appear likeable to myself is crucial ... In short, the difference between how we see ourselves and the point from which we are being observed is the difference between the imaginary and symbolic identification.[83]

This is all predicated on the misrecognition of the Symbolic, as the subject believes in the transparency of language. Thus the Imaginary is not merely the place where the subject allows his imagination to create *imagos*, but the level at which the subject *méconnaît* the nature of the Symbolic, the level of illusion. The Imaginary echoes Freud's concept of the ego.[84]

Lacan and Cinema

Because of the importance that Lacan ascribed to the visual, particularly the *gaze*, it is not surprising that he has also left his mark on cinematic, or film studies. His most notable influence can be seen in the work of Christian Metz, who claims that the cinema draws its viewers into a stance that can only be described through Lacan's Imaginary. The spectator's experience in front of the screen corresponds somewhat to the mirror stage in Lacanian psychoanalysis, susceptible to the Imaginary.

Rather than looking into the nosographic approach to psychoanalytical film reading, which considers the actual films as symptoms to be

82. Sarup, *Jacques Lacan*, p. 103.
83. Sarup, *Jacques Lacan*, p. 103.
84. See Catherine Clément's work, which associates Lacan's concept of the Imaginary with Freud's concept of the ego, the Symbolic with the superego, and the Real with the id; Catherine Clément, *The Lives and Legends of Jacques Lacan* (New York: Columbia University Press, 1983), p. 169.

analysed in order to understand the psychology of the film-maker, I am more interested in the textual approach, which sees film as an independent text, as a signifier. Metz defends this approach by arguing,

> What the child sees in the mirror, what he sees as an other, who turns into 'I', is after all the image of his own body; so it is still an identification with something *seen*. But in traditional cinema the spectator is identifying only with something *seeing*: his own image does not appear on the screen; the primary identification is no longer constructed around a subject-object, but around a pure, all-seeing and invisible subject, the vanishing point of the monocular perspective which cinema has taken over from painting.[85]

In other words, in order to appreciate film, the viewer must understand the captured object as absent, replaced by its image that signifies that very absence. The screen plays the role of a second mirror, a symbolic means of representation, which depends on absence/lack and reflection/significance. Cinema is possible because of the circulation of desire, the desire for that which is forever lost, the mother or wholeness. Drives like scopophilia, or the pleasure of the gaze, voyeurism, are rooted in the our *manque-à-être*, our lack of being, which we forever try to fill and heal.

The work of film theoreticians like Metz regards films as dreams, or dream fragments, and thus capable of communicating elements of the unconscious to the viewers. 'Even with a realistic subject, the cinema is not always totally realistic. Its language, its syntax, its grammar are from the beginning dreamlike and poetic. It carries with it, by its nature, a mysterious and surreal dimension', Joseph Marty observes.[86] As in dreams, we are not always able to recognize directly what it is that we find meaningful in them. The underlying message of dreams, their latent content from within the id, are altered by the intervention of the ego through processes called 'displacement' and 'condensation'.

Dream displacement is the process by which we use a safe character, incident, or object as a stand-in to represent a more hostile character, incident, or object; like, for example, a dream about a friend sexually molesting the subject, when what the unconscious is trying to expose is in fact the trauma of experiencing similar or the same type of molestation from a person who is closer, sometimes even a member of the family. Dream condensation, on the other hand, sees the subject dreaming a single image or incident that is meant to represent numerous unconscious pains or conflicts; for example, when one dreams about losing one's teeth

85. Christian Metz, *Psychoanalysis and the Cinema: The Imaginary Signifier* (London: Macmillan, 1982), p. 97. Italics in the original.
86. Marty, 'Toward a Theological Interpretation and Reading of Film', p. 135.

in order to express the anxieties connected to psychological conflicts regarding losing one's job, position in society, relationships, and so on.

No matter how disturbing dreams are, they are relatively safe means of expressing repressed hurts, fears, guilty desires, or unresolved conflicts, for we always experience them in a veiled manner and so only read them partially. Of course, if the dream takes too frightening a shape, we are able to wake up and thus terminate the experience. By association, contemporary viewers watch violent or disturbing films because they feel that they can simply walk out of the cinema theatre or turn off the TV, video or DVD.

The most important element of dream-work is that thoughts and emotions are expressed through visual images, which are edited by our unconscious through secondary revisions, to follow displacement or condensation or both, in order to deceive the censors, the ego and the super-ego. Lacan expounds Freud's theory by associating metaphor with condensation and metonymy with displacement.[87] Metaphor exists through the relationship between two signifiers, while depending on the presence of one *and* the absence of the other; it condenses the signification process to fewer elements. On the other hand, metonymy exists as the relationship between an unlimited number of signifiers, chained together by the transference of one into the next, and that one into the next still, and so on. As metonymy accommodates metaphor, so displacement accommodates condensation. The purpose of both is to facilitate the experience of a seemingly innocuous fantasy that is not rated or repressed by the censoring board.

While one can see the underlying logic associating films with dreams, one can also perceive obvious differences. For instance, watching a film is generally a voluntary experience, while dreams are not; one is, for most parts, aware that the fictional story presented on screen is only a film (though the surrounding darkness and the perceived immobility of the viewer may resemble dreaming conditions), while dreams are more vivid, if not completely indistinguishable from reality; furthermore, films are usually more structured, or more logical, than dreams.

What psychoanalytical film theory focuses upon are the intricate ways in which the viewer is lured into subjecting him- or herself to the experience of the waking dream. Metz argues that viewers and the cinema are engaged in a passionate tango of disavowal: the film provides an openly fictional narrative, which we are ready to believe as true, thus willingly

---

87. Lacan borrows elements of Roman Jakobson's work in this theory. See R. Jakobson and M. Halle, *Fundamentals of Language* (The Hague: Mouton, 1959).

disavowing our knowledge of the opposite. 'Cinematographic "projection", as its name rightly indicates, always involves a submission to the
images and an unconscious participation. It is, of course, always possible
to escape it, but most time the viewing has impregnated and changed
us.'[88] Thus, the viewer is a split self, a double, inhabiting a domain akin
to that between the conscious and the unconscious.[89]

The territory of the viewer is perceived by psychoanalytical film theory
as a construct of three main forces at work: regression, primary identification and the concealment of those marks of enunciation, or the fingerprints of the cinematic apparatus.[90] Regression to the infant state, which
is characterized by a false sense of wholeness, where the boundaries
between the pre-symbolic infant and the mother—indeed the rest of the
world—are not realized, is predicated upon the desire of/for the Real.
While watching film, the viewer may allow him- or herself to forget, to
disavow, their subjectivity momentarily and return to a pre-symbolic
state, because of their presupposed immobility—and lack of performance,
therefore—within the cinema theatre. The viewer relishes in this illusory
anonymity or lack of individual identity.

Primary identification is, according to Metz, the process by which the
viewer identifies with the act of looking itself. Because all other subsequent identifications (mainly with characters on the screen) are facili-
tated by this process, the act of identification with the gaze is considered
primary. Giving the viewer the illusion that he or she is everywhere at
once,[91] this identification is possible due to the viewer's identity as a
subject (achieved through the experience of the mirror stage) and
therefore different from the Other. The viewer's subjectivity should be
reinforced by film, since the experience may aid in the realization that he
or she is not mirrored by the screen. Yet, because the viewer identifies
with the gaze and its perceived omnipresence and omnipotence, watching film may reinforce the misrecognition performed though the Imaginary. The images on screen are not part of reality; the screen, although
perceived as a mirror, is not.

The process of primary identification is made possible through the
concealment of marks of enunciation, the concealment of film author-
ship. In order to disarm the viewer and neuter the viewer's suspicions,
film-makers must hide their fingerprints on the roll. Playing between

---

88. Marty, p. 135.
89. Metz, *Psychoanalysis and the Cinema*, pp. 69-74.
90. See Sarup, *Jacques Lacan*, p. 151.
91. Metz, *Psychoanalysis and Cinema*, p. 48.

'enunciation' and 'statement'—Metz's use of *énonciation* and *énoncé* (as the act of speaking/language and the content of speech)—film theory insists that there is a psychoanalytical connection between the film's enunciation and voyeurism (seen as the erotic element of the gaze). The eye replaces, or represents, the phallus here, and pleasure of a sexual nature can be obtained through seeing. Metz argues that the perfect illusion that cinema has the task to create is that the film is the dream that the viewer is having; in other words, that it is the viewer's own desires and creations that are represented on the screen. Thus, cinematic editing techniques—like the invisible editing, of which Hollywood is so proud—hide all or most signs of film production (there are no camera persons and no microphones in sight; one cannot see or hear the director shout, 'cut!', and so on).

While the psychoanalytical construction of the viewer is achieved through the play of regression, primary identification and the conceal-ment of enunciation marks, the creation of subject positions for the viewer is achieved though what is known as 'suture'. While suture is mostly connected to film studies, the term itself was coined by Jacques-Alain Miller, one of Lacan's disciples.[92] Miller defines it,

> Suture names the relation of the subject to the chain of its discourse … it
> figures there as the element which is lacking, in the form of a stand-in. For,
> while there lacking, it is not purely and simply absent. Suture, by extension—
> the general relation of lack to the structure of which it is an element,
> inasmuch as it implies the position of a taking-the-place-of.[93]

One can hear the Lacanian influences in Miller's use of 'lack' and 'absence'. Miller quite clearly links his new concept to the Lacanian interpretation of the *fort–da* game of the child, used by Freud to illustrate the impulse to repeat certain acts and the desire of the child to control the mother, and by Lacan the desire for the mother and her substitution by the object in the child's psyche.[94] Thus, a given signifier offers the

92. The term used by Kaja Silverman, 'Suture: The Cinematic Model', in *idem*, *The Subject of Semiotics* (Oxford: Oxford University Press, 1983), pp. 199-215.

93. Jacques-Alain Miller, 'Suture: Elements of the Logic of the Signifier', *Screen* 18.4 (1977–78), pp. 25-26.

94. The infant throws the cotton reel out of its cot repeatedly in a game that is meant to symbolise the presence and absence of the mother; perhaps this represents the first inkling that the child has of 'absence'. While for Freud this game represented the infant's desire to have control over the mother (and thus bring forth her presence by throwing the cotton reel that she will pick up and give back to the infant), Lacan sees the *fort-da* game as the inception of the infant's entry into the symbolic, when the concept of an absent mother brings about the thought of separation and thus individual subjectivity.

subject entry into the symbolic order but at the price of the absence of that which it signifies; the signifier stands-in for the object that is absent.

The theory of suture was introduced to film studies by the French theoretician Jean-Pierre Oudart, in order to address the frequently considered questions of whether or not there is a cinematic equivalent to language in the literary text, and whether or not there is such a thing as cinematic syntax. The two questions converge over the issue of subject-formation.

As shot relationships are seen by some film theoreticians to be the equivalent of syntactic ones in linguistic discourse, the viewing subject is said to be spoken through interlocking shots. Noel Burch comments,

> Although camera movements, entrances into and exits from frame, com-
> position and so on can all function as devices aiding in the organization of the
> film object ... the shot transition [remains] the basic element [of that
> organization].[95]

Thus, it is through shot relationships that meaning is created and a subject position emerges for the viewer. These shot relationships are perceived differently by different critics. Oudart and Daniel Dayan find the particular shot/reverse shot formation to be synonymous with the process of suture, while Stephen Heath insists that the shot/reverse formation is only one in a larger system underlying shared editing techniques.

The shot/reverse shot formation is in fact a cinematic set in which the second shot transgresses the 180° rule and thus reverses the look to show the field of vision from which the first shot is assumed to have originated. The 180° rule refers to the assumed scope of the camera; because the camera itself is concealed (as a mark of enunciation), it is the understanding that the camera only covers an angle of 180°, thus leaving the other half of the circle unexplored. The 180° rule functions on the basis that a complete camera revolution would be unrealistic, defining a space beyond the scope of the naked eye. By denying the possibility of a 360° camera shot, cinematography reinforces the idea that the camera must not enter the field of vision, fostering the illusory impression of an autonomous creation.

However, the shot/reverse shot is meant to disquiet the viewer, who eventually wonders about whose gaze controls what he or she is seeing. A belief in an independent cinematic creation cannot be sustained for long, but the shot/reverse does manage to perpetuate the illusion. Thus, if shot 1 does not violate the 180° rule and shows an area in which there may or

95.   Noel Burch, *Theory of Film Practice* (trans. R. Lane; New York: Praeger, 1973), p. 12. Cited in Silverman, 'Suture', p. 201.

may not be a human figure, shot 2 locates a spectator character in the remaining half of the circle,[96] implying that shot 1 preceding was seen through the eyes of the person in shot 2. The result is that the marks of enunciation remain veiled, hidden from the scrutiny of the subject's own gaze and absorbed into the fictional dimension of the film. Thus, what the viewer perceives is that his or her gaze is directed by a fictional character (and not the camera). In other words, the subject of the speech seems to be the speaking subject.

Stephen Heath comments against a limiting of suture by too strict an association of it with the shot/reverse shot formation. In his 'Notes on Suture', Heath points out that, statistically, this particular shot relationship is symptomatic of only one third of the shots in a classic Hollywood film.[97] Heath insists that more important is the process of cinematic signification and its relationship to the viewing subject. Thus, the importance of the shot/reverse emerges from its reduplication of the history of the subject. Because shot 1 is watched as an imaginary plenitude unmarked by difference, shot 1 is the locus of a *jouissance* similar to the pre-symbolic pleasure that the infant experiences at catching a first sight of him- or herself in the mirror, imagining for a moment that what reflects back is the ideal image. Following the model of brevity that the infant's experience marks (the child does notice his or her boundaries almost immediately), shot 1 also becomes almost immediately the locus of the subject's suspicions of self-limitation and therefore displeasure. Daniel Dayan explains,

> When the viewer discovers the frame—the first step in reading the film—the triumph of his former *possession* of the image fades out. The viewer discovers that the same camera is hiding things, and therefore distrusts it and the frame itself which he now understands to be arbitrary. He wonders why the frame is what it is. This radically transforms his mode of participation—the unreal space between characters and/or objects is no longer perceived as pleasurable. It is now the space which separates the camera from the characters. The latter have lost their quality of presence. The viewer feels dispossessed of what he is prevented from seeing. He discovers that he is only authorized to see what happens to be in the axis of the gaze of another spectator, who is ghostly or absent.[98]

Oudart calls this spectator the 'Absent One'; the Other, who, as Kaja Silverman observes, has 'all the attributes of the mythically potent

---

96. Although in practice this is not observed scrupulously, of course.

97. Stephen Heath, 'Notes on Suture', *Screen* 18.2 (1977–78), pp. 65-66.

98. Daniel Dayan, 'The Tutor Code of Classical Cinema', in Bill Nichols (ed.), *Movies and Method* (Berkley, CA: University of California Press), p. 448.

symbolic father: potency, knowledge, transcendental vision, self-suffi-
ciency, and discursive power'.[99] However, this speaking subject is none
other than the cinematic apparatus. Yet, suddenly aware of his or her
limitations, the viewing subject perceives him- or herself as lacking
everything that the Other appears to have. This perception changes into
a desire to see more, fuelled by the same desire for the Real experienced
in infancy, at the mirror-stage.

Cinematic signification depends entirely on the moment of displeasure, for Oudart. In other words, the shot becomes a signifier only with the
disruption of imaginary plenitude. The suture thus is the complex chain
of signification introduced 'in place of that lack which can never be made
good, suturing over the wound of castration with narrative'.[100] As the gaze
within fiction conceals the controlling gaze outside that fiction, 'a benign
other steps in and obscures the presence of the coercive and castrating
Other'.[101] Thus, the subject of speech is introduced as the speaking subject. Suture is successful when the viewing subject identifies with the
fictional spectator, when the subject allows the fictional subject (the
subject of speech) to stand-in for him or her.

Suture, of course, is about stitching, bringing together cuts that are
meant to form one piece. The stitching line stands-in for the missing
pieces. Thus, in film the camera is meant to show the audience stitched
cuts in order to exercise its pull. The cut is a prime agency of disclosure,
that which divides one shot from the next. The viewing subject is shown
only enough to imply that there is more, which becomes the object of
desire. The absence of the excluded shots is that upon which cinematic
significance is predicated. Absence is that which transforms one shot into
the signifier of the next and the signified of the preceding one. Through
cuts and negations the cinematic discourse is established as the only valid
discourse. Silverman observes, 'This castrating coherence, this definition
of a discursive position for the viewing subject which necessitates not
only its loss of being, but the repudiation of alternative discourses, is one
of the chief aims of the system of suture'.[102] Therefore, for the theoreticians of suture, the viewing subjects desire the fictional dimension of
film, allowing themselves to be spoken through the film's discourse,
because they wish for a re-enactment of their entry into the Symbolic
order. 'We want suture so badly', Silverman exclaims, 'that we'll take it

99. Silverman, *The Subject of Semiotics*, p. 79.
100. Silverman, *The Subject of Semiotics*, p. 79.
101. Silverman, *The Subject of Semiotics*, p. 79.
102. Silverman, *The Subject of Semiotics*, p. 80.

at any price, even with the fullest knowledge of what it entails—passive insertions into pre-existing discursive positions (both mythically potent and mythically impotent); threatened losses and false recoveries; and subordination to the castrating gaze of a symbolic Other'.[103]

Suture, therefore, represents the moment of 'an intersection', as Heath would have it,[104] where the subject is stitched into the flow of discourses. Film cannot in and of itself create a reading that fixes the subject. Valerie Walkerdine sees the interplay between subject positions and filmic representations as transforming the process of viewing into a point of dynamic intersection, or 'the production of a new sign articulated through the plays of significance of the film and those which already articulate the subject'.[105] Identities are points of temporary attachment to the subject positions that discursive practices construct for us.[106] Stuart Hall perceives suture as an *articulation* that emphasizes identification, because the subject invests in the subject position onto which he or she is sutured.[107] Both the visual as well as the narrative filmic discourse participate in the process of identification.

Feminist writing on the subject of identification—primarily in connection to gender identities—has taken two opposing routes, interestingly. One such route is the path paved by Laura Mulvey's 1975 article 'Visual Pleasure and Narrative Cinema',[108] which introduced the ideas of woman as image and man as bearer of the look. Followers of that approach to film criticism are still very suspicious of any kind of feminine role models, heroines or feminine images of identification. Mulvey's own films[109] as well as her theoretical writings have attacked visual pleasure and supported a rejection of conventionally popular representations, not merely due to the filmic constructions of female images but also due to the processes of identification presented to the viewing subjects. Identification is thus perceived as a 'cultural process complicit with the reproduction of

---

103.   Silverman, *The Subject of Semiotics*, p. 85.

104.   Stephen Heath, *Questions of Cinema* (Basingstoke: Macmillan, 1981), p. 106.

105.   Valerie Walkerdine, 'Video Replay: Families, Films and Fantasy', in V. Burgin *et al.* (eds.), *Formations of Fantasy* (London: Routledge, 1986), pp. 167-99.

106.   Stuart Hall, 'Introduction: Who Needs Identity?', in Stuart Hall and Paul du Gay (eds.), *Questions of Cultural Identity* (London: Sage Publications, 1996), pp. 1-17 (6).

107.   Hall, 'Who Needs Identity?', p. 6.

108.   Laura Mulvey, 'Visual Pleasure and Narrative Cinema', *Screen* 16.3 (1975), pp. 6-18.

109.   For example, *Amy!* (1980).

dominant culture by reinforcing patriarchal forms of identity'.[110] Anne
Freidberg explains,

> Identification can only be made through recognition, and all recognition is
> itself an implicit confirmation of an existing form. The institutional sanction
> of stars as ego ideals operates to establish normative figures. Identification
> enforces a collapse of the subject onto the normative demands for sameness,
> which, under patriarchy, is always male.[111]

The woman of cinematic discourse is seen as perpetuating the Law of the
Father within the viewing woman.[112]

Different from those marching on this path of suspicion, some feminist
cultural theoreticians have endeavoured to avoid such harsh criticism
and thus salvage the process of identification as possibly the means of
empowerment within certain levels of consumption of popular culture.
This position is exemplified by Valerie Walkerdine's 1986 article 'Video
Replay: Families, Films and Fantasies', which argues that identification
can be a rather desirable element of cultural development.[113] In her article she provides an analysis of the means by which different members of a
working-class family read *Rocky II*, and she concludes that their reading
had the potential of developing fighting, or rebellious attitudes that could
focus on the dominant system of their experience. Walkerdine suggests
that gender differences do influence the process of identification, and
resistance to prescribed identities is made possible through identification.

Thus, while Mulvey's school would criticize identification of any kind
for its perpetuating sameness, fixity and the confirmation of existing
identities, Walkerdine's take would see potential redeeming qualities in
the process of identification as an empowering tool, encouraging resistance. These two perspectives converge, however, over accepting the
psychoanalytical dimension as formative of their understanding of identification in the visual media.[114]

---

110.   Jackie Stacey, 'Feminine Fascinations: Forms of Identification in Star-Audience Relations', in Christine Gledhill (ed.), *Stardom: Industry of Desire* (London:
Routledge, 1991), pp. 141-63.
111.   Anne Freidberg, 'Identification and the Star: A Refusal of Difference', in
Christine Gledhill (ed.), *Star Signs* (London: BFI Publishing, 1982), p. 50.
112.   For an analysis of audience–star relations see Andre Tudor, *Image and Influence: Studies in the Sociology of Film* (London: Allen & Unwin, 1974) and Stacey,
'Feminine Fascinations'.
113.   Walkerdine, 'Video Replay'.
114.   For detailed psychoanalytical accounts of the psychic processes of identification see, for example, Rose, *Sexuality in the Field of Vision*; Mary Anne Doane, *The
Desire to Desire: The Woman's Film of the 1940s* (Bloomington: Indiana University Press,

I will come back to issues pertaining to the relationship between feminism and cinema later, but let us look now at the way Lacan perceives the play between authority and subjectivity, that is, at the Law and Name of the Father and the phallus.

The Name of the Father and the Phallus

Within the Symbolic Order, or language, it is the Name of the Father—associated with the Law of the Father and the phallus—that holds prime position. According to Lacan, the development of the Oedipal drama depends on the emphasis that castration is given, thus by being linked strongly with the concept of paternal law.

Lacan focuses on the nature of the subject's being by establishing the subject's primal desire for, and dependence on, the Other. The Other can be seen as the subject's 'guarantor' of existence. The Other is the place where the subject's birth takes place. The role of the mother as the Other is explained through the dyadic mother-infant relationship: she become the M-Other, who creates the subject, nurses and affirms the child in his or her existence. Yet, the mother herself is a subject with a lack-of-being, not whole, therefore, and thus insufficient.

According to Lacan, the lack that the child perceives in the mother is signified by the phallus. The child desires to be the phallus, in order to complete the mother; or rather, the child identifies with the phallus, perceived as the object lacking to, and desired by, the mother. The role of the father, his categorical 'no', is that of forbidding and successfully stopping the imaginary *jouissance*, this symbiosis between the child and the mother. The Law of the Father is the law of symbolic castration, which demands that the mother is castrated and remains so, in order to desire the Father's phallus.

Lacan sees the phallus not only as representative of the authority or/and the Law of the Father, but also as the signifier of sexual difference. Lacan borrows the myth of Aristophanes from Plato's *Symposium* when he calls humans 'sexed partial beings'. As in the myth, we are all looking for that which, we imagine, complements or completes us; in Lacanian terms, for that part of us which is lost and without which we are partial and not complete sexual beings. As signifier of sexual difference, the phallus takes the position of the privileged signifier.[115]

1987); Teresa de Lauretis, *Alice Doesn't: Feminism, Semiotics, Cinema* (London: Macmillan, 1984).

115. Jacques Lacan, 'La signification du phallus', in Jacques Lacan, *Ecrits* (Paris: Seuil, 1966), p. 692; also as 'The Signification of the Phallus', p. 287; and 'The Meaning of the Phallus', in Rose and Mitchell (eds.), *Feminine Sexuality*, p. 82.

There is considerable controversy over the meaning of the phallus. While some critics believe the claim that the phallus is supposedly neutral, many others fail to concur. Lacan himself is not particularly helpful, either. On the one hand, he makes quite a clear statement differentiating the phallus from the penis: 'The phallus in Freudian doctrine is not a fantasy ... Nor is it as such an object ... It is even less the organ, penis or clitoris, which it symbolizes.'[116] Thus, the phallus can easily take on the symbolization of either penis or clitoris, which may render it neutral. However, Lacan also refers in his writings to 'a real phallus' when seemingly referring to a penis: 'This ordeal of the desire of the Other, clinical experience shows us that it is not decisive inasmuch as the subject there learns whether he himself has or does not have a real phallus, but inasmuch as he learns that the mother does not have it'.[117] This statement throws a great deal of confusion over the matter, as quite clearly the phallus does not symbolize the mother's clitoris here. Even in their guide to reading *Ecrits*, John Muller and William Richardson state that 'the term "phallus" ... assumes a new ambiguity, oscillating as it does between its role as signifier and its role as real or imagined organ'.[118] Of course, Lacan could have used a different term for his privileged signifier, particularly in light of his own focus on the Symbolic Order. Perhaps Lacan, too, is not a master in his own house, not master of language; instead, he is tortured by it.

Interestingly, Lacan not only falls prey [unconsciously?] to the allures of metonymy (penis–phallus), he also follows his own given cultural context when developing his theories. The family unit is seen as the norm:

> The primordial law is therefore that which in regulating marriage ties superimposes the kingdom of culture on that of a nature abandoned to the law of mating. The prohibition of incest is merely its subjective pivot ... This law, then, is revealed clearly enough as identical with an order of language. For without kinship nominations, no power is capable of instituting the order of preferences and taboos that bind and weave the yarn of lineage through succeeding generations. And it is indeed the confusion of generations which, in the Bible as in all traditional laws, is accused as being the abomination of the Word (*verbe*) and the desolation of the sinner.[119]

---

116.   Lacan, 'La signification du phallus', p. 690; 'The Signification of the Phallus', p. 285; 'The Meaning of the Phallus', p. 79.

117.   Lacan, 'La signification du phallus', p. 693; 'The Signification of the Phallus', p. 289; 'The Meaning of the Phallus', p. 83.

118.   John P. Muller and William J. Richardson, *Lacan and Language: A Reader's Guide to Ecrits* (New York: International Universities Press, 1982), p. 337.

119.   Lacan, 'The Symbolic Order', p. 185.

In aid to the symbolic function within the Symbolic Order comes the Name of the Father, or the proper name of the family unit. In order for the family to survive generation after generation, in order to ensure the survival of the Name of the Father, the Law of the Father is imposed. Thus, paraphrasing Rabelais, Lacan explains that by securing the Name of the Father, 'the voyage on which wives and goods are embarked will bring back to their point of departure in a never-failing cycle other women and other goods, all carrying an identical entity'.[120] This identical entity is meant to be what Lévi-Strauss calls a zero-symbol (*symbole zéro*),[121] the point where the sacred, inviolable Great Debt towards the symbolic function, towards perpetuating the Name of the Father in this case—and Lacan identifies it with 'the sacred *hau* or the omnipresent *mana*'—is fulfilled and passed on to the next generation in the same instance.

Lacan's position towards the family, sexuality and the Name and Law of the Father has attracted different reactions from feminist critics. Although not an easy task, some have categorized these responses into two camps.[122] The Father's 'dutiful daughters' defend Lacan and Freud and their take on the Oedipus complex and castration and the role of the phallus as supreme signifier. This faction includes, for instance, Barbara Johnson, Ellie Ragland-Sullivan, Monique Plaza, Catherine Clément, Juliet Mitchell, and, to some extent, Jane Gallop. This group support Lacan against the accusations of phallocentrism by arguing that, in Lacanian terms, subjectivity and sexuality are cultural constructs and the product of nature or development; the mirror stage initiates the Oedipal drama, which explains the 'psychological dimensions of the social construction of subjectivity'.[123] Outside his or her cultural context, the child has no determinate subjectivity or sexuality. The phallus is only the term around which the social construction of *both* sexes is orientated. The phallus is a neutral signifier, affecting both sexes equally, representing lack and law for both, and thus subjecting them both to the symbolic. The phallus is *necessary*.

The other group of feminist critics, whose take on Lacanian psychoanalysis is quite different, is that of the 'Mother's daughters'. These critics

---

120.   Lacan, 'The Symbolic Order', p. 186.

121.   See Claude Lévi-Strauss, *The Elementary Structures of Kinship* (trans. James Harle Bell, John Richard von Sturmer and Rodney Needham; Boston: Beacon Press, 1969).

122.   See, for example, Sarup, *Jacques Lacan*, pp. 131-32; and Elizabeth Grosz, *Jacques Lacan: A Feminist Introduction* (London: Routledge, 1990), pp. 140-50.

123.   Grosz, *Jacques Lacan*, p. 142.

move away from the theories of Freud and Lacan and reject the primacy of the role of the Father and phallus in the Symbolic Order. This second faction numbers among its members thinkers like Luce Irigaray, who is possibly the clearest example, Hélène Cixous and Julia Kristeva.[124] More about this group next.

124.　　Kristeva is sometimes categorised as a Father's 'dutiful daughter'. See the difference between the categorising of Sarup and Grosz, for instance. Even more strange is that Jane Gallop accuses Luce Irigaray of being a Father's 'dutiful daughter', which is an interesting though quite debatable position.

4

THE 'I'S OF THE FEMININE AND THE VEILED WORD

Post-Lacanian Continental Feminisms

Feminism's affinity with psychoanalysis rests above all … with this recognition
that there is resistance to identity which lies at the very heart of psychic life

—*Jacqueline Rose*[1]

Feminist theory remains fascinated by Lacan's work, although reactions
to them, as I have mentioned, are divided. Much can be said in favour of
Lacan. His work has been hailed as a much needed 'counterbalance to
the naturalisms, humanisms, essentialisms, etc., so common in theories of
human subjectivity'.[2] His work on the unconscious and rejection of ego-
and object-relations psychologies give Freudian theories a more attractive
hue for feminist thought. Lacan's ideas bring into the light concepts that
are generally ignored, like subjectivity/identity, desire, discursive disruption, reading and interpretation, which play important roles within
feminism. It is with Lacanian psychoanalysis that the 'I' is perceived as a
cultural, socio-linguistic construct, and no longer as a biologically pre-
ordained, pre-given and unified subject. Furthermore, Lacanian psychoanalysis ushered in sexuality as a legitimized academic discourse. At the
core of Lacan's theories lies the idea that, in order to become 'I', the
subject must take on the sexualized position, or identify with the gendered role, assigned to the subject by society. This and the resulting concept of 'resistance to prescribed identities' is what feminism welcomes.

Not everything within Freudian and Lacanian psychoanalysis is so
easily accepted, however, and now I shall try to outline briefly the individual positions of the 'Mother's daughters' before turning to feminine
identity and John's Prologue.

---

1. Jacqueline Rose, cited by Valerie Walkerdine, 'One Day my Prince Will Come:
Young Girls and Preparation for Adult Sexuality', in A. McRobbie and M. Nava (eds.),
Gender and Generation (London: Macmillan, 1984), p. 181.
2. See further Grosz, *Jacques Lacan*, p. 145.

Julia Kristeva

Julia Kristeva and Luce Irigaray share a commitment to Lacan's take on the primacy of language in psychical life, his anti-humanism and his resolute theory of the sexualized role of the subject within the symbolic. They emerge from similar backgrounds (Irigaray influenced by Lacan's own seminars) and are both psychoanalysts. The focus of their work is to encourage the development of analysis that focuses on the production of sexualized identities. Furthermore, they both try to cover areas that Freud's and Lacan's theories overlook, areas that have much to do with the pre-Oedipal phase: in Kristeva's case, the relationship between the mother and the child, and for Irigaray, that between the mother and the daughter.[3] However, they also resist certain aspects of Lacanian psychoanalysis, and they do that somewhat differently.

Julia Kristeva is a literary theorist and semiologist, and as such she focuses on texts and discourses and the exchanges between transgressive discourses and subjectivity, or the psycho-sexual development. The subject is, for Kristeva, the speaking subject, yet this subject is divided and decentred, never fixed, a subject in process, or *sujet en procès*. While relying largely on Lacan's understanding of the Symbolic, Kristeva refines its role by introducing the Semiotic:

> We shall call *symbolic* the logical and syntactic functioning of language and everything which, in translinguistic practices is assimilable to the system of language proper. The term *semiotic*, on the other hand, will be used to mean: in the first place, what can be hypothetically posited as preceding the imposition of language, in other words, the already given arrangement of the drives in the form of facilitations in the form of rhythms, intonations and lexical, syntactic and rhetorical transformations. If the *symbolic* established the limits and unity of a signifying practice, the *semiotic* registers in that practice the effect of that which cannot be pinned down as sign, whether signifier or signified.[4]

Kristeva distinguishes between the symbolic as governing order and the semiotic as the pre-lingual, repressed and disruptive pool of energy within the child's body. Kristeva borrows elements from Melanie Klein's work on the instinctual economy of infancy, so one can imagine the semiotic in the pre-verbal sounds—echolalia and vocalic and intonational differences—cries and gestures of the infant. In the discourses of the adult the semiotic is expressed by prosody, musicality, poetry, 'paragrams'

---

3. See the excellent analysis of Kristeva and Irigaray that Elizabeth Grosz offers in her *Jacques Lacan*.

4. Julia Kristeva, 'Signifying Practice and Mode of Production', *Edinburgh Review* 1 (1976), pp. 65-78 (68).

(Saussure's term, which Kristeva prefers to 'anagrams'), the no-sense of sense, laughter.

The semiotic expresses itself through interruptions of the symbolic, as pulsating, uncontrollable excess. Kristeva's interest in the semiotic manifests itself in her fascination with avant-garde texts, namely works by Mallarmé, Lautréamont, Artaud, Schoenberg, Joyce, Stockhausen, Cage, Bellini and others.[5] Irrespective of their genre—poetic, novelistic, musical, dramatic, visual—these texts disturb because of their unique ability to express the semiotic more freely than generally achievable within the conventional symbolic representational systems. Kristeva argues that the symbolic relates directly to a certain moral code established by the structures of human relations, and that literary texts are perfect examples of symbolic products. The textual elements that do dance to the tune of the symbolic fiddle pertain to what Kristeva calls 'phenotext', to be distinguished from 'genotext', or the textual traces of semiotic modalities. The genotext is characterized therefore by *le mystère dans les lettres*, the mysterious, enigmatic, anterior, musical and rhythmical between the lines.

The symbolic is seen, therefore, as an 'order superimposed on the semiotic', that which regulates libidinal energies and transforms them into signifying items, discourses and practices.[6] This process, this control, is not altogether a smooth and easy one. According to Kristeva, there are thus privileged moments, when the semiotic erupts and overflows its symbolic boundaries, and 'madness, holiness and poetry' form as subversive drives.[7] The subject is seen as external to the engendering of meaning and the significance of the genotext, and remains therefore almost exclusively symbolic. Kristeva notes, 'being neither structured nor structuring, the genotext does not know the subject. Exterior to the subject, it is not even its nihilist negative.'[8] Thus the 'I' of the subject is no longer seen as being divided into mind and body but as producing the body-as-*jouissance*,

---

5. Kristeva is highly criticised over her choice of writers, for they are all male. Elizabeth Grosz and Gayatri Chakrovorty Spivak in particular accuse Kristeva for being 'anti-feminist' because of her interest in the male avant-garde. See Elizabeth Grosz, 'Philosophy, Subjectivity and the Body: Kristeva and Irigaray', in Carole Pateman and Elizabeth Grosz (eds.), *Feminist Challenges: Social and Political Theory* (Sydney: Allen & Unwin, 1986), pp. 125-44; *idem*, *Sexual Subversions* (Sydney: Allen & Unwin, 1989); Gayatri Chakrovorty Spivak, 'French Feminism in an International Frame', *Yale French Studies* 62 (1981), pp. 159-79.

6. Julia Kristeva, *The Revolution in Poetic Language* (New York: Columbia University Press, 1984), p. 47.

7. Julia Kristeva, 'Signifying Practice and Mode of Production', p. 64.

8. Julia Kristeva, 'L'engendrement de la formule', p. 284, cited in John Lechte, *Julia Kristeva* (London: Routledge, 1990), p. 128.

the material, unrepresentable support of language; the body-as-*jouissance* becomes linked with the semiotic. 'This "I" has one possible place: that of the main axis which pulverizes every body thinkable by a narcissistic and metaphysical subject.'[9] In other words, the body-as-*jouissance* becomes the locus of the *chora*.

The *chora* is rather difficult to describe, since it is meant to exist beyond representation. As John Lechte puts it, 'To speak about the *chora* at all is paradoxical, given that to do so is to give it a place in the symbolic'.[10] Kristeva explains the *chora* as 'a nonexpressive totality formed by the drives and their stases in a motility that is as full of movement as it is regulated ... [an] extremely provisional articulation constituted by movements and their ephemeral stases'.[11] Thus, the *chora* is the semiotic precursor to language, the unconscious and pre-Oedipal organization of drives. However, Kristeva sees the *chora* as closely associated with the feminine in disrupting the Name of the Father and the Symbolic. Thus, the *chora* is linked to the poetic in language, and Kristeva perceives poetry as a means to repudiate the 'flight into madness'.[12] It is the *signifiance* that bridges the masculine symbolic and the feminine semiotic/ poetic (which is perceived as marginalized).

Most importantly, Kristeva understands the *chora* as closely associated with the mother's body. In fact, as Lechte observes, the 'mother' and the 'body' as such go together for Kristeva.[13] The body of the mother becomes connotative of the pre-symbolic, the pre-Oedipal, and, therefore, the semiotic. Kristeva does use Lacan's mirror stage in explaining the development of the subject, and so the mother and the *chora* are linked in their suppression by the Father and the Symbolic. However, the pre-Oedipal mother for Kristeva (as much as for Freud, in fact) does not represent the feminine, for it does not become a sexed object until the child realizes the difference between the mother and the father as sexual. The semiotic, therefore, is not to be associated with the feminine. The body of the mother becomes the object of desire, yet when focused upon, its materiality is part of the symbolic, even though elements such as laughter, intonation and timbre of voice, the ephemeral movements and gestures of the body—elements upon which art focuses—fall within the scope of the semiotic. Everything that can be represented, imagined, conceptualized,

9. Kristeva, 'L'engendrement de la formule', pp. 351-52; cited in Lechte, *Julia Kristeva*, p. 128.
10. Lechte, *Julia Kristeva*, p. 128.
11. Kristeva, *Revolution*, p. 25.
12. Kristeva, *Revolution*, pp. 81-84 (82).
13. Lechte, *Julia Kristeva*, p. 129.

explained and regulated is part of the symbolic, but there are small tones and gestures that are easily overlooked due to the over-powering nature of linguistic communication.

Within the realm of the mother, Mary, the Mother of Christ, holds for Kristeva a certain fascination. She sees her as inspiring a level of 'baroqueness' in art, namely a plethora of signs, expressed through 'metaphors of nonspeech, a "semiotics" that linguistic communication does not account for'.[14] Kristeva's theory on the symbolic and the semiotic displaces Lacan's distinction between the symbolic and the imaginary. Where Lacan places a great deal of emphasis on the verbal and the visual, Kristeva opens the stage for other means of communication and all senses. Kristeva allows for a certain continuity between the semiotic and the symbolic, whereas Lacan would insist on a clear separation of the symbolic and the imaginary.

As Lacan would have it, and as a *sujet en procès*, 'woman' for Kristeva does not exist. That is, there is no such homogenous, centred entity. So woman becomes 'that which cannot be represented, that which is not spoken, that which remains outside naming and ideologies'. Instead Kristeva focuses on 'femininity', which she perceives as 'that which is marginalized by the patriarchal symbolic order'. Kristeva, therefore, favours an understanding of femininity that is expressed artistically, and which 'would have as many "feminines" as there are women'.[15] That is why she resists the suggestion of an *écriture féminine*, highlighting the risk that feminine writing would return to a concept of 'essential/inherent femininity', which does not exist. For her, women cannot truly write (other than fantasies that take the place of a real family), because women are bound to their body (and its rhythms). She says,

> In women's writing, language seems to be seen from a foreign land; it is seen from the point of view of an asymbolic, spastic body ... Estranged from language, women are visionaries, dancers who suffer as they speak.[16]

Hence Kristeva's interest in male texts, something that has attracted much criticism from fellow feminists. Though fighting for the Mother, Kristeva seems rather close to the Father and his Language/Law/Symbolic.

14. Julia Kristeva, *Histoires d'amour* (Paris: Denoel, 1983); ET: *Tales of Love* (trans. Leon S. Roudiez; New York: Columbia University Press, 1987), p. 249.

15. Toril Moi, *Sexual/Textual Politics: Feminist Literary Theory* (London: Methuen, 1985), p. 169.

16. Julia Kristeva, 'Interview—1974', *m/f* 5/6 (1974), p. 166. Cited in Grosz, *Jacques Lacan*, p. 165.

Luce Irigaray

The advocates of *écriture féminine* are Hélène Cixous (who coined the term) and Luce Irigaray, and they are more openly against Freudian and Lacanian psychoanalysis than Kristeva. So much so that one of them, namely Irigaray, was dismissed by Lacan himself (from *Ecole Freudienne*) after the publication of her doctoral dissertation, *Speculum of the Other Woman*, in 1974.

While Irigaray also defines femininity—and feminism, for that matter—as plural and polymorphous[17] as women themselves are, she does not share paths with Kristeva. Irigaray sees 'woman' as a patriarchal construct, co-opted into the male/female oppositions within metaphysics. Woman is thus exiled and excluded from language, or the symbolic order (which belongs to the Father), unable to express the feminine, whatever form it may take. Therefore, by proposing feminine speech, Irigaray tries to allow for a female symbolic, a 'home' for women. She does not suggest a *new* language for women, but rather a new *syntax*, or the means by which women could appropriate systems of meaning and signification that already exist; a syntax that would *blur*, or destabilize—through 'disruptive excess'—the oppositional boundaries and hierarchical structures within phallocentric texts.[18] So, *écriture féminine* for Irigaray means *parler-femme*, or speaking/writing *woman* (into being) or speaking/writing *as woman*.

Analytically, Irigaray relates the idea that some women do not achieve a full separation from the mother (a matter of clinical evidence) to the concept that women lack individuation; they form relationships within which they themselves are not clearly contoured (the presence of the mother threatens the boundaries of self). Furthermore, women are not individuated metaphysically; because of the Freudian theory of sexual difference (which is highly influenced by the visible difference between the sexes, namely that man has an obvious sexual organ, while woman has not), woman appears as absence. Irigaray believes that Freud was subject to his cultural context, in which misogynist attitudes were rife. Woman is conceived within that discourse as castrated, the negative mirrored image of man, the dark continent, man's other. So, for Irigaray, the entire culture of the West is monosexual, by which she means that women are perceived as 'lesser men', defective through their being castrated.

17. Luce Irigaray, *This Sex Which Is Not One* (trans. Catherine Porter and Carolyn Burke; Ithaca, NY: Cornell University Press, 1985), p. 164.
18. Irigaray, *This Sex Which Is Not One*, pp. 77-78.

Furthermore, all that appears to be neutral or universal in society, like the discourse of philosophy or of science, is in fact gendered. Irigaray insists that it is all the discourse of the male subject. The reason why this state of affairs is not challenged is the very reason that sustains it: the absence of a female discourse. Since *parler n'est jamais neuter*, one should pursue an openly *sexuate* discourse. Hence her case for *parler-femme* and thus speaking/writing the body, or creating for women 'that house of language [*langue*] which for man even constitutes a substitute for his home in a body'.[19]

Irigaray aims to facilitate through the *parler-femme* the coming-to-be of the woman-as-subject in language. That is not easily achieved, however (hence Irigaray's 'struggles'), because women find it very difficult to perceive themselves as subjects. At the Oedipal stage, the crux of the identity-formation process, the daughters learn to identify with their mothers, who become the other, the object. Because mothers and daughters share the same sex, Irigaray maintains that daughters will forever consider themselves objects rather than subjects, even when sporting a pseudo-subjectivity within the symbolic.[20] The entry into language offers women a choice between remaining (with the mother) outside signification and accepting the patriarchal genealogy, in which her *object*-position is already established. Thus, the woman's economy is that of the between subjects and not that of the subject-object relation, in which the woman is directly in intersubjectivity with the mother.[21] Irigaray wishes to create a medium through which women can enter language as subject and by which female identification with the mother is possible without objectifying them:

> It is necessary for a woman to be able to speak her identity in words, in images, and in symbols within this intersubjectivity with her mother, then with other women, in order to enter a relation with men that is not destructive.[22]

Women need to represent their difference. The link between their subjectivity and language can be achieved through a different syntax, within which women are not the universal predicate. If Kristeva's subject was the subject-in-process, for Irigaray there is the subject-in-dialogue; that is the concept that women achieve an identity through dialogue with the other (women as well as men) once they have a language house of their

---

19.   Luce Irigaray, *An Ethics of Sexual Difference* (trans. Carolyn Burke and Gillian C. Gill; London: Athlone Press, 1993), p. 105.
20.   Luce Irigaray, *Sexes et parentés* (Paris: Minuit, 1987), p. 210.
21.   Irigaray, *Sexes et parentés*, p. 211.
22.   Irigaray, *Sexes et parentés*, p. 211.

own. The two poles of dialogue for Irigaray are the 'I' and the 'you', and so it is imperative that women also acquire an 'I' that is not limited to the monological and monosexual characteristics of the language of men.

The female imaginary, however, is understood by Irigaray as linked to the unconscious, mobile and fluid, 'a proper(ty) that is never fixed in the possible-to-self of some form or another. It is always fluid'.[23] It is for this reason that the female imaginary does not subject itself to the male logic of identity, which requires a sense of stability, of oneness, and which is phallomorphic, that is, constructed on the premise of one organ, the phallus. Thus, considering the female sexual organs, which know 'the contact of at least two (lips) which keeps woman in touch with herself',[24] Irigaray suggests that female individuation is absent, for woman 'is neither one nor two'.[25] So, like the womb, the maternal/feminine is conceived as supporting all possibilities of determining identity, already a split self, as the two lips. Furthermore, woman's identity is *in-fini*, both infinite and unfinished. This concept of fluid, ever-changing, female identity is also shared by Hélène Cixous.

Hélène Cixous

Cixous and Irigaray have a lot in common. Cixous coined the term *écriture féminine* in her 1975 'Le rire de la Méduse' ('The Laugh of the Medusa'). Like Irigaray with her *parler-femme*, Cixous suggests *écriture féminine* as means for women's identity, which is itself multiple and fluid. They both agree that 'woman' is a cultural construct, systematically exiled to the margins of narrative and history, and Cixous sees this exclusion reinforced by myth, legend and literature.

Influenced by Derrida, Cixous' work underlines the concept that women's oppression is predicated in language through binary oppositions that favour patriarchy and its symbolic system of representation. Thus, activity/passivity, day/night, sun/moon, culture/nature, head/emotions, father/mother, logos/pathos and so on, perpetuate the negative and powerless female position, always associated with the secondary opposites (passivity, nature, emotions and so on). Woman does not exist unless she is passive. Cixous is critical of this oppression, which is perceived as denying or repressing difference, colonizing the other.

Therefore, Cixous wishes to promote a change in the means of representation that are co-existent with patriarchy, and she suggests elements

23. Irigaray, *This Sex Which Is Not One*, p. 79.
24. Irigaray, *This Sex Which Is Not One*, p. 26.
25. Irigaray, *This Sex Which Is Not One*, p. 26.

that instead celebrate sexual difference and move away from the phallo-morphic 'oneness'. Unavoidably, the body plays an important role in Cixous' understanding of female subject-formation. As Irigaray conceives corporeal morphological elements into her concept of feminine syntax, so Cixous advocates ambivalent and ambiguous, bisexual *jouissance* as the key to feminine writing.

For Cixous, *écriture féminine* is not just woman's. Yet, while it is poten-tially achievable by men also, Cixous believes that women are simply closer to a certain economy of the gift (the giving of themselves) that is presupposed by *écriture féminine* and to the pre-symbolic experience with the mother. Cixous understands *écriture féminine* as

> a place ... which is not economically or politically indebted to all the vileness and compromise. This is not obliged to reproduce the system. That is writing. If there is somewhere else that can escape the infernal repetition, it lies in that direction, where *it* writes itself, where *it* dreams, where *it* invents new worlds.[26]

It is the value of new experiences, unique experiences to women that Cixous appreciates.

Sexual difference is important for Cixous not because of its anatomical characteristics *per se*, but because it influences the determining of gender behaviour and its capacity to sustain the existing system. However, as sexuality is living, an exchange of experience may help find alternative ways of understanding the world. Cixous argues that women's experiences (many of which pertain to the body, like pregnancy and childbirth) can fashion new and radically different means of relating to the other. Thus,

> It is not only a question of the feminine body's extra resource, this specific power to produce some thing of which her flesh is the locus, not only a ques-tion of a transformation of rhythms, exchanges, of relationship to space, of the whole perceptive system ... It is also the experience of a 'bond' with the other, all that comes through in the metaphor of bringing into the world ... There is a bond between woman's libidinal economy—her jouissance, the feminine Imaginary—and her way of self-constituting a subjectivity that splits apart without regret.[27]

Since feminine writing gives voice to new means of relation and expres-sion, to new ways of perceiving the world, it is in this sense that Cixous considers feminine writing as revolutionary. She envisages this writing as disrupting the binary logic of patriarchal and phallocratic order and thus bearing cultural, social and political results.

26. Hélène Cixous, *The Newly Born Woman* (trans. Betsy Wing; Minneapolis: Minnesota University Press, 1986), p. 72. Italics in original.
27. Cixous, *The Newly Born Woman*, p. 90.

Like Kristeva and Irigaray, Cixous is greatly interested in literature. She has been influenced by Kafka, Shakespeare, Joyce, Dostoevsky, and others, while her strongest literary influence remains the Brazilian writer Clarice Lispector. Cixous sees in Lispector's texts 'a return of the living, a dazzling revaluation of primary values', where one finds not the economy of opposition but the 'economy of the gift. And of love. Of how to give.'[28] Philosophically, Cixous acknowledges a great debt to Derrida:

> Derridian deconstruction will have been the greatest ethical critical warning gesture or our time. Careful! Let us not be the dupe of logocentric authority. We are not 'pure' I. A gesture dictated by humility, and which recalls us to humility.[29]

Like Kristeva and Irigaray, Cixous insists on the idea of the multiple, fluid, decentred I, on a concept of identity not predicated on the premise of (male) oneness and unity, but the correspondence between the 'I' and 'play', the *Je* and *jeu*, the terrain of female creativity.

I will return later for a closer look at the individual types of feminisms that these Post-Lacanian thinkers adopt when reading John's Prologue in relation to feminine identity. It is quite interesting to note, however, that, whether they kick him or embrace him, feminists still want to have a relationship with Lacan. He is quite a seducer, as Elizabeth Grosz notes,[30] quite a 'ladies' man'. Lacan embodies both the Law and the delinquent. In trying to succeed where Freud failed, namely in understanding women's desires, Lacan can be perceived as both phallocentric and anti-phallic. Jane Gallop writes,

> Feminists have been hard on the ladies' man, presuming that his intentions are strictly dishonourable. They're right. But should not feminism be working to undo the reign of honour, and all those virile virtues? In as much as feminists are hard on anyone, they betray an inappropriate (which is to say, all too appropriate and proper) phallicization ... [Lacan] is no mere father figure out to purvey the truth of his authority; he also comes out seeking his pleasure in a relation that the phallocentric universe does not circumscribe. To designate Lacan at his most stimulating and forceful is to call him something more than just phallocentric. He is also phallocentric. Or, in more pointed language, he is a prick.[31]

28. Taken from a transcript of 'Au bon plaisir d'Hélène Cixous', broadcast in 1987. Trans. Deborah Jenson, 'At Hélène Cixous' Pleasure', cited by Susan Sellers (ed.), *The Hélène Cixous Reader* (London: Routledge, 1994), p. xxx.

29. Hélène Cixous, 'Preface', in Sellers (ed.) *The Hélène Cixous Reader*, pp. xv-xxiii (xviii).

30. Grosz, *Jacques Lacan*, p. 184.

31. Jane Gallop, 'Nurse Freud: Class Struggle in the Family', *Hecate* 3.1 (1982), pp. 35-36.

It is because Lacan is perceived in an ambivalent light—as both phallus and prick, authority and delinquency—that he has managed to captivate and infuriate feminists for quite some time now.

A Veil of One's Own? Feminine Identity, John's Prologue and The Pillow Book

Considering self-disclosure/knowing and un-veiling, Derrida writes, 'There's no chance of ... belonging to oneself enough ... and of succeeding in turning such a gesture toward oneself. You'll end up in imminence—and the un-veiling will still remain a movement of the veil.'[32] By regarding the body as veil and seeing as means of knowing, I investigate next the notions of 'becoming' and 'self-identity' in John's Prologue and Peter Greenaway's film *The Pillow Book*. Is it true that, as Hélène Cixous writes, 'eyes are lips on the lips of God'?[33] This section explores the implications of the Word becoming a male body in John and of a woman becoming a writer by using male bodies in Greenaway.

Veils and Sails

> Just now everybody wants to talk about 'identity' ... identity only becomes an issue when it is in crisis, when something assumed to be fixed, coherent and stable is displaced by the experience of doubt and uncertainty.
>
> —*K. Mercer*[34]

What does it mean *to know*? And know *what* exactly?

In her poem 'Savoir' ('to know') Hélène Cixous writes about her newly found sight after a lifetime of severe myopia, and she attaches a great deal of importance to 'seeing', and seeing the world. Thus,

> Is *seeing* the supreme enjoyment? Or else is it: no-longer-not-seeing? ... It was *seeing-with-the-naked-eye*, the miracle. That's what was transporting her. For she had already seen all that behind glass with spectacles and without exaltation: borrowed vision, separated sight. But at this dawn without subterfuge she had seen the world with her own eyes, without intermediary, without the non-contact lenses. The continuity of her flesh and the world's flesh, touch then, was love, and that was the miracle, giving. Ah! She hadn't realized the

32. Jacques Derrida, 'A Silkworm of One's Own', in Hélène Cixous and Jacques Derrida, *Veils* (trans. Geoffrey Bennington; Cultural Memory in the Present; Stanford: Stanford University Press, 2001), pp. 20-92 (28).

33. Hélène Cixous, 'Savoir', in Cixous and Derrida, *Veils*, pp. 1-16 (9).

34. K. Mercer, 'Welcome to the Jungle', in J. Rutherford (ed.), *Identity: Community, Culture, Difference* (London: Lawrence and Wishart, 1990), p. 4.

day before that eyes are miraculous hands, had never enjoyed the delicate tact
of the cornea, the eyelashes, the most powerful hands, these hands that touch
imponderably near and far-off heres. She had not realized that eyes are lips on
the lips of God.[35]

Cixous writes in the third person in this poem, but she refers to herself
and her own experience. The initial exuberance at being able to function
without contact lenses, which separated her from the world around, is so
powerful that Cixous celebrates seeing as touching and thus knowing.
The result of her losing her myopia is intimacy with God. In what starts
as a celebratory piece, however, where seeing is possibly the 'supreme
enjoyment', and myopia, this 'native veil' (as she calls it)[36] is gone and
good riddance, Cixous takes self-exploratory steps that lead her to a sense
of mourning, to bidding a 'cruel and tender farewell to the veil she had
cursed so much', her myopia.[37] She mourns the loss of 'what the seers
have never seen: presence-before-the-world',[38] the limbo, also the loss of
anger, of truth, of the behind-and-with-the-veil.

For Cixous, it seems, the veil separates and unites simultaneously: it
separates her from the world as is but unites her with the non-seers, those
who enjoy the freedom of not seeing themselves being seen, of being
without the interruptions of the world, the freedom from other faces.
Gaining the seeing-with-the-naked-eye *miracle* means losing the veil as
part of self, the secret part of self, always there, comforting in its constant
presence now lost forever. Irreversibly gone. The eye is naked. Unveiled.
'The continuity of her flesh and the world's flesh, touch then, was love,
and that was the miracle, giving. Ah!', Cixous sighs with pleasure. 'She
had not realized that eyes are lips on the lips of God.'[39]

Responding to Cixous, Jacques Derrida warns, however:

> We'll have to give up touching as much as seeing … For you must know right
> now: to touch 'that' which one calls 'veil' is to touch everything. You'll leave
> nothing intact, safe and sound, neither in your culture, nor in your memory,
> nor in your language, as soon as you take on the word 'veil'. As soon as you let
> yourself be caught up in it, in the word, first of all the French word, to say
> nothing yet about the thing, nothing will remain, nothing will remain
> anymore.[40]

Allowing for echoes of the torn Temple curtain/veil that accompanied
Christ's death, Derrida struggles with the concept of separation as linked

35. Cixous, 'Savoir', p. 9. Italics in original.
36. Cixous, 'Savoir', p. 3.
37. Cixous, 'Savoir', p. 11.
38. Cixous, 'Savoir', p. 13.
39. Cixous, 'Savoir', p. 9.
40. Derrida, 'A Silkworm of One's Own', p. 24.

to the veil; in this case, the separation between the holy and the holy of holies. In fact, Derrida focuses on the temple curtain as the quintessential separator; he declares that he 'know[s] of no other separation in the world, or that would be commensurable with that one, analogous, comparable to that one which allows us to think nonetheless every other separation, and first of all the separation that separates from the wholly other'.[41] However, Derrida is not willing to allow for this separation because it would presuppose the act of tearing the veil as an act of unveiling, of revealing, or revelation. He does not dare to claim that the veil is not still hung between the holy and holy of holies; playfully, Derrida settles for 'perhaps', the inbetweenness of choice, decentred truth and meaning.[42]

I will return to the idea of divine revelation later and stay with the concept of self-revelation for now. Cixous' poem and Derrida's response to it betray clear autobiographical elements, though Cixous talks *of* herself (the 'she' and 'her') and Derrida talks *to* himself (through a dialogue that takes place between the 'I' and the 'you'). While Cixous' veil is a part of self, her myopia, her fault, her truth (as true self), for Derrida the veil is more complex. He declares the 'semantic motifs of the veil' to be 'revelation, unveiling, unburying, nudity, shame, reticence, halt, what is untouchable in the safe and sound, of the immune or the intact, and so the holy and the sacred, *heilig*, *holy*, the law, the religiosity of the religious, etc'.[43] Moreover, Derrida declares himself '[f]ed up with veils and sails'[44] and tired, **'fatigued of the truth**, *voilà*, fatigued like truth, exhausted from knowing it, for too long, that history of the veil, and all the folds [*plis*], explications, complications, explicitations of its revelations and unveilings'.[45] And yet, Derrida continues,

> But I'm not exhausted at all, me, myself, I'm as young as can be, as though on the eve of a resurrection that has not yet spoken its name. You still don't know me by my name. I am only tired by the veil, it is the veil that is exhausted for me, *in my place*. It has stolen my name from me. I am pretending to confess: failing to have been able to do too well what is beginning to get a bit much with veils of all sorts, as if apparently the fate of humanity, of so-called humanity supposedly born with shame, reticence, *Verhaltenheit*, nudity, evil-knowledge, the knowledge of evil, the tree of knowledge, sin, fall or *Verfallen*,

41. Derrida, 'A Silkworm of One's Own', p. 29.
42. Derrida, 'A Silkworm of One's Own', pp. 29-30, 37.
43. Derrida, 'A Silkworm of One's Own', p. 55. Italics in original.
44. Although Derrida declares this in English, he plays on the French meaning of his words. In French, the masculine *les voiles* means 'veils', while the same term in the feminine means 'sails'.
45. Derrida, 'A Silkworm of One's Own', pp. 38-39. Bold and italics in original.

therefore the veil, as though the fate of humanity were again going to depend on whoever holds the power over women about the veil.[46]

So, what exactly constitutes the veil for Derrida? Knowledge? Truth? Knowledge of truth? And why the terrible warning that associates touching the veil with death and destruction? Why is the veil the 'forbidden fruit' in Derrida's wisdom? And why is he so tired of it?

According to his own confession, Derrida has 'already written on the veil, about it, thematically, inexhaustibly, and woven *right on* the veil'.[47] In 'The Double Session', for instance, Derrida connects the *hymen* with the veil, and he warns again, 'to pierce the hymen or to pierce one's eyelid … to lose one's sight or one's life, no longer to see the light of day … is the fate of the simulacrum'.[48] I believe that, for Derrida, the body and the veil are united, for the sake of life and identity. The long and deeply autobiographical notes on the tallith—the Jewish prayer shawl—that Derrida inherited from his grandfather, in memory of the Law, are telling in its connection to identity. Derrida proposes,

> The secret of the shawl envelops one single body. One might think that it is woven *for* this one body, or even *by* it, from which it seems to emanate, like an intimate secretion, but this is less through having engendered it thus right up close to oneself than through having already opened it or given it birth into the divine word that will have preceded it. For a secretion, as is well known, is also what separates, discerns, dissociates, dissolves the bond, hold to the secret. One says 'my shawl' only by obeying Yahweh's order. And by beginning to wonder: who am I, I who have already said 'here I am'? What is the self?[49]

Of course, the self is linked to one's veils. And sails. To one's *skins*.[50] Where the sense of possession—the 'my'—establishes the ruling order, the law. The questions that surface are: Does one, or can one, possess oneself? or Does/Can one, possess oneself enough to reveal oneself? Possession presupposes knowledge; having a self means knowing that self. What is *my* veil/sail/skin/self? Who is *my* self? But can one say *my* veil/

---

46.   Derrida, 'A Silkworm of One's Own', p. 41. Italics in original.

47.   '… for example in all the texts on Heidegger … in *Dissemination* (… especially in "The Double Session", short treatise of the veil, the hymen, the wing, and the eyelid, etc.…), on *Spurs*, stuck in the "veils of all sorts", and in *Glas*, *La carte postale*, *D'un ton apocalyptique* …, *Mémoires d'aveugle*, etc.' Derrida, 'A Silkworm of One's Own', p. 99 n. 18. Italics in original.

48.   Derrida, 'The Double Session', p. 214.

49.   Derrida, 'A Silkworm of One's Own', p. 44. Italics in original.

50.   See Derrida's thoughts on the tallith as 'another skin', in 'A Silkworm of One's Own', p. 43.

skin/self truthfully? Derrida, of course, denies that possibility. He writes, 'There's no chance of that happening, of belonging to oneself enough (in some *s'avoir*, in you want) and of succeeding in turning such a gesture toward oneself. You'll end up in imminence—and the un-veiling will still remain a movement of the veil.'[51]

The Pillow Book, *or Exhibiting Veils*

> Text, my body ...
>
> —*Hélène Cixous*[52]

> The link between writing and the search for identity has been underlying feminist thought and practice for a long time ... As the concept of a unified identity is put into question, writing is more often tied to the impossibility, or even undesirability, of such a goal and becomes the mirror of a split erratic subjectivity.
>
> —*Lidia Curti*[53]

Since I have written on Peter Greenaway's film *The Pillow Book* above, I will not go into too much detail about the story that unfolds in the film. Suffice it to say that Greenaway explores complex themes in this film, and identity, becoming, writing and gender are some of them. What preoccupies me here are mainly the issues surrounding the principal character's identity; her *becoming* or, as many would say, her journey of self-discovery.

Nagiko, the protagonist of *The Pillow Book*, is the little girl who grows up with writing, namely, the birthday blessings that her father would write on her skin every year and the writings of Sei Shonagon, the Heian lady-in-waiting, whose pillow book is constant reading material for Nagiko. Out of love and reverence for her father and Sei Shonagon, to whom she feels connected by virtue of carrying the same name, Nagiko develops a particular affinity to writing. As a woman, she desires it deeply, and writing comes to her first from her carefully chosen calligrapher lovers. Her body becomes the object of different men's sexual affections and of her own literary ones. She is the paper, the passive recipient of writing. However, after being challenged by one of her lovers who proves to be a 'scribbler' in her judgement, Nagiko picks up the brush and begins to write herself. Her first choice of paper is an easy one: the body of her

51. Derrida, 'A Silkworm of One's Own', p. 28.
52. Hélène Cixous, *'Coming to Writing' and Other Essays* (Cambridge, MA: Harvard University Press, 1991), p. 12.
53. Lidia Curti, *Female Stories, Female Bodies: Narrative, Identity and Representation* (London: Macmillan, 1998), p. 108.

lover, Jerome. Thus she reciprocates both love and writing. After a sequence of events, however, Nagiko writes on random men's bodies, each a different 'book'. After Jerome's tragic death, his skin is used by Nagiko's unyielding publisher as true parchment and is bound in a pillow book.[54] This Nagiko recovers by enticing the publisher with new written bodies, or books, and by eventually killing him. A truly fascinating story. What I would like to explore here is the transformation of Nagiko from passive paper to active brush, from what is generally perceived as a feminine role to a masculine one.

In her essay 'The Newly Born Woman', Hélène Cixous follows the thread of such a transformation, or what she calls 'woman's bisexuality'. She exposes the well-known dual, hierarchical oppositions between 'feminine' and 'masculine' poetically:

> Where is she?
> Activity/passivity
> Sun/Moon
> Culture/Nature
> Day/Night
> Father/Mother
> Head/Heart
> Intelligible/Palpable
> Logos/Pathos
> Form, convex, step, advance, semen progress/
> Matter, concave, ground—where steps are taking, holding- and dumping-ground.[55]

In Cixous' opinion, '[e]ither woman is passive or she does not exist. What is left of her is unthinkable, unthought.'[56] Yet Cixous does not accept this state of affairs and proposes a reconsideration of bisexuality. Rather than accepting it in its conceptualized form as neuter, she offers two contrasting ways of conceiving bisexuality: (i) bisexuality as a 'fantasy of a complete being ... Ovid's Hermaphrodite ... two within one'; and (ii) 'the *other bisexuality*, the one with which every subject, who is not shut inside the spurious Phallocentric Performing Theatre, sets up his or her own erotic universe'.[57] Of course, this theory is meant to show woman as the principal beneficiary of this bisexuality, through woman's openness to

---

54. For more on this, see 'The Seduction of Words and Flesh and the Desire of God' above, where I offer a poststructuralist reading of the inscription of the flesh in *The Pillow Book* and the incarnation of the word in John's Prologue.

55. Hélène Cixous, 'The Newly Born Woman', in Sellers (ed.), *The Hélène Cixous Reader*, pp. 36-55 (37).

56. Cixous, 'The Newly Born Woman', p. 39.

57. Cixous, 'The Newly Born Woman', p. 41. Italics in original.

difference, to the other. So, as Cixous would have it, woman is bisexual, while man is the (other) victim of phallocratic ideology. She explains, 'As a woman, I could be obsessed by the sceptre's great shadow; and they told me: adore it, that thing you don't wield. But at the same time, man has been given the grotesque and unenviable task of being reduced to a single idol with clay balls. And terrified of homosexuality, as Freud and his followers remark. Why does man fear *being* a woman? Why this refusal (*Ablehnung*) of femininity?'[58]

So, why, or rather 'how', this relocation of woman? Cixous is informed by psychoanalysis (the formation of self, in particular) when she suggests that, because woman is allowed a close connection to the mother—and the Other, therefore—'in her becoming-woman, she has not erased the bisexuality latent in a girl as in a boy'.[59] Femininity and bisexuality are seen as developing together. Furthermore, Cixous claims that writing is quintessential in this development. Thus,

> I will say: today writing is woman's. That is not a provocation; it means that woman admits there is an other ... Writing is the passageway, the entrance, the exit, the dwelling place of the other in me—the other that I am and I am not, that I don't know how to be, but that I feel passing, that makes me live— that tears me apart, disturbs me, changes me, who?—a feminine one, a masculine one, some?—several, some unknown, which is indeed what gives me the desire to know and from which all life soars. This peopling gives neither rest nor security, always disturbs the relationship to 'reality', produces an uncertainty that gets in the way of the subject's socialization. It is distressing, it wears you out; and for men this permeability, this non-exclusion is a threat, something intolerable.[60]

Cixous perceives writing as independent of its author, autonomous, alive in and by itself. Her argument is based on the idea that women find it within themselves to release writing from all obligations towards its (m)other; women's writing thus is presented by Cixous as lacking in possessiveness. Or as Derrida would say, 'to write is to draw back. Not to retire to one's tent, in order to write, but to draw back from one's writing itself. To be grounded far from one's language, to emancipate it or lose one's hold on it, to let it make its way alone and unarmed.'[61]

What is essential in understanding Cixous' theory is that she considers there to be two different economies or attitudes to giving. Echoing Derrida's own take on the gift but coloured by her own theory on sexual difference, Cixous argues that the masculine attitude to giving is

58.   Cixous, 'The Newly Born Woman', p. 41. Italics in original.
59.   Cixous, 'The Newly Born Woman', p. 42.
60.   Cixous, 'The Newly Born Woman', pp. 42-43.
61.   Derrida, 'Edmond Jabès and the Question of the Book', p. 70.

concerned with return as in 'revenue', and thus man's gift is a 'gift-that-takes', echoing Derrida's 'gift that is not'. By contrast, the feminine gift, while not a free gift (which does not exist) is different qualitatively. As Cixous would have it, it is all in 'the why and the how of the gift'.[62] Unlike man's giving, which is seen as linked to some social status, woman's giving, according to Cixous, is predicated by pleasure, happiness, and increased value of and for her self and the other. Cixous' woman 'doesn't try to "recover her expenses"'.[63]

While I salute Cixous' attempts to create a dimension that does not revolve around the penis, a bisexual universe where woman finds a home, I am troubled by the terms of this new creation. The 'newly born woman' is idealized and thus limited by her own liberation contract. Cixous concludes her essay,

> I am spacious singing Flesh: onto which is grafted no one knows which I—which masculine or feminine, more or less human but above all living, because changing I.[64]

Like Luce Irigaray, who proposes the developing of a specifically feminine mode of expression (*parler-femme*) and suggests the 'two lips' in exchange for Freud's and Lacan's 'phallus', Cixous is connected to flesh/matter all too closely for comfort for many feminist critics. It seems that what both Cixous and Irigaray have in common is a homogenous take on men and women, man and woman. While woman is allowed to embrace difference, man is condemned to being 'an idol with clay balls'. For instance, as woman is allowed her bisexuality, why is she not allowed an 'I' which asks for a good return on her gifts? Again, hues of biological essentialism hover gloomily over otherwise creative and daring feminism.

On the other hand, Cixous does allow for a pleasurable return on the women's gifts. She sees the link between the lack of stability in sexual identity and writing as occurring through the female body. While defending a female separateness in writing, she speaks of 'a subjectivity that splits apart without regret ... without the ceaseless summoning of the authority called Ego'.[65] This split subjectivity joins the female body to writing:

> There is a link between the economy of femininity—the open, extravagant subjectivity, that relationship to the other in the gift doesn't calculate its influence—and the possibility of love; a link today between this 'libido of the other' and writing.[66]

62. Cixous, 'The Newly Born Woman', p. 43.
63. Cixous, 'The Newly Born Woman', p. 44.
64. Cixous, 'The Newly Born Woman', p. 45.
65. Cixous, 'The Newly Born Woman', p. 90.
66. Cixous, 'The Newly Born Woman', pp. 91-92.

Both the body and writing are off centre: they do not experience margins, they come and go and come again, they are one and the other and many others.

Cixous and Irigaray take on the risk of being bundled up within flesh and matter because they are also proposing the act of mimicry as subversive of the Law of the Father. By employing the prescribed, 'proper' language and identity of woman—that linked to the body—they try to defeat the rule of the Father at his own game. By proposing woman's bisexuality while shouting 'I am spacious singing Flesh: onto which is grafted no one knows which I', Cixous presents an image that is unsettling. It is one in which woman's identity is not fixed, not unified, not assured. Though presented through the language of the Father, woman's identity has no fixed contours and is thus beyond control. It lacks definition, the very aim of the Law and Logic of the Father, and so it is not easily classified within the prescribed system.

In her *Pouvoir du discours/subordination du féminin*, Luce Irigaray also argues that 'subordination can become women's power, and mimicry the main instrument of this transformation, the same mimicry that is historically assigned to women'.[67] However, 'it is a question of assuming this role deliberately. Which already means turning subordination into affirmation, and therefore subverting it.'[68] Irigaray understands *écriture féminine* (feminine/ female writing) as the means of disrupting the unity of subject and object, on which the definition of what is female is based. For her, women's writing violates the phallocratic order of writing in denying its unitary character, its emphasis on oneness: 'what a feminine syntax might be is not simple nor easy to state, because in that "syntax" there would no longer be either object or subject, "oneness" would no longer be privileged, there would no longer be proper meanings, proper names, "proper" attributes'. It is a tactile, simultaneous, fluid style, resisting and exploding 'every firmly established form, figure, idea or concept'.[69] As Trinh Minh-ha would say,

> When i say 'I see myself seeing myself', I/i am not alluding to the illusory relation of subject to subject (or even object) but to the play of mirrors that defers to infinity the real subject and subverts the notion of an original 'I' ... [W]riting, like a game that defies its own rules, is an ongoing practice that may be said to be concerned, not with inserting a 'me' into language, but with creating an opening where the 'me' disappears while 'I' endlessly come and go.[70]

67. Curti, *Female Stories*, p. 3.
68. Luce Irigaray, 'The Power of Discourse', in *idem, This Sex Which is Not One*, p. 76.
69. Irigaray, 'The Power of Discourse', p. 79; Curti, *Female Stories*, p. 109.
70. Trinh T. Minh-ha, *Woman Native Other: Writing Postcoloniality and Feminism* (Bloomington: Indiana University Press, 1989), p. 28.

The most important element in Cixous' own theory is that of the 'changing I', the multi-faceted identity. For Cixous, therefore, identities are
always 'living', fluid, chosen for a while then changed for others. The
flow of identities is not simply linear, in a progressive sense, as this would
indicate the possibility of a bettering and thus a hierarchical system. The
changes in identity take place in a relational system, where difference
plays a meaningful game.

Thus, identities are never complete, never unified; instead, they are
the stage on which many conflicts and negotiations play out. As a result,
in a society that insists on fixed identities, there will be perceived
moments of, what Jacqueline Rose calls, 'failure' of identity. She argues,

> Failure is not a moment to be regretted in a process of adaptation, or develop-
> ment into normality, which ideally takes its course ... Instead, 'failure' is
> something endlessly repeated and relived moment by moment throughout our
> individual histories. It appears not only in the symptoms, but also in the
> dreams ... Feminism's affinity with psychoanalysis rests above all ... with this
> recognition that there is resistance to identity which lies at the very heart of
> psychic life.[71]

For Rose, it is the unconscious that is constantly revealing, through errors
and displacements, the *failure* of identity.[72] This resistance to identity, or
rather resistance to prescribed identity is the creative ground upon which
Cixous, Irigaray and Kristeva launch their theories. It is there that the
two I's/eyes—the 'eyes' and the 'I's—come into conflict, or, what Laura
Mulvey calls the 'long love affair/despair between image and self-image'.[73]

The power of the image in identity development, or self-formation, is
widely recognized in psychoanalysis. From Freud's *Interpretation of Dreams*
to Lacan's development of the mirror stage, the image—either seen with
the eyes or conjured up in one's mind—shapes the 'I'. The image is
essential for the process of identification, namely, the formation of an
identity through 'equations made between oneself and external objects
through the internalization of images or models of those objects'.[74] As
in Lacan's Imaginary, subject formation, image and identification are
strongly interdependent.

Returning to *The Pillow Book*, the principal, female character is the
product of Peter Greenaway, a man. As her creator, Greenaway allows
Nagiko to become a writer. He gives her a name, which appears to be
liberating. If Sei Shonagon managed to become a writer though a woman

71. Jacqueline Rose, cited in Walkerdine, 'One Day my Prince will Come', p. 181.
72. Rose, *Sexuality in the Field of Vision*, pp. 90-91.
73. Mulvey, 'Visual Pleasure and Narrative Cinema', p. 10.
74. Rivkin and Ryan, 'Strangers to Ourselves: Psychoanalysis', pp. 119-27 (122).

a whole thousand years before her, why should Nagiko fail? I should like to explore the process of Nagiko's becoming.

When God made the first clay
model of a human being

Figure 10. *Nagiko receives her father's written blessing on her birthday.*

Nagiko's self emergences through a series of events that seem to play rather well within the bounds of an Oedipal drama. She adores her father, who is a writer and who performs his art on Nagiko's skin ritualistically each year, on her birthday. He writes her name on her face while reciting, 'When God created the first clay model of a human being, he painted in the eyes, the lips, and the sex. Then he painted in the name of each person, lest its owner should forget it. If God approved of his creation, he signed his own name' (Fig. 10). At this point, Nagiko turns, and the father signs his own name, the Name of the Father (à propos Lacan), on the back of her neck. There they are: the male god, with full authority, and *his* female subject, who in entranced by him. This father god becomes Nagiko's object of desire. Soon it is writing that substitutes the father, and she desires it intensely. She needs writing, she declares at one point, echoing thus Cixous herself, who declares, 'I need writing; I need to surprise myself living; I need to feel myself quiver with living ... I need writing to celebrate living'.[75] Nagiko does not need just any writing, but writing performed on skin. Her skin, in the beginning. To say that she trades sex for writing is to limit Nagiko's character, and it does not seem to be the case (at least, not consistently).

75. Hélène Cixous, *(With) Ou l'art de l'innocence*, in Sellers (ed.), *The Hélène Cixous Reader*, pp. 95-104 (95).

Of course, Nagiko's mother is Sei Shonagon. The actual mother character is mostly absent (apart from a brief encounter towards the end of
the film), and it is quite strongly suggested by Greenaway that the lady-
in-waiting who lived and wrote a thousand years before Nagiko is the
Proper mother. She appears systematically in Nagiko's imagination, to
guide and spur on the younger woman (Figs. 11 and 12).

Figure 11. *Sei Shonagon and her Pillow Book, as imagined by Nagiko.*

Figure 12. *Sei Shonagon and her Pillow Book, as imagined by Nagiko.*

Like Sei Shonagon, Nagiko begins to write her own pillow books, filled with 'all manner of observations'; she creates lists of things that she likes or does not like. She is not the dutiful wife; in fact, she sets fire to her unhappy marital home and runs away, pursuing her own path, independently of her husband and owner. Nagiko welcomes the idea of having many lovers, as Sei Shonagon had done. When Nagiko reaches adulthood—both in body and mind—Greenaway treats his viewers to a powerful sequence of juxtaposed images of the adult Nagiko and Sei Shonagon, with their lovers. What seems to unite the two is sex and writing. Nagiko subscribes willingly, if not happily, to Sei Shonagon's philosophy that 'there are two things which are dependable in life: the delights of the flesh and the delights of literature' (Section 172).

Nagiko *develops*; she *becomes*. She becomes a woman and writer. For all intents and purposes, she is a heterosexual woman—Freud's normative model—so the Oedipal phase is successfully transited. She manages to imitate, indeed identify with, her 'mother' and channel her attraction to her father onto other adult males. Furthermore, she becomes a mother herself, the ending note of the film, seen as the climax of Nagiko's life. Yet, as we all know, Freud's Oedipal model does not work very easily for girls. Boys have the relatively easier task of relocating their attraction away from the mother and onto other adult females and identify with the father, a male adult with authority, in the process. On the other hand, girls must first learn to displace their desire from the mother onto the father, and only then learn to adopt the identity of a female adult within new sexual contexts, where the father is replaced by other adult males. Hence Cixous' theory of female bisexuality, due to the initial (and sometimes prolonged) close relationship with the mother.

In Nagiko's case, when we are introduced to her as a little girl she seems fascinated with her father already. Yet the presence of Sei Shonagon is very powerful. Nagiko's aunt reads to her from Sei Shonagon's writings, and Nagiko is determined to have her own pillow book. It is quite possible that what appears to be a significant attraction to the father is in actual fact a taste for writing. Could it be that what she truly desires is writing? She begins to despise her husband for his lack of literary interests and his inability to perform writing on her body. After she escapes him and finds herself in Hong Kong, she types her birthday blessing and glues the paper onto her chest, which proves to be bitterly disappointing and only leads her into the arms of calligrapher lovers. It seems that writing is indeed the object of desire for Nagiko.

If initially she adopts a passive role, where she is the paper, the recipient of writing, Nagiko later does pick up the brush herself and steps into an active role. In actual fact, Greenaway presents this as the 'identity' that awaited Nagiko; a writer is what she was always meant to be. Just like Sei Shonagon.

It is my opinion that writing becomes a signifier here, and not just any signifier; writing is the Phallus. Nagiko's father is himself a writer, and Nagiko thinks him all-powerful until the day she witnesses his father's subjection by his own publisher. In order for Nagiko's father's books to be published, he becomes the unwilling lover of his homosexual publisher, and so it is the publisher who holds the authority, the Phallus. In her struggles to become a writer, Nagiko desires recognition not from her father, but his publisher. She chooses him as the recipient of her writing, because she wants her acquiring of a phallus to be recognized by someone of equal, if not superior, phallic weight. The fact that mere photographs of her work on male bodies are rejected as worthless by the publisher hurts Nagiko. So, in her active role as writer, Nagiko decides to use a different kind of paper, that of male skin, first her lover's and then random people's.

In *Coming to Writing*, whose title is intended to highlight the connection between writing and orgasm, Hélène Cixous argues,

> Writing is to touch with letters, with lips, with breath, to caress with the tongue, to lick in its remoteness … The texts I ate, sucked, suckled, kissed … To write: to love, inseparable. Writing is a gesture of love … Read-me-lick-me, write-me love.[76]

Cixous' writing endeavours to blur the border between book and body.

> To write—the act that will 'realize' the uncensored relationship of woman to her sexuality … that will return her goods, her pleasures, her organs, her vast bodily territories kept under seal … Write yourself, your body must make itself heard.[77]

It is no wonder that Jane Gallop thinks of *écriture féminine* of being 'not only female but somehow French, a passage from the phallic paradigm to oral sex'.[78]

Nagiko sends forth her first book, written on her lover's body. As expected, the publisher succumbs to the beauty of both Nagiko's writing and her lover carrying it, taking them both. It is at that point that

---

76. Cixous, *'Coming to Writing' and Other Essays*, pp. 4 and 12.
77. Cixous, 'Sorties', p. 97.
78. Jane Gallop, *Around 1981* (London: Routledge, 1992), p. 42; Gallop wishes to indicate that French feminist theory evokes a certain sensuality that is linked to the somewhat 'sinful' image that Paris denotes for the English-speaking world.

Nagiko is forced to accept an identity as writer that is separate from her identity as woman; writing and sex are divided, distinguished, separate, it would seem. From that point on, all the male bodies that her brush touches are to be perceived as mere paper. These bodies are more than pages, however. They are veils, Nagiko's skins. The viewer sees these written bodies and understands little from what is written (it is all either in Chinese or Kanji, and the subtitles are fragmented and fugitive). One is torn between admiring the aesthetics of writing and learning its meaning, with the former exercising a stronger pull. The act of writing, therefore, and specifically writing-on-male-bodies, is more prominent than what is written, at least for a while. The frequency of naked male bodies appearing in the film creates in the viewer a certain disinterest in them eventually (even though their exposure is a little shocking and thus captivating at the beginning). It is as if Nagiko is exhibiting her writing, her skins, her veils.

Furthermore, all these naked male bodies are sent as gifts by Nagiko, in order for her to recover the body of her lover. Is her writing spurred on by the lack of, and desire for, Jerome? Alas, when she next writes on her lover's body, he is dead, so beyond the sexual/sensual realm. As a unique occurrence, Nagiko writes on dead skin. As Cixous would say, 'one can only begin to advance along the path of discovery, the discovery of writing or anything else, from mourning and in the reparation of mourning'.[79]

Nagiko is recognized as a true writer by the publisher eventually. Even more so, he adores her work and has every word typed by his secretaries for fear of an early disappearance of it from the bodies sent to him. The publisher also begins, therefore, to distinguish between writing and the body, and he pursues sex with none of the subsequent messengers. After Jerome's funeral, the publisher has his body exhumed and skinned, in order for the writing performed on his body to remain as a pillow book, the publisher's pillow book. Greenaway shows the flesh under the skin scraped away, expelled.

Greenaway's methods are similar to those of one of Kristeva's favourite avant-garde writers, C.-F. Céline, who is not afraid to write of horror, to speak it, the very element shunned by Romanticism. Céline writes, for example,

---

79.   Hélène Cixous, 'De la scène de l'Inconscient à la scène de l'Histoire: Chemin d'une écriture', in Francoise van Rossum-Guyon and Myriam Diaz-Diocaretz (eds.), *Hélène Cixous, chemins d'une écriture* (Saint-Denis: Presses Universitaires de Vincennes, 1990), pp. 18-23 (19). This translation is by Deborah Jenson, as cited by Susan Sellers, 'Introduction', in *idem* (ed.), *The Hélène Cixous Reader*, pp. xxvi-xxxi (xxvi).

He sticks his finger into the wound ... He plunges both hands into the meat ...
He digs into all the holes ... He tears away the soft edges ... He pokes around ...
He gets stuck ... His wrist is caught in the bones ... Crack! He tugs ... He
struggles like in a trap ... Some kind of pouch bursts ... The juice pours out ... it
gushes all over the place ... all full of brains and blood ... splashing ...[80]

In the same fashion, Greenaway treats his viewers to bloody images of
flesh being removed meticulously from its skin, gathered together in a
bucket and thrown into the gutter.[81] The entire corpse should be considered as abject, having been expelled ritualistically through burial. Having
the corpse exhumed is sacrilegious, because it brings back the abject that
has already been released into the exterior, similar to re-consuming that
which has been excreted. In the publisher's actions, it is the flesh belonging to the corpse that becomes abjection and thus removed, while the
written skin becomes sacred. The flesh is ambiguous, without definitions,
while the skin becomes paper and thus clearly defined and can relish in a
new identity: the sacred pillow book.

Yet, the fact that the book is written on skin destabilizes its identity as
book. It is not like Christ's dead body, which does not remain a corpse
and abject. Through his resurrection, Christ not only can remain within
the accepted and familiar, within the living, but he also ascends into the
sacred, by the very divine nature of his return to life. His sacred book, the
Bible, can have an unquestionable identity as a book because it is made
of paper throughout. In *The Pillow Book*, the skin still threatens the
boundaries of its newly found self, and it is for this reason that Nagiko
buries the pillow book after she recovers it by having the publisher killed.
The skin of the corpse cannot truly be removed from its dead flesh; in
fact, the dead skin is still dead flesh, σὰρξ, and so it is only proper that it
should be removed, buried. Writing cannot exist together with the abject.
And yet, the burial site is not far; it seems that Nagiko cannot let go of
either her writing or the skin of her lover. The pillow book remains with
Nagiko though buried, under the roots of an indoor bonsai tree. Derrida's
question remains, Do 'you ... become "yours" with your own death, the
mourning of your body in ash or buried, with your own winding sheet

80. L.-F. Céline, *Death on the Instalment Plan* (trans. Ralph Manheim; New York:
New Directions, 1966), p. 560; in Julia Kristeva, *Powers of Horror: An Essay on Abjection*
(trans. Leon S. Roudiez; New York: Columbia University Press, 1982), p. 150.
81. Greenaway is renowned for his shocking the viewer with images of horror, of the
grotesque. See, for instance, his *The Cook, the Thief, His Wife and Her Lover*, in which
the lover is cooked and eaten.

until the presumed end of time, with the imprint of your face on the linen of a shroud, until the end of time'?[82]

The Pillow Book concludes with Nagiko giving birth to a daughter. She writes the blessing on her daughter's forehead while imagining Sei Shonagon and remembering her own path to writing (Figs. 13 and 14). Nagiko is a writer; she has the ability for a type of *écriture féminine*, performed in and through love, on bodies. If the father of Nagiko's child is absent, we find in his place writing, a pillow book.

Why is Nagiko's coming to writing paved with death, though? Why is 'every text implicitly a monstrous, female double self'?[83] Is it true that, as Lidia Curti observes, 'the monster at the end of it all is women's writing, writing as the female body, ink and milk and blood'?[84] Cixous' poem 'A Woman's Coming to Writing' reads,

> Who
> Invisible, foreign, secret, hidden, mysterious, black, forbidden
> Am I ...
> Is this me, this nobody that is dressed up, wrapped in veils, carefully kept distant, pushed to the side of History and change, nullified, kept out of the way, on the edge of the stage, on the kitchen side, the bedside?
> For you?[85]

By proposing an *écriture féminine*, women are seen as wanting the phallus. Within the Law of the Father, and like the patricide and incest of Oedipus, a phallic woman—not castrated—is bad grammar, monstrous, horrifying. The phallic woman disturbs and disrupts the identity of man, which he, in his illusion, perceives as (phallo)centred and unified. A phallic woman betrays hybrid sexuality and failed identity, where she no longer asks, 'Where am I? Where is my sexual identity?' 'The fragmentation of identities is also spatial and temporal dissemination.'[86] *The Pillow Book* is itself presented in fragments, juxtaposed frames, alluding thus to its story and its principal characters as being fragmented, *sujets en procès*. In his allowing Nagiko to become the phallic woman—in this case, the writer *using* male bodies as paper—Greenaway's film is unveiling fears; writing horrors.[87]

---

82. Derrida, 'A Silkworm of One's Own', p. 42.
83. Jane Gallop, cited in Curti, *Female Stories*, p. 108.
84. Curti, *Female Stories*, p. xiii.
85. Cited in Curti, *Female Stories*, p. 108.
86. Curti, *Female Stories*, p. 128, alluding to Jeanette Winterson's *Written on the Body* (London: Jonathan Cape, 1992).
87. If not (unconscious?) *desires*.

Figure 13. *Nagiko realises, like Sei Shonagon before her, that 'happiness is writing of love and finding it' (note Sei Shonagon inset).*

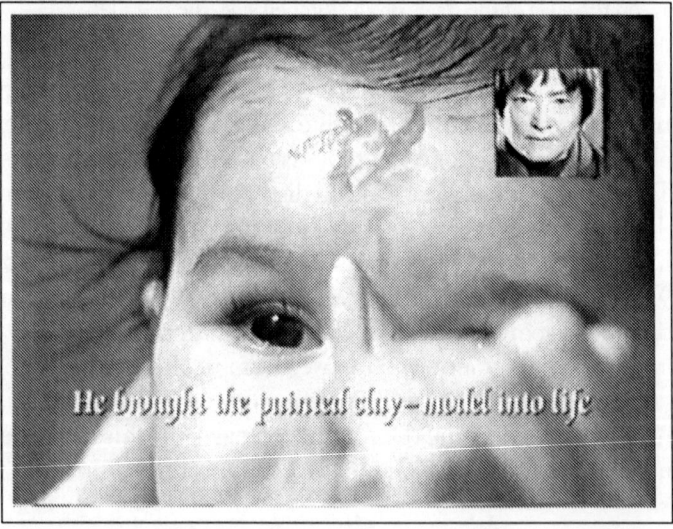

Figure 14. *Nagiko has become both writer and mother, and she performs the father's blessing onto her new born baby girl (note Father inset).*

John's Prologue, or the Veiled Word

In him was life, and the life was the light of people. The light shines in the darkness, and the darkness has not grasped it ... It was the true light that enlightens every person coming into the world. He was in the world, and the world was made through him, yet the world knew him not. He came to his own, and his own people received him not. But to all who received him, who believed in his name, he gave authority to become children of God; who were born not of blood, nor of the will of the flesh, nor of the will of man, but of God ... No one has ever seen God; the only Son, who is in the bosom of the Father, he has made him known (Jn 1: 4-5; 9-13; 18).[88]

The Logos—life and light, here—is said to have been unknown to humankind until the Logos came to them in an embodied form. This bodily performance has a dual effect: to give a new identity to believers and to reveal God.

I have chosen this outline for the text's interpretation based on my understanding of καὶ ἡ σκοτία αὐτὸ οὐ κατέλαβεν, in which οὐ κατέλαβεν takes on the 'has not grasped' meaning.[89] Somewhat similar to Moffatt's version of 'mastered', it is meant to combine—though a little unequally—the two principal possibilities for καταλαμβάνω, 'to comprehend/perceive' and 'to overtake/overcome', with a slight preference for the former.[90] As I mentioned at the beginning of this work,[91] there is much to be said about the oscillations between 'comprehend' and 'overtake'. Briefly, they display two different scores. In 'overtake', where darkness 'has not overtaken/overcome' light, it is the darkness that is the stronger, more muscular element; the light is the trembling candle flame, cornered, assaulted, sabotaged by the hounding lightlessness, the all-consuming black hole. The light is caught in the flickering defensive/offensive/defensive/offensive motion. The 'comprehend' version, on the other hand, where darkness 'has not comprehended/understood' light, offers a translation that is flavoured with irony, which is indeed one of

88. I prefer this translation of v. 9 to 'The true light that enlightens everyone *was* coming into the world', because of the participle, ἐρχόμενον, and the context; v. 10 confirms that 'he was [already] in the world', ἐν τῷ κόσμῳ ἦν, so there is no apparent need for v. 9 to announce that the light/he *was* coming into the world, when he had been there already since, or before, creation.

89. Though the verb is aorist, I believe that κατέλαβεν may not be referring to a specific moment in the past when darkness 'did not' grasp light. Should that have been the case, the text may have elaborated on it, which it does not. So, perhaps this is a so-called 'gnomic' aorist, allowing for a translation closer to the present perfect, 'has not grasped'.

90. Cyril of Alexandria, the Vulgate, Lagrange, Macgregor, Braun and others have opted for the 'comprehend' translation, as the intellectual ability to understand. Others, like Bultmann, Dupont and Wikenhauser have favoured the 'receive, accept, appreciate' translation for its echoes with the original Aramaic *lā qabbleh qablâ*. However, Origen, most of the Greek Fathers, Westcott, Schlatter, Boismard and Brown have chosen the 'overcome' translation because of the parallels that they see between the Johannine Prologue and the *Odes of Solomon* xviii.6; *Wis.* vii. 29-30; and *Acts of Thomas* 130.

91. See above.

the strongly distinguishable elements of Johannine style.[92] Thus, the inferior ignorance, the thick denseness cannot see what is staring it brightly in the face. Furthermore, the duality between light as knowledge and darkness as ignorance is pursued elsewhere in the Johannine writings. John 12.46, for example, has Jesus saying, ἐγὼ φῶς εἰς τὸν κόσμον ἐλήλυθα, ἵνα πᾶς ὁ πιστεύων εἰς ἐμὲ ἐν τῇ σκοτίᾳ μὴ μείνῃ: 'I have come as light into the world, that whoever believes in me may not remain in darkness'. Before this, v. 45 explains that 'he who sees me [Jesus] sees him who sent me', καὶ ὁ θεωρῶν ἐμὲ θεωρεῖ τὸν πέμψαντά με, later qualified as 'the Father who sent me', ὁ πέμψας με πατήρ (v. 49). Thus, vv. 45-46 and 49 in John 12 form a recognizable echo to Jn 1.18. 1 John 1.5 also introduces God as light: ὁ θεὸς φῶς ἐστιν καὶ σκοτία ἐν αὐτῷ οὐκ ἔστιν οὐδεμία, 'God is light, and in him there is no darkness at all', while in Jn 8.12 and 9.5, Jesus declares, ἐγώ εἰμι τὸ φῶς τοῦ κόσμου· ὁ ἀκολουθῶν ἐμοὶ οὐ μὴ περιπατήσῃ ἐν τῇ σκοτίᾳ, ἀλλ' ἕξει τὸ φῶς τῆς ζωῆς: 'I am the light of the world; he who follows me will not walk in darkness, but will have the light of life'. John's theme seems to be quite clear: the Son, Jesus, comes as light into the world to reveal God, the Father, in his person and remove those who believe in his revelation from darkness into the light of life.

Many scholars have tried to show that the Prologue finds convincing parallels in Gnostic and Hermetic literature (precisely in the Coptic *Trimorphic Protennoia*, the Syriac *Odes of Solomon* and the *Corpus Hermeticum*).[93] Others, however, have argued that some of these texts are not even Gnostic,[94] and that there is no interdependent relationship between them and the prologue of John's Gospel.[95] Many more, however, put

92. See Brown, Culpepper, Ashton and others.
93. See, for example, R. Bultmann, 'The History of Religions Background of the Prologue to the Gospel of John', in John Ashton (ed.), *The Interpretation of John* (London: SPCK, 1986), pp. 27-46; R. Reitzenstein, *Das iranische Erlösungsmysterium* (Bonn: Marcus & Weber, 1921); C. Colpe, 'Heidnische, jüdische und christliche Überlieferung in den Schriften aus Nag Hammadi. III', *JAC* 17 (1974), pp. 109-25; C.K. Barrett, *The Gospel of John and Judaism* (London: SPCK, 1975); R. Schnackenburg, 'Logos-Hymnus und johanneischen Prolog', *BZ* 1 (1957), pp. 69-109; H. Ridderbos, 'The Structure and Scope of the Prologue to the Gospel of John', *NovT* 8 (1966), pp. 180-201; I. de la Potterie, 'Structure du Prologue de Saint Jean', *NTS* 30 (1984), pp. 354-81; C.H. Dodd, *The Interpretation of the Fourth Gospel* (Cambridge: Cambridge University Press, 1953).
94. See J.H. Charlesworth, 'The Odes of Solomon—Not Gnostic', *CBQ* 31 (1969), pp. 357-69.
95. J.H. Charlesworth and R.A. Culpepper, 'The Odes of Solomon and the Gospel of John', *CBQ* 35 (1973), pp. 298-322; J.T. Sanders, 'Nag Hammadi, Odes of Solomon,

forward a very convincing argument according to which the parallels between other biblical texts as well as Jewish tradition and the Prologue are more telling.

As I have mentioned before, and as it is widely recognized, there is a clear correspondence between John's Prologue and Genesis 1–2, and, within the creation account, it is the role of Wisdom that is most prominent. Thus, Wisdom and Logos are associated by their agency in creation.[96] Nowhere else is this more apparent than in the parallels between Philo's exegesis, which precedes the Johannine writings, and the Prologue.[97] Philo's λόγος is also '[in] the beginning' (Conf. ling. 28 §146 // Jn 1.1); is 'within no intervening distance' from God (Fug. 19 §101 // Jn 1.1b; 18); is called 'God' (Somn. 1.39 §230; Fug. 18 §97; Quaest. in Exod. 2.68 // Jn 1.1c); through Philo's logos the world is created (Cher. 35 §127; Op. mund. 5 §20; 6 §24 // Jn 1.3, 10). Furthermore, Philo also makes it clear that no one, not even Moses, has seen God (Poster. C. 48 §169 // Jn 1.18a), and that the logos was God's first born (Conf. Ling. 14 §62-63; 28 §146-47 // Jn 1.18a), the faithful image (εἰκών) of God (Fug. 19 §101), who was God, θεός (Somn. 1.39 §228-30).[98]

Most importantly for my purpose, Philo's logos plays, through the incarnation, the role of intermediary and reconciler between God and humanity. Philo's exegesis mentions that 'the Divine Logos, inasmuch as

and New Testament Christological Hymns', in J.E. Goehring et al. (eds.), Gnosticism and the Early Christian World: In Honour of James M. Robinson (Sonoma, CA: Polebridge Press, 1990), pp. 51-66. G.D. Kilpatrick, 'The Religious Background of the Fourth Gospel', in F.L. Cross (ed.), Studies in the Fourth Gospel (London: Mowbrays, 1957), pp. 36-44; Brown, John; D. Burkett, The Son of the Man in the Gospel of John (JSNTSup, 56; Sheffield: JSOT Press, 1991).

96. See G.R. Beasley-Murray, John (WBC, 36; Dallas: Word Books, 1987), p. 10; Brown, John, pp. 4-5; D.A. Carson, The Gospel According to John (Grand Rapids: Eerdmans, 1991), pp. 113-14; E. Haenchen, John 1: A Commentary on the Gospel of John (Hermeneia; Philadelphia: Fortress Press, 1984), p. 109; E.C. Hoskyns, The Fourth Gospel (ed. F.N. Davey; London: Faber & Faber, 2nd edn, 1947), pp. 135-36; B. Lindars, The Gospel of John (NCB; London: Marshall, Morgan & Scott, 1972), p. 82; R. Schnackenburg, The Gospel According to St John, I (New York: Crossroad, 1987), p. 232. See also the excellent study of Craig A. Evans, Word and Glory: On the Exegetical and Theological Background of John's Prologue (JSNTSup. 89; Sheffield: JSOT Press, 1993).

97. See Dodd, Interpretation of the Fourth Gospel, pp. 54-73; L. Hurtado, One God, One Lord: Early Christian Devotion and Ancient Jewish Monotheism (Philadelphia: Fortress Press, 1988), pp. 44-50; R.L. Duncan, 'The Logos: From Sophocles to the Gospel of John', Christian Scholar's Review 9 (1979), pp. 121-30; T.H. Tobin, 'The Prologue of John and Hellenistic Jewish Speculation', CBQ 52 (1990), pp. 252-69.

98. See parallels between Philo's use of the logos and John's Prologue cited in Evans, Word and Glory, pp. 100-103.

it is appropriately in the middle (μέσος), leaves nothing in nature empty, but fills all things and becomes a mediator (μεσίτης) and arbitrator for the two sides which seem to be divided from each other, bringing about friendship and concord, for it is always the cause of community (κοινωνίας) and the artisan of peace (εἰρηνης)' (*Quaest. in Exod.* 2.68 [on Exod. 25.21]). He also mentions that 'the incorporeal world is set off and separated from the visible one by the mediating Logos (ὑπὸ τοῦ μεθορίου λόγου) as by a veil' (*Quaest. in Exod.* 2.94 [on Exod. 26.33]).[99]

Thus, the 'veiled' Word unites and separates 'peacefully' the visible and the invisible, humanity and God. On Jesus, God writes himself and becomes visible, legible text. In *The Pillow Book*, God is said to have written *only* his name on his created human beings that were 'pleasing'. On Jesus, one could say that God writes *himself*. It is through the embodied logos that humans see the revealed God, and those who believe it— namely, that what they perceive with their eyes *is* indeed God—take on a new identity, a new subject position, that of children of God.

However, it is not God that they see in the logos; it is rather the veiled God. Through his writing, God veils his very revelation. As Derrida would insist, 'there's no chance of that ever happening, of belonging to oneself enough … and of succeeding in turning such a gesture toward oneself. You'll end up in imminence—and the un-veiling will still remain a movement of the veil.'[100] The embodied Word is the veiled God, and the body of Christ is the veil of God. Those believing that they see God do not truly see God, and so they do remain in a darkness of sorts, the darkness of the veil. Is this the price for their achieving their new identity, their subjectivity?

Louis Althusser claims that it is ideology that interpellates individuals as subjects, making reference also to what he calls 'the Christian religious ideology'. Althusser's thesis is that God is the Subject, and Moses and all the other of God's people are the Subject's interlocutors-interpellates, his mirrors, his reflections. God needs human beings for his own subjectivity to be established; thus, the Subject needs subjects, irrespective of the risk of an inversion of his image in them—when the subjects, the human beings, indulge in something contrary to God's image, that which is labelled 'sin'. Better still, Althusser argues,

> God duplicates himself and sends his Son to the Earth, as a mere subject 'forsaken' by him (the long complaint in the Garden of Olives which ends in the Crucifixion), subject but Subject, man but God, to do what prepares the

99. Cited in Evans, *Word and Glory*, p. 106.
100.   Derrida, 'A Silkworm of One's Own', p. 28.

way for the final Redemption, the Resurrection of Christ. God thus needs to 'make himself' a man, the Subject needs to become a subject, as if to show empirically, visibly to the eye, tangibly to the hands (see St Thomas) of the subjects, that, if they are subjects, subjected to the Subject, that is solely in order that finally, on Judgement Day, they will re-enter the Lord's Bosom, like Christ, i.e. re-enter the Subject.[101]

Althusser goes as far as saying that the 'dogma of the Trinity' is in fact the theory of the duplication of the Subject (the Father) into a subject (the Son) and of their mirror-connexion (the Holy Spirit). The result of this duplication is that the subjects 'work by themselves', seemingly freely, at establishing the Subject's existence. Thus, the individuals are interpellated as free subjects in order that they submit themselves freely to the commandments of the Subject, in order that they accept freely their subjection. Thus, 'there are no subjects except by and for their subjection'.[102] What comes into question, therefore, is the mechanisms of the mirror recognition of the Subject and the subjects, by which reality is ignored, misrecognized, *méconnue*. Althusser sees the Christian ideology as constructed upon this misrecognition, upon the moment of the veil, the mirror masquerading as reality.

Althusser's theory does, of course, echo elements of Lacan's mirror stage in the development of the subject. However, Lacan presents the mirror stage as a positive formative process, where the child becomes a subject, an individual, separate from the Mother, who becomes Other. What emerges, however, at the mirror stage with the infant's specular ego is the Imaginary order, which develops throughout the life of the individual, playing an important role in the subject's adult experience of others and the world in general.

It is this, the Imaginary, that Lacan sees as a veil, an item of clothing, functioning as armour. By understanding the mirror stage as an *identification* process, namely, the transformation that takes place in the subject when he or she assumes an image, Lacan brings in the use of the term *imago*, the same term that expresses the creation of human beings as *imago dei*, as/in the image of God.[103] The Imaginary, in similarity with Althusser's ideology, stands for misrecognition (*méconnaissance*) in opposition to knowledge (*connaissance*). Like the mirror, the Imaginary plays on the interdependence between image, identity and identification.

101.   Louis Althusser, 'Ideology and Ideological State Apparatuses', in *idem*, *Lenin and Philosophy and Other Essays* (London: New Left Books, 1971), pp. 170-86 (82).

102.   Althusser, 'Ideology and Ideological State Apparatuses', p. 83.

103.   Lacan, 'The Mirror Stage', p. 382.

Perhaps the Prologue is—or rather reading the Prologue offers—the locus of such activity, of the Imaginary and the subject's identification, where believers become 'children of God' by identifying themselves freely with the embodied Word, because they misrecognize him as God through the play of the Imaginary. God the Father, as the ultimate Other, takes the place of the lost mother, thus perceived as accommodating his children back into himself, in a false sense of united and unified identity. They are promised light, but are left in a new kind of darkness predicated on misrecognition, the darkness of Lacan's impossible Real, or the fulfilment of all desire and the illusion—the ultimate fantasy—of a centred and unified identity.

Another element that presents itself as a problem is that of the Word taking the form of a *male* body. The fact that the Father wants the role of the mother is not necessarily a surprise, and I will look at that aspect of the Prologue later—namely, the removal of the mother and the appropriation of her role by the Father. As Hélène Cixous would say, things always come back to man's 'desire to be the origin', so they always come back to the father.[104] What is problematic here is the mechanism of identification with the embodied Word available to women. How does the Imaginary work in this case for us? The Prologue does allow, after all, for female τέκνα τοῦ θεοῦ, 'children of God'.

In *The Shining Garment of the Text: Gendered Readings of John's Prologue*, Alison Jasper makes a convincing case as to why women should read the prelude to the Gospel of John.[105] I am not quite sure whether there are any arguments why they should not. Jasper concludes her work by declaring that it is 'perfectly possible to read the text of the Prologue from a woman-centred perspective'.[106] While I am not convinced that one can offer a 'centred' reading of any text (be that within a woman's realm or not), Jasper does touch on a very important issue: whether it is possible for a woman to read John's Prologue and undergo a process of identification with the word become flesh, when that flesh happens to take the form of a male body. To her aid, Jasper calls Kristevan psychoanalytical theories, particularly those surrounding the concept of abjection, thus emphasizing the role that difference plays within subject formation.

In her essay on abjection, *Pouvoirs de l'horreur*, or *Powers of Horror*, Kristeva describes abjection as the psychoanalytical amplification of

104.   Cixous, 'The Newly Born Woman', p. 39.
105.   Alison Jasper, *The Shining Garment of the Text: Gendered Readings of the Prologue* (JSNTSup, 165; Gender, Culture Theory, 6; Sheffield: Sheffield Academic Press, 1998), in particular pp. 242-47.
106.   Jasper, *The Shining Garment of the Text*, p. 246.

universal 'horror', which creates a link between the subject and what he or she recognizes as 'times of dreary crisis'. It is easily understood that, because of the horror element, the abject is all the more powerful while it remains hidden, unknown. Analytically, however, while that happens, what also remains hidden is the 'other side of religious, moral, and ideological codes on which rest the sleep of individuals and the respites of societies. Such codes are abjection's purification and repression.'[107]

Kristeva maintains that the Symbolic is not strong enough to cause or impose the separation from the mother on its own. Thus, before the child's entrance into the Symbolic order, there exists the experience of certain impulses and drives towards rejecting, or expelling, the mother; towards making the mother into the abjected object. 'The abject would thus be the "object" of primal repression.'[108] It is possible, Kristeva explains, that, through changing nappies, toilet training, and other cleanliness-related habits, the mother becomes associated, at the pre-symbolic level, with that which is expelled. Thus, abjection could be understood as an undesirable part of ourselves, something that we do not wish to face, 'the mud of Narcissus' pool', as John Lechte puts it,[109] 'the moment of narcissistic perturbation'.[110]

Analytically, the abject is the ambiguous element that disrupts the confines of the ego, that which resists unity and disturbs the formation of identity on a unified premise, that which resists system and order. Examples of the abject number not only material filth and waste (corpses, too), but also elements of moral and political hypocrisy, like 'the traitor, the liar, the criminal with a good conscience, the shameless rapist, the killer who claims he is a saviour',[111] where corruption is the most conventional 'socialized aspect of the abject'.[112]

In contrast to this, the sacred is formed, in Kristeva's opinion, as a 'two-sided sacred',[113] on the premise of the subject-object dyad and the resulting subjects and social codes, which are constructed on the division between murder (the murder of the father) and incest (engaging the mother). This theory corresponds to Freud's own take on 'totem and

107. Julia Kristeva, *Pouvoirs de l'horreur. Essai sur l'abjection* (Paris: Seuil, 1980); ET: *Powers of Horror: An Essay on Abjection* (trans. Leon S. Roudiez; New York: Columbia University Press, 1982), p. 209; translation modified by John Lechte, 'Horror, Love, Melancholy', in *Julia Kristeva*, pp. 157-98 (158).

108. Kristeva, *Powers of Horror*, p. 12.
109. Lechte, *Julia Kristeva*, p. 160.
110. Kristeva, *Powers of Horror*, p. 15.
111. Kristeva, *Powers of Horror*, p. 4.
112. Kristeva, *Powers of Horror*, p. 16.
113. Kristeva, *Powers of Horror*, pp. 57-58.

taboo', which sees the existence of the sacred predicated on murder and incest, more precisely on its difference *from* murder and incest. As the separation from the mother is a feared moment—the same moment when unified identity is exposed as illusory—it is associated with other elements that threaten the unity of the 'I', elements that exist on the border of identities, namely filth and defilement.[114]

Elements like bodily waste, nail clippings, menstrual blood, etc., which create a hazy contour for the body, ambiguous and undefined, become subject to ritualistic habits, so that the abjection linked to them is warded off. Corpses undergo similar treatment for the same reasons. These rituals, however, while intending to affirm identities, emphasize the existence of, and separation between, subject and object. This is similar to the removal of the mother (and the threat that she brings to identity contours), which only establishes the mother as the Other.

Kristeva, however, remarks that through the links to the maternal and/ or the feminine, two of the defiling elements, namely menstrual blood and excrement, are not perceived as polluting, as a corpse would be, for example. While the case for menstrual blood may be an easy one to figure out, excrement presents a slightly more difficult riddle here. According to Kristeva, excrement is seen as part of the maternal realm because of the cleansing rituals undergone by the infant, associated thus with the pre-symbolic *corps proper*, or clean body. Excrement is seen as marking out the body at the level of the pre-symbolic, the pre-linguistic, and of the semiotic authority of the mother (who is still perceived as having the phallus at that stage). Kristeva maintains,

> Through frustrations and prohibitions this authority shapes the body into a *territory* having areas, orifices, points and lines, surfaces and hollows, where the archaic power of mastery and neglect, of the differentiation of proper-clean and improper-dirty, possible and impossible, is impressed and exerted.[115]

In the light of this territorial demarcation, excrement is perceived as improper/dirty, not part of the self, but belonging to a different *territory*. Through excrement, the infant realizes the difference between an 'inside' and an 'outside', which later becomes linked to the separation from the mother. Thus, the mother, as the expelled element, becomes associated with the abject. For Kristeva, defilement marks the separation between the semiotic authority and the symbolic law,[116] between the realm of the mother and that of the father.

---

114.   See on this the work of Mary Douglas, *Purity and Danger* (London: Routledge & Kegan Paul, 1979).

115.   Kristeva, *Powers of Horror*, p. 71. Italics in original.

116.   Kristeva, *Powers of Horror*, p. 73.

How does Kristeva's theory of the abject influence our reading of the Prologue, however? If the maternal, indeed the feminine, is removed, expelled from the Prologue, then it follows that the biblical text submits to the Law of the Father, where the mother/feminine is abjection. What is left to the female self in terms of subject-formation? The flesh, σάρξ? Perhaps the Word does not take the shape of a woman because that would be perceived as horrifying. God cannot write himself on the body of a woman! A woman cannot carry his Phallus. That would be feminine perversion, père-version.[117] Perhaps Lidia Curti is right when she notes that 'the monster at the end of it all is women's writing, writing as the female body, ink and milk and blood'.[118] Contrary to these, the gifts of the embodied Logos are grace and truth, χάρις καὶ ἀλήθεια (Jn 1.17b). Again, this betrays the metaphysics of phallogocentrism, which presupposes the superiority of spirit over matter, of brain over womb, of man over woman. Is there a way out of this binary world?

Jasper does not dwell on the apparent dichotomy between the mother/woman as abjection and the father as the Law, since she tries to erase the borders between binary oppositions. Yet she does highlight a powerful link between abjection and darkness. By associating darkness with a certain *exteriority to God*, Jasper argues that darkness could be perceived as the 'outside' that characterizes Kristeva's abjection. What the subject—who always remains a *sujet en procès* after all—experiences in the path of self-formation is

> a sudden emergence of uncanniness, which, familiar as it might have been in an opaque and forgotten life, now harries me as radically separate, loathsome. Not me. Not that. But not nothing either. A 'something' that I do not recognize as a thing. A weight of meaninglessness, about which there is nothing insignificant, and which crushes me.[119]

Abjection forces the subject to move out of the maternal semiotic and on towards the paternal symbolic, towards accepting the existence of the Other and the outside. The Word becomes a Subject by successfully rejecting the mother, whose semiotic authority joins the darkness of the unconscious, and by accepting to identify with the Father, whom he himself reveals, or whose person/nature/authority he represents. The transition is so accomplished, and the Word perceives his birth as from the 'bosom' of the Father (cf. Jn 1.18).

117.   See Kristeva's essay 'Stabat Mater', in Toril Moi, *The Kristeva Reader* (Oxford: Basil Blackwell, 1986), pp. 160-86 (183).

118.   Curti, *Female Stories*, p. xiii.

119.   Kristeva, *Powers of Horror*, p. 2; cited by Jasper, *The Shining Garment of the Text*, p. 224.

Kristeva does not support the idea of an *écriture féminine*, and is thus *contra* Irigaray and Cixous. She believes that there is indeed a danger of essentializing woman in promoting a feminine writing while trying to oppose the phallic sign; that there may be a relapse back into feminine mysticism through it; and that the symbolic enclosure in which the problem arose would not change by simply privileging woman's *signifiance* (be that 'lips' or 'writing') over man's phallus. These are valid concerns, and I have addressed some of them already. Jasper insists on emphasizing, within Kristevan psychoanalysis, the mechanisms supporting the formation of, not *male* or *female*, but *human* subjectivity. As such, she also may perhaps be called a dutiful daughter, willingly revealing the Father and accepting his Law, where women do not exist but are happy to accept their veiling as 'human'.[120] While the intention to dispose of the borders imposed by sexual difference is laudable, the process of achieving it is perhaps impossible.

Where Cixous and Kristeva agree is in accepting that

> all speaking subjects have within themselves a certain bisexuality, which is precisely the possibility to explore all the sources of signification, that which posits meaning as well as that which multiplies, pulverizes and finally revives it.[121]

The difference is that Kristeva sees this happening in art—she still sees 'the very dichotomy man/woman ... as belonging to *metaphysics*',[122] and only certain aesthetic practices able to transcend it. Thus, for Kristeva, the (male) avant-garde text 'mimes' not the feminine, not the woman, but the 'constitution and deconstitution of the subject; a subject in process/on trial.[123] For both Kristeva and Cixous, however, identity is always in process, in formation; never stable, never fixed. Kristeva argues,

> What inconceivable ambition it is to aspire to singularity, it is not natural, hence it is inhuman; the mania smitten with Oneness ... Within this strange feminine see-saw that makes 'me' swing from the unnameable community of women over to the war of individual singularities, it is unsettling to say 'I' ... A woman discourse, would that be it? Did not Christianity attempt, among

120.   Primarily Freudian, it seems, Jasper is still fond of the concept of a transcendent God/Word and thus of a centred identity for the children of God. See Jasper, *The Shining Garment of the Text*, pp. 214-15, 228-33.

121.   Julia Kristeva, 'Oscillation between Power and Denial', in Elaine Marks and Isabelle de Courtivron (eds.), *New French Feminism* (Brighton: Harvester Press, 1985), p. 165.

122.   Julia Kristeva, 'Women's Time', in Moi (ed.), *The Kristeva Reader*, pp. 188-213 (209). Italics in original.

123.   Kristeva, *Revolution in Poetic Language*, p. 616.

other things, to freeze this see-saw? To stop it, tear women away from its rhythm, settle them permanently in the spirit? Too permanently ...[124]

If one agrees with Jasper and accepts the universal veil, is not desiring the facelessness of 'human' the same as desiring to be whole and united with the Other? It this not desiring, or 'writing the Real'?[125] I think it may be.

Therefore, and if we can still allow for gendered readings, what is it that remains in the Prologue for the female subject ('bisexual' or not)? Ironically, while women are not openly identified with the body in the Prologue, since *the* body is male, the absence of the mother is nevertheless traced back to σάρξ, which substitutes and represents her (and I shall return to this later). If one were to move away from corporeality, however, what would be woman's in John's Prologue?

Should one read with Kristeva 'in the beginning was love'[126] and thus allow for a different identification path for women? Kristeva muses,

> What is loving, for a woman, the same thing as writing. Laugh. Impossible. Flash on the unnameable, weaving of abstractions to be torn. Let a body venture at last out of its shelter, take a chance with meaning under a veil of words. WORD FLESH. From one to the other, eternally, broken up visions, metaphors of the invisible.[127]

Love, as writing, however, only reinforces the separation from, and the desire for, the mother. In *Tales of Love*, Kristeva makes it quite clear that love is impossible without that separation and without the resulting idealization of the mother in primary narcissism. She looks at Christianity for the perfect example of idealization: in the myth of the Virgin Mother, whom she sees as embodying the perfect femininity. As a mother, Mary is perfect because she facilitates rather than contest her own removal. Christ's separation from his mother is complete, and he makes a perfect entry into the Symbolic and the Law of the Father. (The fact that he is perceived as having no sin confirms this.) Furthermore, Christ does not desire (only) the mother; instead God as the Ideal replaces her. By her coupling with the Ideal (the Holy Spirit), the Virgin remains a virgin. In giving up her body and her son out of love for God, the Father, she becomes the ideal feminine.

124. Kristeva, 'Stabat Mater', pp. 182-83.

125. À propos Kristeva's understanding of acts of purification that aim to encapsulate the cathartic energy of the pre-linguistic/symbolic semiotic, the return to the mother. See Kristeva, *Powers of Horror*, p. 74.

126. À propos Kristeva's essay *Au commencement était l'amour. Psychanalyse et foi* (Paris: Hachette, 1985); ET: *In the Beginning Was Love: Psychoanalysis and Faith* (trans. Arthur Goldhammer; New York: Columbia University Press, 1987).

127. Kristeva, 'Stabat Mater', p. 162. Capitals in original.

However, this ideal is not an object of identification for women. The position of the mother of Christ is unique, and she is 'alone of all her sex'.[128] The myth of the Virgin Mother is meant to portray separation and not union, a model followed by none. She is the impossible ideal feminine. If the mother of the Gospels is not available for identification processes, are women to follow a different love? Mystical love?

Lacan himself looks at mystical love in trying to elucidate his understanding of *jouissance*, particularly at St Teresa's expressions of it:

> Beside me on the left appeared an angel in bodily form ... very beautiful ... In his hands I saw a long golden spear and at the end of the iron tip I seemed to see a point of fire. With this he seemed to pierce my heart several times so that it penetrated my entrails. When he drew it out I thought he was drawing them out with it and he left me completely afire with a great love for God. The pain was so sharp that it made me utter several moans; and so excessive was the sweetness caused me by this intense pain that one can never wish to lose it, nor will one's soul be content with anything less than God. It is not bodily pain, but spiritual, though the body has a share in it—indeed, a great share. So sweet are the colloquies of love which pass between the soul and God that if anyone thinks I am lying I beseech God, in His goodness, to give him the same experience.[129]

Using it inversely, and quite adamant not 'to reduce the mystical to questions of fucking',[130] Lacan understands women's sexuality, more precisely their *jouissance*, as similar to the climaxing moment within a relationship with God (whatever that may be). However, Lacan does insist that although they experience it, and that mystical love is an 'act of enjoying', mystics do not understand their own attraction; they 'do not know anything about it'.[131]

Kristeva also tries to understand the mystics, and she focuses on the writings of Bernard of Clairvaux. She is of the opinion that Christian love goes beyond passion. If analytically the separation from the mother is 'a painful and passionate affair', so is the 'way to tranquillity in the Father's love'.[132] For Christians, says Kristeva,

---

128.   See Marina Warner, *Alone of All Her Sex: The Myth and Cult of the Virgin Mary* (London: Picador, 1985).

129.   St Teresa, cited by Georges Bataille, *Eroticism* (London: Marion Boyars, 1987), p. 224. See Fig. 15, Bernini's sculpture of *The Ecstasy of St Teresa* (1647–52; Cornaro Chapel, St Maria della Vittoria, Rome), which inspired Lacan.

130.   Lacan, 'God and the Jouissance of Woman', p. 142.

131.   B. Benvenuto and R. Kennedy, *The Works of Jacques Lacan: An Introduction* (London: Free Associations Book, 1986), p. 192.

132.   Lechte, *Julia Kristeva*, p. 173.

the love of God and for God resides in a gap: the broken space made explicit by sin on the one side, the beyond on the other. Discontinuity, lack and arbitrariness: topography of the sign, of the symbolic relation that posits my otherness as impossible. Love, here, is only for the impossible.[133]

Kristeva sees mystic love as a 'saintly violence' that aims to conquer the resistance of the flesh while being dependent on it. She insists that the flesh is both inevitable and necessary, because 'the flesh gives body to spirit, just as the spirit sanctifies the body'.[134] Mystic love, therefore, is ambivalent and ambiguous; the mystic tries to be united with God, while at the same time realizing and fighting her (or his) divided subjectivity. 'Love, here, is only for the impossible',[135] for the united and centred S/subject.

Irigaray also is quite taken with mysticism—or rather, the 'mysteric'— and she sees it as the means by which women, while under the patriarchal symbolic, can discover elements of pleasure, *jouissance*. The mysteric is the discourse in which masculine consciousness and self-consciousness are no longer the controlling and regulating factor. Referring to Lacan's take on St Teresa's ecstasy, Irigaray observes,

This is the only place in the history of the West in which a woman speaks and acts so publicly. What is more, it is for/by woman that man dares to enter the place, to descend to it, condescend to it, even if he gets burned in the attempt.[136]

If Teresa is excessive in her mystical *jouissance*, she is so beyond the phallus, and her ecstasy is perceived by male speculation as beyond signification. Further still, it is the means by which men may want to approach (their) God, too. However, while 'illuminating' male speculation, this ecstatic state may also burn.

And if 'God' has already appeared to me with face unveiled, so my body shines with a light of glory that radiates it. And my eyes have proved sharp enough to look upon the glory without blinking. They would have been seared had they not been that simple eye of the 'soul' that sets fire to what it admires out of its hollow socket. A burning glass is the soul who in her cave joins with the source of light to set everything ablaze that approaches her hearth. Leaving only ashes there, only a hole: fathomless in her incendiary blaze.[137]

133.   Kristeva, 'Stabat Mater', p. 184.

134.   Lechte, *Julia Kristeva*, p. 173.

135.   Kristeva, 'Stabat Mater', p. 184.

136.   Luce Irigaray, *Speculum: Of the Other Woman* (Ithaca, NY: Cornell University Press, 1985), p. 191.

137.   Irigaray, *Speculum*, p. 197.

St Teresa's ecstasy, eulogized by Lacan, represents for Irigaray the *ex-stasis*, the 'outside-itself' that in fact is constructed by male speculation; thus, it represents the phallic refusal to tolerate an otherness that is not modelled on the phallus, or on the Same.[138] Irigaray insists that mystical love is not beyond signification, after all. It is only that women speak differently from men, emitting what men perceive as a flowing, fluctuating, blurring language,[139] so men simply cannot hear their voices. Mystical, ecstatic, love is not beyond the male signification system and thus not woman's. This love is expressed for the impossible, which is exactly what escaping the symbolic, or having an identity not limited to it, seems to be.

Figure 15. *Giovanni Lorenzo Bernini*, The Ecstasy of St Teresa
(*1647–42; Cornaro Chapel, St Maria della Vittoria, Rome*).

138.   See Grosz, *Jacques Lacan*, p. 175.
139.   Irigaray, *Speculum*, pp. 112-13.

So what can be woman's—or rather, women's—in the Prologue of John? The answer is: the Word, Writing. In her 'bisexuality', woman can identify with the father here, namely, the Father who writes himself onto a body. The mother is not only absent, but she is also ideal and alone, beyond the scope of identification. Her σάρξ is not the attractive identification target. In understanding her multiple, decentred and fluid identity, the female reader comes to writing, much like Nagiko. She enters the Symbolic, yet, in her identifying with the Father and not the Mother, she disturbs the Law of the Father and threatens his identity as master writer. Perhaps it is true that 'today writing is woman's'.[140] Moving away from abjection, for woman writing can be *écriture féminine*, or love, or motherhood, or writing as liberation of the *chora*, or heterogeneous subjectivity, or whatever type of self-creative *écriture féminine* or *parler femme* she (as any of her 'I's) chooses.

Perhaps it is true that 'the Word became flesh' can indeed be read as the arrival of the subject (in this case the Subject as subject), the entry of human beings into the Symbolic, into language, into light. If, therefore, the Incarnation of God signifies the success of the Symbolic and the Law of the Father, then does the pre-symbolic Word belong to the semiotic mother? Who is she? If the light of the Word is language, does that mean that the pre-lingual is darkness? That would make the children of God *as* subjects of the Symbolic, subjects coming to writing. The process that ensures their arrival to language presupposes the subjects' having experienced the mirror stage, realized their boundaries, and separated successfully from the darkness of the pre-lingual semiotic mother (who is completely removed from the Prologue). God as the Father replaces the Mother by exercising his authority in a veiled manner while promising, not the Law (of Moses), but tranquillity, or grace and truth (Jn 1.17, 18).

Yet to accept the veil of human subjectivity, of seeming neutrality and universality (which is only an illusion, since all discourses *are* gendered), is to remain hidden, dwelling in darkness. As Irigaray laments,

> We lack, we women with a sex of our own, a God in which to share, a word/language to share and to become. Defined as the often obscure, not to say hidden, mother-substance of the word/language of men, we lack our *subject*, our *noun*, our *verb*, our *predicates*: our elementary sentence, our basic rhythm, our morphological identity, our generic incarnation, our genealogy.[141]

140.   Cixous, 'The Newly Born Woman', p. 42.

141.   Irigaray, *Sexes et parentés*, p. 83; this is Margaret Whitford's translation in *Luce Irigaray: Philosophy in the Feminine* (London: Routledge, 1991), p. 45.

The term 'human' veils the sexual differences that ensure our survival as humankind, and perhaps we desire the 'human' identity only as a return to the Garden, to the innocence of unity with God, who is both Mother and Father in the beginning. Perhaps that is why Derrida warns of

> the thing itself *behind* the veil or the thing itself the phantasm of which is itself an effect of the veil, as much as to say *thing* as *veiled cause*—of nudity, of modesty, of shame, of reticence (*Verhaltenheit*), of the law, of everything that hides and shows the sex, of the origin of culture and so-called humanity in general, in short of what links evil, radical evil, to *knowledge*, and knowledge to avowal, knowing-how-to-avow [*le savoir-avouer*] to knowledge avowed [*le savoir avoué*].[142]

Perhaps *écriture feminine/parler femme* could, however, pursue unconscious impulses, play with the veil but never own it (thus circumventing the need to pierce it and then loose one's *sight*); it could 'go on and on without ever inscribing or distinguishing contours', undergoing these 'dizzying passages in other, fleeting and passionate dwellings within him, within the hims and hers *she* inhabits';[143] through feminine writing, women may escape the eternal repetition and invent new worlds, where eyes are lips on the lips of God. All that remains is for women to realize whether they experience split subjectivities without regret.

What of women's discourse(s), however?

---

142.   Derrida, 'A Silkworm of One's Own', pp. 98-99 n. 18. Italics in original.

143.   Cixous, 'The Newly Born Woman', p. 87. My emphasis, à propos Margaret Davies's use of 'she' and 'her' for God in her reading of John's Prologue. See Margaret Davies, *Rhetoric and Reference in the Fourth Gospel* (JSNTSup, 69; Sheffield: JSOT Press, 1992).

5

OPENING MOUTHS AND LEGS, OR WOMEN'S TALK: GENDER, JOHN'S PROLOGUE AND *THE FIFTH ELEMENT*

In Brief on Body and Self

A woman is trapped within the frontiers of her body and even of her species, and consequently always feels exiled by the general clichés that make up a common consensus and by the very powers of generalization intrinsic to language. This female exile in relation to the General and to Meaning is such that a woman is always ... the fragmentation, the drive, the unnameable.

—*Julia Kristeva*[1]

It is for a long time that women have endeavoured to achieve an identity that is not predicated on the body. This is one of the important elements in the shared discourse between feminism and postmodernism, among the decline of an undivided subjectivity, the rejection of canonized structures, the resistance to a morality of consensus ('it is not a question of obtaining a consensus that others have had for too long but of creating a space for dissent'), the focus on the marginal and the hidden. The distinctions between subject and object, centre and margins, sameness and difference, and, ideally, oppressor and oppressed are blurred and uncertain.[2]

Like all marginalized groups, feminism has fought and continues to fight against this condition, but the answer does not lie in exchanging the margins for the centre; as with deconstruction, a mere inversion would only reinforce old dualities and a hierarchical order of the world and thus would not be truly valuable to women. As Gayatri Spivak notes, 'by pointing attention to a feminist marginality, I have been attempting, not to win the centre for ourselves, but to point at the irreducibility of

---

1. Julia Kristeva, 'A New Type of Intellectual: The Dissident', in Moi (ed.), *The Kristeva Reader*, pp. 292-300 (296). Italics in original.
2. Curti, *Female Stories*, p. 2.

the margin in all explanations'.[3] This philosophy is shared by Lidia Curti, who suggests, 'Margins cannot be included, or appropriated or used as tokens; the movement between centre and periphery is a narration of displacement'.[4]

The issue at hand is that of the formation of the 'I' in rapport with the body. What is the relationship between individual identity and individual corporeality? In *Volatile Bodies: Towards a Corporeal Feminism*, Elizabeth Grosz structures feminist responses to this question in a number of categories, which while, as she maintains, are not hard and fast, seem to present a 'tidy' picture of developments.[5] We shall look at this very briefly.

One category would be Egalitarian Feminism, as seen in the works of Simone de Beauvoir, Shulamith Firestone, Mary Wollstonecraft and other liberal, conservative and humanist feminists (even ecofeminists). This position is characterized by a veiled acceptance of the patriarchal and misogynist view that women's bodies are somehow more material, closer to nature. Thus, some feminists in this category look at the body as a cumbersome burden for women; its specific physiology—menstruation, pregnancy, childbirth, lactation—limits women's access to *equality* and thus the privileges that men enjoy. Other feminists, such as the ecofeminists, regard the body as a means of knowledge and understanding (of the world in general and the ways of nature in particular).

As a result of their understanding of the role of the body in the formation of feminine identity, these feminists have focused on the relationship between motherhood and society. The introduction of regulatory techniques of motherhood (such as the pill, abortion and so on) has been hailed by some (Beauvoir and Firestone in particular) as a wonderful means of progress towards an egalitarian society. On the other hand, the same developments have been criticized as means by which patriarchy extends its control over women's bodies and the ultimate goal of femininity that is motherhood. Strangely, while these feminists see the female body as an impediment to the furthering of the mind, the male body is not at all considered an impediment to the furthering of men's intellectual abilities, to their perceived transcendence. It seems, therefore, that an egalitarian way would choose the option of a biological transformation of women. Into men.

3. Gayatri Chakrovorty Spivak, *In Other Worlds: Essays in Cultural Politics* (London: Methuen, 1987), p. 107.

4. Curti, *Female Stories*, p. 3.

5. Elizabeth Grosz, *Volatile Bodies: Towards a Corporeal Feminism* (Bloomington: Indiana University Press, 1994), pp. 15-19.

The second category that Grosz delineates is that of Social Construc-
tionism, which can be traced through the works of many, if not all, contemporary feminist theorists: Juliet Mitchell, Julia Kristeva, Michele
Barrett, Nancy Chodorow, Marxist feminists, psychoanalytic feminists
and all those who subscribe to the idea of the social construction of the
subject. The position towards the body in this category is less negative
than that of the Egalitarianists. The body is no longer perceived as cumbersome. Instead the body is perceived as merely signifying the difference
between males and females by means of its political representation and
functioning. In other words, the male/female opposition is no longer
associated directly with mind/body (although that duality is kept), but
with the ideology/production-reproduction distinction, seen through the
difference between biology and psychoanalysis. This position opens the
gates for the concept of 'gender' as the performed sexual difference. Thus,
this kind of feminism feels no commitment to biology but to the representation of biology within socio-political language. Thus, the transformation that Social Constructionists desire is one of values, beliefs and
attitudes and not that of the body itself.

Strikingly different from either of the two groups above, a third category focusing on Sexual Difference emerges with the works of Luce Irigaray, Hélène Cixous, Gayatri Spivak, Jane Gallop, Moira Gatens, Vicki
Kirby, Judith Butler, Naomi Schor, Monique Wittig and others. These
feminists consider the body as the lived body, no longer an ahistorical,
biologically fixed, acultural object. Through sexual difference the body is
constituted through, and constitutive of, systems of meaning, signification
and representation. The body occupies simultaneously two positions: (1)
the signifying and signified body and (2) an object of social coercion,
legal inscription and sexual and economic exchanges. The mind/body
opposition is rejected in favour of a monism of interdependence. The
body is no longer the raw and passive nature subjected by culture; it is
not a biological *tabula rasa* that bears masculine or feminine identities
indifferently. The body is perceived as 'social and discursive object, a body
bound up in the order of desire, signification and power'.[6] It is for this
reason that the body has become the site of contestation for a number of
economic, political, intellectual and sexual discourses.

Through his study on genealogy, Foucault meant to 'expose the body
totally imprinted by history and the processes of history's destruction of
the body'.[7] Foucault makes a radical statement when suggesting that

6. Grosz, *Volatile Bodies*, p. 18.
7. Michel Foucault, 'Nietzsche, Genealogy, History', in P. Rabinow (ed.), *The
Foucault Reader* (Harmondsworth: Penguin Books, 1984), p. 63.

'[n]othing in man—not even his body—is sufficiently stable to serve as a basis for self-recognition for understanding other men'.[8]

Stuart Hall and other cultural critics disagree with this theory, not because the body is sufficiently stable a basis for self-recognition, but because the body has indeed 'served to function as the signifier of the condensation of subjectivities in the individual'.[9] Furthermore, some critics think that the body acquired a totemic value in post-Foucauldian work because of the seemingly talismanic status that it enjoyed in Foucault's own work. 'It is almost the only trace we have left in Foucault's work of a "transcendental signifier"', Hall suggests.[10]

What is more striking in Foucault's work (*Discipline and Punish*, *The History of Sexuality*) is his theory of power discourses, which perceives the subject as 'docile body'. Within the disciplinary, confessional and pastoral modalities of power that Foucault discusses there emerges no probable cause of disruption of the power discourse. What is offered is in fact a refiguring of the body's materiality, a reinforcing of the body's submission through the soul. In Foucault's opinion, the subject is entirely the product of discursive forces. There is no subject before or outside the Law. The juridical 'machinery transforms individual bodies into a social body. It brings to bear in these bodies the text of a law.'[11]

Although Foucault himself did not promote psychoanalysis (instead he focused on producing a phenomenological approach to subject formation and a genealogy of the technologies of self-production, to which I will return later), Judith Butler connects his work with Lacan and post-Lacanian feminism. Butler is concerned with the transactions between the subject, the body and identity, particularly as displayed within the performativity of gender roles. Butler's work

> accepts as a point of departure Foucault's notion that regulatory power produces the subjects it controls, that power is not only imposed externally but works as the regulatory and normative means by which subjects are formed. The return to psychoanalysis, then, is guided by the question of how certain regulatory norms form a 'sexed' subject in terms that establish the indistinguishability of psychic and bodily formation.[12]

This argument connects the question of identification with the process of assuming a sex and with the discursive means by which the heterosexual

8.   Foucault, 'Nietzsche, Genealogy, History', p. 63.
9.   Hall, 'Who Needs Identity?', p. 11.
10. Hall, 'Who Needs Identity?', p. 11.
11. Michel de Certeau, 'Des outils pour écrire le corps', *Traverses* 14–15 (1979), pp. 4-5. See Grosz, *Volatile Bodies*, p. 118.
12. Judith Butler, *Bodies that Matter* (London: Routledge, 1993), p. 23.

norm enables certain sexed identifications while foreclosing and/or disavowing others. At the basis of Butler's argument is the concept that

> sex is, from the start, normative; it is what Foucault has called a 'regulatory ideal'. In this sense, then, sex not only functions as a norm, but is part of a regulatory practice that produces (through the repetition or iteration of a norm which is without origin) the bodies it governs, that is, whose regulatory force is made clear as a kind of productive power, the power to produce—demarcate, circulate, differentiate—the bodies it controls ... 'sex' is an ideal construct which is forcibly materialized through time.[13]

Refiguring the body's materiality in terms of power, Butler accommodates Foucault's concept of the subject as a social construct. However, the subject's performativity, though grounded in language, is presented as divorced from personal choice and volition. In *Bodies that Matter* (and meant as a clarification of some misreadings of her earlier *Gender Trouble*), Butler offers a definition of performativity 'not as the act by which a subject brings into being what she/he names but rather as that reiterative power of discourse to produce the phenomena that it regulates and constrains'.[14]

Because Butler makes her case within the frame of feminism, her theory is the more challenging then, because she suggests that all identities operate through exclusion, or 'the production of an "outside", a domain of intelligible effects'.[15] This outside corresponds to Kristeva's abject, indicating that identities are formed through repulsion and rejection (processes that are directed both ways). What Butler's work primarily does is to problematize identity categories, even those of women. It seems that Butler's position from within feminist theory—particularly feminist identity politics—brings into question the 'adequacy of a representational politics whose basis is the presumed universality and unity of its subject—a seamless category of women'.[16] That is why I also feel somewhat uncertain about using the representation term 'woman'.

As with all theorists that emphasize sexual difference, Butler also is weary of using the sex/gender duality, since it is somewhat unclear a distinction (as we have just seen). There is, therefore, a lot of value in recognizing the role of the lived body—be it male, female, masculine, feminine or any combination of these—in subject formation. In terms of gender, if one were to consider *penetrability* and *passivity* or *submission* as

13. Butler, *Bodies that Matter*, p. 1.
14. Butler, *Bodies that Matter*, p. 2.
15. Butler, *Bodies that Matter*, p. 22.
16. Hall, 'Who Needs Identity?', p. 15.

corresponding to the feminine performance/normative role, even Jesus shows his feminine gender by allowing himself to be penetrated on the cross, followed by all his male disciples—even the often perceived as misogynist Paul—who show their feminine gender by submitting to the male God as the male master.[17]

Grosz suggests that bodies are to be understood not simply in their biological concreteness, but in their historic and cultural context. In fact, there is no body as such (as much as there is not woman as such). 'There are only *bodies*—male or female, black, brown, white, large or small—and the gradations in between.'[18] Rather than pursuing a schemata that places bodies on a linear continuum that identifies its polar extremities as male and female, Grosz argues for a 'field, a two-dimensional continuum in which race (and possibly even class, caste, or religion) form body specifications'.[19]

While Grosz herself admits that 'knowledges, like all other forms of social production, are at least partially effects of the sexualized positioning of their producers and users; [that] knowledges must themselves be acknowledged as sexually determined, limited, finite',[20] her suggestion of a two-dimensional structure for bodies seems rather simplistic to me. When there are so many different elements that constitute, engage, transform the body and are in turn constituted, engaged and transformed *by* the body, and when the relationship between body, identification and identity is such a complex and still mysterious one, proposing a mere two-dimensional vision for that picture is inadequate.

Indeed, the question is exactly whether we can, or should, sustain a structure at all. If we allow for the lived body—or, indeed, lived bodies— why do we strive for a language that would limit and categorize them? It is true that such a language exists already—that of the summoning Law, the prescribing power that sutures subjects *through* their bodies to pre-constituted subject positions. Yet, would not the point be to resist it? By formulating further categories—be they two- or multi-dimensional—we perpetuate the power and control exercised over subjects already. It is the sign of our willing subjection to the Law.

---

17.   A lot more can be said on this, of course, although not much has been written on it. For further reading, see Stephen D. Moore, *God's Beauty Parlor: And Other Queer Spaces in and around the Bible* (Contraversions: Jews and Other Differences; Stanford: Stanford University Press, 2001).
    18.   Grosz, *Volatile Bodies*, p. 19.
    19.   Grosz, *Volatile Bodies*, p. 19.
    20.   Grosz, *Volatile Bodies*, p. 20.

The Female Saviour and The Fifth Element:
Can One Hear the Mother of Christ in John's Gospel and Leeloo in Luc
Besson's The Fifth Element?

Playing on the tension between biologistic and linguistic grounds for gender construction, I would like to read afresh the Johannine presentation of the mother of Christ in relation to Luc Besson's creation of the Leeloo character, or 'The Fifth Element', in the film with the same name. Both women are instrumental in the salvation of humankind: Mary opens her legs and gives birth to the divine Saviour, to Christ, the Word, the light and life of humankind; and Leeloo opens her mouth and releases the Fifth Element, or the saving light and energy of all life. Yet the actual voices of the two female characters are either silenced or sabotaged. In preference for an all-male cast, John excludes the mother of Christ from his unique birth narrative, the Prologue (although he allows brief echoes of her voice elsewhere in his Gospel), while Besson has Leeloo speak an unintelligible yet divine language that requires male-performed interpretation. Here I ask whether these women's discourses are dutifully performed 'in the Name of the Father' or whether they are subversive in their nature; whether these characters are rooted within the confinements of the masculine, phallocentric, symbolic order or indeed outside of it.

Opening Legs, or the Discourse of the Mother
'The whole of our Western culture is based upon the murder of the mother', declares Luce Irigaray in her 1981 paper 'Women-Mothers, the Silent Substratum of the Social Order'.[21] Irigaray's theory comes in direct conflict with that of Jacques Lacan (conflict which attracted her dismissal by Lacan),[22] who remains faithful to Freud in this regard and thus sees the murder of the father as the pivotal act of civilization. What Irigaray does is to reinterpret the same Greek tragedies used by Freud for his *Totem and*

---

21.   Luce Irigaray, 'Women-Mothers, the Silent Substratum of the Social Order', in Margaret Whitford (ed.), *The Irigaray Reader* (Oxford: Basil Blackwell, 1991), pp. 47-52 (47).

22.   Irigaray occupied a teaching position in Lacan's Department of Psychoanalysis at Viencennes, but she was dismissed after the publication of her second book, *Speculum*, in 1974. After she lost her post, Irigaray described herself as 'put into quarantine' by the psychoanalytic establishment (as cited by Elaine Hoffman Baruch and Lucienne Serrano, *Women Analyze Women in France, England, and the United States* [London: Harvester Wheatsheaf, 1988], p. 183).

Taboo, namely Aeschylus's *Oresteia*.[23] Irigaray rereads the trilogy as a myth of triumphant patriarchy at the sacrifice of the mother and her daughters. The focal point of her work is to expose one of the great cultural taboos, the relationship with the mother. It seems that the focus that psycho-analysis places on the Oedipus complex should be turned from the castra-tion motif onto another, different, type of incision: the severing of the umbilical cord, the removal of the mother.

In his unique birth narrative, John removes the mother of Christ in favour of an all male cast: God the Father, Logos the Son/Jesus the Christ, John the Witness, even Moses the Lawgiver. In Jn 1.1-18 there is no reference to the mother of Christ. Her birth pains are not mentioned; her screams are not heard; her caresses not felt. The mother has been removed (and some have commended John for doing it—so Luther, for example). John tells that the Word becomes flesh, full of grace and truth and glory. No blood, no placenta, no umbilical cord. All the physical ele-ments of the actual birth are also expelled with the mother, as the abjec-tion. The Word becomes flesh all by himself, one would think. Well, no: the Word is born with a little help from his Father. The Logos is πρὸς τὸν θεόν. Jesus is the Christ, come from God the Father. One does not quite know what the Father's exact involvement is in the matter (John leaves that out, too), but we are told that he makes his Son, who is in his bosom, known to the world as a revelation of himself (1.18). Rather than investigating, or re-investigating, the Christology of this passage, the

23. In this trilogy (first presented in 458 BCE), Aeschylus tells the story of the Greek king Agamemnon and his family. In the first tragedy, *Agamemnon*, King Agamemnon returns triumphant from the Trojan war accompanied by his mistress, the prophet Cassandra. Rather than getting a hero's reception, Agamemnon is humiliated and violently killed by his wife, Clytemnestra, and her lover, Aegisthus. Clytemnestra is driven by a desire for revenge for the death of her daughter Iphigenia, whom Aga-memnon had sacrificed for the sake of the war. At the end of the play, Clytemnestra and her lover rule over Argos. In the second play, *The Libation Bearers* (Gk *Choephoroi*), Orestes, the son of Agamemnon and Clytemnestra, returns from abroad (where he had been sent as a child) with the intention of avenging his father's death, at the god Apollo's bidding. Orestes is reunited with his sister, Electra, and they plan together the murder of Aegisthus. However, after killing Aegisthus, Orestes also kills his own mother, Clytemnestra. The act fills him with deep remorse and confusion, and he becomes insane as a result. The same madness befalls Electra. The play finishes with Orestes being pursued by the Furies (Erinyes), as ghostly incarnations of his dead mother. The third play, *Eumenides*, sees Orestes recovered from his madness, tried and acquitted for the two murders, all through the interventions of the gods Apollo and Athena. The Furies are persuaded to leave Orestes alone also, in exchange for a home and a cult in Athens (where they live as the kind goddesses of the title of the play). Orestes is the founder of the new order.

theological implications of the two natures of Christ, the human–divine or flesh–spirit apposition/opposition or other related topics, which have been the subject of much scholarship already, I am preoccupied with discursive elements in this text; in particular the mother's discourse. I find the mother's absence in John's unique birth narrative rather conspicuous. The only trace that John allows of her here is the flesh/σάρξ, the 'unnamed flesh' (as Plato would have it).

Throughout time, feminist philosophers have been known to endeavour to expose and criticize the fact that flesh, the body, is always perceived as feminine; in other words, that, while men are associated with reason, logic and science, women are always associated with materiality—either inert and therefore already dead, or fertile, so procreative. Or, the way Elizabeth Grosz puts it,

> Patriarchal oppression … justifies itself, at least in part, by connecting women much more closely than men to the body and, through this identification, restricting women's social and economic roles to (pseudo) biological terms. Relying on essentialism, naturalism and biologism, misogynist thought confines women to the biological requirements of reproduction on the assumption that because of particular biological, physiological, and endocrinological transformations, women are somehow *more* biological, *more* corporeal, and *more* natural than men. The coding of femininity with corporeality in effect leaves men free to inhabit what they (falsely) believe is a purely conceptual order while at the same time enabling them to satisfy their (sometimes disavowed) need for corporeal contact through their access to women's bodies and services.[24]

This represents the classic feminist liberational discourse aimed at exposing the fallacy of the natural inequality thesis that has justified unequal social positions for men and women for centuries. Because the female body is different (weaker?), women are perceived as incapable of the same achievements as men. Grosz evidently works on the premise of the male/ female opposition.

In contrast, Luce Irigaray claims that the feminine is in fact exactly what is excluded in and by such a binary opposition.[25] In *Marine Lover* (*Amante marine*), Irigaray argues that 'woman neither is nor has an essence', because 'woman' is precisely what is excluded from the discourse of metaphysics.

24. Grosz, *Volatile Bodies*, p. 14. Italics in original. Also, for a further study of these issues, see Elizabeth Spelman, 'Woman as Body: Ancient and Contemporary Views', *Feminist Studies* (1982), pp. 8 n. 1, 109-31.

25. See Judith Butler, 'Bodies That Matter', in Carolyn Burke, Naomi Schor and Margaret Whitford (eds.), *Engaging with Irigaray* (Feminist Philosophy and Modern European Thought; New York: Columbia University Press, 1994), pp. 141-74 (149-61).

Echoing Derrida's denouncement of Logocentrism, or the metaphysics of presence, Irigaray deplores the fact that, even within philosophical discourse, seeing is privileged, encouraging Phallocentrism: what is seen is allowed presence and Being. Although Lacan would insists that 'the phallus can only play its role when veiled',[26] the perceived lack of penis in the woman leads Irigaray to the conclusion that '[n]othing to be seen is equivalent to having no thing. No being and no truth.'[27] Thus, when one discusses 'matter' philosophically, one substitutes for and displaces the feminine with one stroke. Perhaps like John's σάρξ, which both substitutes and displaces the mother.

In a similar vein, Cixous links the absence of woman with her passivity:

> Ultimately, the world of 'being' can function while precluding the mother. No need for a mother, as long as there is some motherliness; and it is the father, then, who acts the part, who is the mother. Either woman is passive or she does not exist. What is left of her is unthinkable, is unthought. Which certainly means that she is not thought, that she does not enter the oppositions, the she does not make a couple with the father (who makes a couple with the son).[28]

Cixous refers here to Mallarmé's dream (when faced with his son's tragic end), 'For Anatole's Tomb', in which he keeps/hides his son so that death does not reach him; or, as Cixous interprets it, the 'dream of marriage between father and son'. Therefore, the mother is banished. 'She does not exist, she can not-be; but there has to be something of her. He keeps, then, of the woman on whom he is no longer dependent, only this space, always virginal, as matter to be subjected to the desire he wishes to impart.'[29] Thus, as Cixous laments, it always comes back to man's 'desire to be (at) the origin', back to the father.[30] Lacan himself attributes life to the phallus: 'One can … say that [the phallus] is by its turgidity the image of the life flow [*flux vital*] inasmuch as it passes in generation'.[31]

Echoing Heidegger's house of language, in her *L'oubli de l'air*, Irigaray insists that women lack a home. By that she means that women are forced to operate within the constraints of male, phallocentric language (phallogocentrism), thus unable to express the feminine. Lacan makes

26. Lacan, 'La Signification du phallus', p. 692.
27. Irigaray, *Speculum*, p. 48.
28. Cixous, 'The Newly Born Woman', p. 39.
29. Cixous, 'The Newly Born Woman', p. 39.
30. Cixous, 'The Newly Born Woman', p. 39.
31. Lacan, 'La signification du phallus', p. 692, as quoted in Gallop, *Reading Lacan*, p. 154.

the phallus 'the kingpin in the bowling alley of signification', as Maud Ellman would describe it, the signifier that 'takes the place of God as the absolute guarantee of meaning' (and life, it would seem); as signifier of the difference between the sexes, the phallus comes to stand for all the differences that structure the symbolic order.[32] Of course, the phallus is not meant to represent the penis, as I have already discussed above, but the choice on Lacan's part seems less than opaque and fails to convince many of its neutrality. As Jane Gallop succinctly puts it, 'Phallus/Penis, same difference'.[33] It follows, for Irigaray, that the feminine sex can only be perceived as the castrated category; thus, there is only one sex, which is male, the female being nothing but a mutilated and corrupted copy of the Same.[34]

Rather than looking for equality between the two sexes, however, Irigaray wants to emphasize the difference between male and female, the masculine and the feminine. That is why Irigaray suggests the introduction of a feminine syntax as a new means of representing the specificity of womanhood. The feminine sex would no longer be perceived as 'a lack, a wound, or a black hole' (all phallogocentric terms, in as much as they find meaning through the signification of the phallus),[35] but rather as 'two lips ... neither identifiable nor separable from one another ... strangers to dichotomy'. Irigaray argues,

> It is the touch which for the female sex seems to me as primordial; these two lips are always joined in an embrace ... Superimposed, moreover, these lips adopt a cross-like shape that is the prototype of crossroads, thus representing both *inter* and *enter*, for the lips of the mouth and the lips of the female sex do not point in the same direction. To a certain extent, they are not arranged as one might expect: those 'down below' are vertical.[36]

In what has been called Irigaray's utopia, where women would enunciate their own sex, their language would defy grammatical divisions, making words as warm and slippery as lips.[37]

32.   Maud Ellman, 'Introduction', in *idem* (ed.), *Psychoanalytic Literary Criticism* (London: Longman, 1994), pp. 1-35 (19).

33.   Jane Gallop, 'Phallus/Penis: Same Difference', in *Men by Women: Women and Literature* (New York: Holmes and Meier, 1981); reprinted in Jane Gallop, *Thinking through the Body* (New York: Columbia University Press, 1988).

34.   Irigaray, *The Sex Which is Not One*, p. 78. Irigaray, *Speculum*, pp. 48-49.

35.   Ellman, *Psychoanalytic Literary Criticism*, p. 24.

36.   See Luce Irigaray, 'Interview', *Ideology and Consciousness* 1 (1977), pp. 64-65; *idem*, 'Sexual Difference', in Whitford (ed.) *The Irigaray Reader*, pp. 165-77 (175).

37.   Ellman, *Psychoanalytic Literary Criticism*, p. 24.

Furthermore, Irigaray insists on 'a genesis of love between the sexes', where 'man and woman may once more or finally live together, meet and sometimes inhabit the same place'.[38] Irigaray envisions,

> The link uniting or reuniting masculine and feminine must be both horizontal and vertical, terrestrial and celestial. As Heidegger, among others, has written, this link must forge an alliance between the divine and the mortal, in which a sexual encounter would be a celebration, and not a disguised or polemic form of the master-slave relationship. In this way, it would no longer be a meeting within the shadow or orbit of a God the Father who alone lays down the law, or the immutable mouthpiece of a single sex.[39]

So, *contra* Lacan's Name of the Father or Law of the Father, according to which Oedipus's incest was simply bad grammar, Irigaray proposes a theory that some feminists find difficult to welcome, as it comes close to biological essentialism. 'Get in touch with your body', 'Speak through your vulva' are not messages that women like to hear, since they appear to associate women with the body, matter and the irrational, which has already been happening since the pre-Socratics. Some feminists defend Irigaray's stance, however. Jan Montefiore, for instance, argues rather convincingly that Irigaray's metaphor of the two lips should not be taken literally, because it is '*not* a definition of women's identity in biological terms … [but] a counter-proposal to the psychoanalytic association of the right to speech with the possession of the phallus … a possible vocabulary for the female imagination other than the Freudian opposition "phallic/castrated"'.[40] Jane Gallop also reads the two lips as both *synecdoche* and *catachresis*, which would make Irigaray's biological essentialism into rhetorical strategy. Thus, Irigaray's figural language constitutes the feminine in language as the persistent linguistic impropriety.[41] And, of course, it is not the first time that the female body has offered philosophers useful terms for symbolic concepts. Derrida uses 'hymen', for instance, to describe the inbetweenness of meaning, the margin so essential for *play*, for *différance*. Irigaray insists that 'language, however formal it may be, is sustained by blood, by flesh, by material elements'.[42] However, as Maud Ellman observes, it would be a pity if 'Irigaray's ethics of "mucosity" displaced the keener energies of women's wit'.[43]

---

38. Irigaray, 'Sexual Difference', p. 174.
39. Irigaray, 'Sexual Difference', p. 174.
40. Jan Montefiore, *Feminism and Poetry* (London: Pandora, 1987), p. 149.
41. Gallop, *Thinking through the Body*.
42. Irigaray, *An Ethics of Sexual Difference*, p. 122. Here Irigaray argues that the body that sustains language is the fantasised body of the mother.
43. Ellman, *Psychoanalytic Literary Criticism*, p. 25.

It is a shame indeed that the mother of Christ is allowed only that, her physicality, in fact, in John's Prologue. Only the nameless flesh is present, and only for its procreative discourse, the gush of birth. There is only one word—*the* Word—that comes forth, and not from the mother but from the Father. The mother is silenced, gagged with her placenta, with her body. Her discourse is only allowed within the realms of materiality, equalled with bodily functions, her *mucosity* entirely physical. Furthermore, the mother is banished. For, as Irigaray points out, 'the social order, our culture, psychoanalysis itself, want it this way: the mother must remain forbidden, excluded. The father forbids the bodily encounter with the mother.'[44]

The point that Irigaray tries to make even through her reinterpretation of *Oedipus Rex* and the *Oresteia* is that the murder, the removal, the banishing, of the mother is performed under the aegis of a benefit for society. Irigaray says,

> The maternal function underpins the social order and the order of desire, but it is always kept in a dimension of need. Where desire is concerned, especially in its religious dimension, the role of the maternal—feminine—power is often nullified in the satisfying of individual and collective needs.[45]

Irigaray illustrates her point with the *Oresteia*, by showing that, in an act meant not only to bring the rule of the law and civic justice (?) but also to seize power, Orestes kills his mother and remains unpunished for it. Needless to say, justice for Clytemnestra and her daughters, Iphigenia (whom Agamemnon had sacrificed to the gods for the sake of the Trojan war) and Electra (who is left in/to her madness), is never called for by the order of the polis. Perhaps Clytemnestra's greatest sin is that of remaining a passionate woman while being a mother; hers is neither a virginal nor a saintly aura. She has a lover and she kills. Irigaray defends Clytemnestra by allowing for her motives: jealousy, fear, frustration, pain at the loss of a child, all on the account of Agamemnon's prolonged absence and silence (Clytemnestra thought he was dead), his many infidelities (he even returns home accompanied by one of his mistresses) and his paternal indifference (read 'lack of love') as reflected in his sacrificing Iphigenia to 'the conflict of men'.[46]

44. Luce Irigaray, 'The Bodily Encounter with the Mother' ('Le corp-à-corp avec la mère'), in Whitford (ed), *The Irigaray Reader*, pp. 34-46 (39).
45. Irigaray, 'The Bodily Encounter with the Mother', pp. 35-36.
46. The expression used by Irigaray. See Irigaray, 'The Bodily Encounter with the Mother', p. 37.

Commenting on Christianity, Irigaray deplores the fate of the woman-goddess, who is not murdered per se, but demoted to a mortal state; she is a mere woman who carries the father's fecundating breath, so that God, together with the Holy Spirit, may take full credit for the act of procreation. 'The problem is that', Irigaray insists,

> by denying the mother her generative power and by wanting to be the sole creator, the Father, according to our culture, superimposes upon the archaic world of flesh a universe of language [*langue*] and symbols which cannot take root in it except as in the form of that which makes a hole in the bellies of women and in the site of their identity.[47]

In other words, women are reduced to being 'guardians of the flesh', 'guarantors of [men's] bodies', 'keepers of men's bodies',[48] while being refused the right to language, to speech, to rational discourse.

Teresa de Lauretis in *Technologies of Gender* criticizes Derrida for using women as mere instruments for theoretical discourse. 'Just as Nietzsche positioned woman as the symbol of Truth, the discourse of woman becomes the discourse of male philosophers, and her problem becomes man's problem. Philosophers speak about "woman", never about real women.'[49] Cixous also argues that woman is a cultural construct, an entity reinforced by myth, legend and literature, or the elements that structure symbolic thought. She insists that throughout history woman has been marginalized, simply for lack of adequate means of representation. Cixous' argument identifies the feminine as that mode of writing and thought which has been repressed and which, like the repressed unconscious, becomes disruptive as a result.

Traditionally, Western representations of the mother of Christ in the arts show her holding either her baby (the newly born, his umbilical cord freshly cut), or the dead body of the grown Jesus (as in Michelangelo's and Bellini's *La Pietà*, for example). The mother is virginal and saintly (even when openly breast-feeding[50]), and the corporeality of her relationship with her son is almost absent; the hold is never an embrace, always reverent and distant. The child, we are never allowed to forget, is divine, precious, different, other. Representations like Munch's Madonna (Fig. 16), in which the mother is allowed her passions, are rare and considered

47. Irigaray, 'The Bodily Encounter with the Mother', p. 41.
48. Irigaray, 'The Bodily Encounter with the Mother', p. 43.
49. Teresa de Lauretis, *Technologies of Gender: Essays on Theory, Film and Fiction* (Bloomington: Indiana University Press, 1987), p. 71.
50. See, for example, representations of 'La Madonna del Latte' by Pisano (1360s), Correggio (ca. 1500), Masolina de Panicale (ca. 1383), etc.

controversial, if not improper. Munch's Madonna has loose, wild dark hair; her breasts are bare and her halo red. Yet, her child is not present yet. It seems that our culture insists on a trade-off: the removal of the child in exchange for the mother's passions.

Figure 16. *Edvard Munch*, Madonna *(1894–1895)*.

Marina Warner attempts to evaluate this imposed transaction by ascribing it to the 'fear that the natural bond excludes men',[51] in other words, that the creative energy of women/mothers that goes unruled, without sanction or governing, posits a threat to a man's world. Hence Warner's theory on yet another opposition, the virginal/monstrous motherhood. Moving from Marian iconography to Greek mythology—Warner's study is based on the perpetuated role of myth in society—she develops her theory by making reference to Medea, the mother who kills her own children. Another mother with passions.[52] Warner says,

51.   Marina Warner, *Managing Monsters: Six Myths of Our Time* (The Reith Lectures; London: Vintage Books, 1994), p. 25.

52.   Euripides' tragedy *Medea* tells the story of a strong woman with the same name who, through murder and intrigue, helps her husband to win the golden fleece. How-

> Her maternity is the terrain of her authority, or rather the authority left to her. Among bad mothers of fantasy, she is the worst; as such, she speaks to our times when the bad mother is always present as an issue, as a threat, as an excuse, as a pleasurable self-justification and as political argument ... Medea the child murderer contravenes the most fundamental criterion of femininity—maternal love. She shares this with many fantasies of female evil: the inquisition condemned witches for cannibal feasts on children; in Judaic myth, the succubus Lilith was believed to haunt the cradles of new-born infants to carry them off.[53]

As Irigaray insists, 'Give or take a few additions and retractions, our imaginary still functions in accordance with the schema established through Greek mythologies and tragedies'.[54]

Going back to Warner, the bad mother can only have an identity in opposition to the good mother, who is perceived to be good to the point of self-sacrifice. Or rather, *imposed* self-sacrifice, under the Law of the Father. Of course, one notices that the height of irony resides in the paradoxical fact that the 'perfect mother' is a virgin and asexual mother. As Katherine Gieve puts it, motherhood is predicated on the notion that 'nature is expected to come to the aid of women to transform themselves from individuals to ideals'.[55] This ideal, in line with Irigaray, is expressed by the Law of the Father (all fathers, that is, all men with authority), according to which the mother is the prohibited, forbidden element.

In fact, the mother is forbidden until death. 'O, woman, what have you to do with me? My hour has not yet come', Jesus underlines in Jn 2.4, the first encounter with the mother of Christ in John's Gospel. It seems that only at the point of dying is the son allowed to have contact with his mother, the unnamed woman, the giver and keeper of his flesh. Yet the mother is kept silent by John even when faced with that, the most horrific event a 'good mother' can experience, the death of her child. Without a name and without a voice, she is refused the cry of pain. Michelangelo's *La Pieta*, for instance, shows a serene mother, a (surprisingly) young and submissive woman, who accepts the death of her son and ultimately the Law of the Father tacitly. She holds the body of her dead son with one hand, the folds of her garment making a soft bed for him. He lies on her knees, close to the womb from which he came, back with the mother to whom he never returned during his life. Yet, if

---

ever, after achieving his goal, he abandons Medea. She kills their children as an act of revenge.

53. Warner, *Managing Monsters*, p. 25.

54. Irigaray, *This Sex Which is Not One*, p. 75.

55. Katherine Gieve (ed.), *Balancing Acts: On Being a Mother* (London: Virago, 1989), p. viii.

Michelangelo takes the creative liberty of portraying this re-encounter, John does not return the body of Christ to his mother. It seems that even in death she is forbidden. She is banished to another who is not her son (cf. Jn 19.25-27), while Joseph of Arimathea is given her son's body. Note that Joseph is a not only a man, but a man with a proper name. He is the one to take Christ's dead body and bury it in his tomb, his womb. (Does his status as a follower of Jesus make him a keeper of Jesus' body? A queer economy.)

Irigaray proposes that the mother's imposed silence is responsible for perpetuating fearful fantasies (precisely that of the woman as devouring monster), which are generated by what Whitford calls 'the unanalysed hatred from which women as a group suffer culturally'.[56] Irigaray argues that there is a deplorable lack of female genealogies within the religious and civil myths and that such exclusions, particularly of the mother-daughter rapport, are responsible for influencing psychoanalysis itself (one of her significant criticisms of psychoanalysis today). What she proposes is that mothers must occupy a subject-position separate from that of women in order for them to have a voice. As Whitford explains, this 'maternal genealogy'

> symbolized the relation between the girl-child and her mother in a way which allowed the mother to be both a mother and a woman so that women were not forever competing for the unique place occupied by the mother, so that women could differentiate themselves from the mother, and so that women were not reduced to the maternal function.[57]

In other words, psychoanalysis should allow for a different discourse, separate from the grammar of the Father, where women and mothers have distinct voices. Irigaray also claims that psychoanalysis itself is the victim of unconscious fantasies, which it cannot acknowledge and therefore analyse, thus continuing in a patriarchal fashion, excluding that which is feared and marginalized.

We have seen that in John's Gospel the mother of Christ is not allowed a 'proper' name; (in) the name of the Father, she is allowed only brief traces of a presence or identity marked by σάρξ/μήτηρ/matter. She is silenced; her voice is heard only once (Jn 2.3-5) submissively, regarding body- or housekeeping matters and attracting a rebuke. As Irigaray would contend, 'the woman who enveloped man before his birth, until he could live outside her, finds herself encircled by a [language] of places that she

56. Whitford, *The Irigaray Reader*, p. 25.
57. Whitford, *The Irigaray Reader*, p. 89.

cannot conceive, and from which she cannot exit'.[58] The only discourse that the mother of Christ is allowed (or should one call her Mary?) is through opening her legs; she speaks through her vulva. Her *mucosity* links and separates her from her child, and she herself is removed. The mother is and remains 'castrated' linguistically also.

Let us now turn to another type of discourse, this time from between the lips of a woman's mouth rather than a woman's sex.

Opening Mouths, or the Discourse of the Woman Saviour

Luc Besson's Leeloo character is an interesting one. At first sight, she is a female role model: beautiful, intelligent, fit, indeed perfect, as she is described. And she saves the world. She is the Fifth Element (complementing the other four elements: earth, wind, fire and water), The Supreme Being, the Ultimate Warrior. Still, Besson manages to reduce Leeloo to a child; a sweet little girl who can indeed do kick boxing rather well but who cannot speak intelligibly. Her language is said to be divine, but nobody understands it, so it requires male-performed interpretation; her speech is erratic if not hysterical, flavoured with onomatopoeic sounds ('badaboom!'); she enjoys putting on make-up; she cries a lot; she gets herself almost killed a few times; and in the end she cannot even do her job properly: she cannot save the world unless a man helps her.

Interestingly, Luce Irigaray has recently started a series of essays on the four elements of life. She has written *Amante marine*, *Passions élémentaires* and *L'oubli de l'air*, to which I have referred earlier. These philosophical books are the result of Irigaray's desire 'to make a study of our relation to the elements: water, earth, fire, air'. 'I wanted', Irigaray confesses, 'to return to these natural materials which constitute the origin of our body, our life, our environment, the flesh of our passions'.[59]

Although Leeloo's entire salvific mission is based on her opening her mouth (Figs. 17, 18), her discourse is fleshly, material rather than symbolic. What she releases is not moving splendour (which is left to the diva, whose song is not only charming but also inspiring, religious), not logic and strategy (which is left to Korben Dallas, whose war tactics recommend him and not Leeloo for the ultimate, die-hard warrior medal), not knowledge or wisdom (which is left to Cornelius, the priest, whose erudition impresses even the High Council), not even entertainment

---

58. Luce Irigaray, *Ethique de la différence sexuelle* (Paris: Minuit, 1984), as cited in Whitford, *Luce Irigaray*, p. 165.

59. Irigaray, *Sexes et parentés*, p. 89. This is Margaret Whitford's translation in her edited volume, *The Irigaray Reader*, p. 8.

(which is left to Ruby Rhod—or Ruby with a rod?—whose confusing gender identity and character comics steal the show). Leeloo is just another element; her identity is elementarily connected to matter. She belongs to the material, to the corporeal, next to the other four elements: earth, wind, fire and water (Fig. 19).

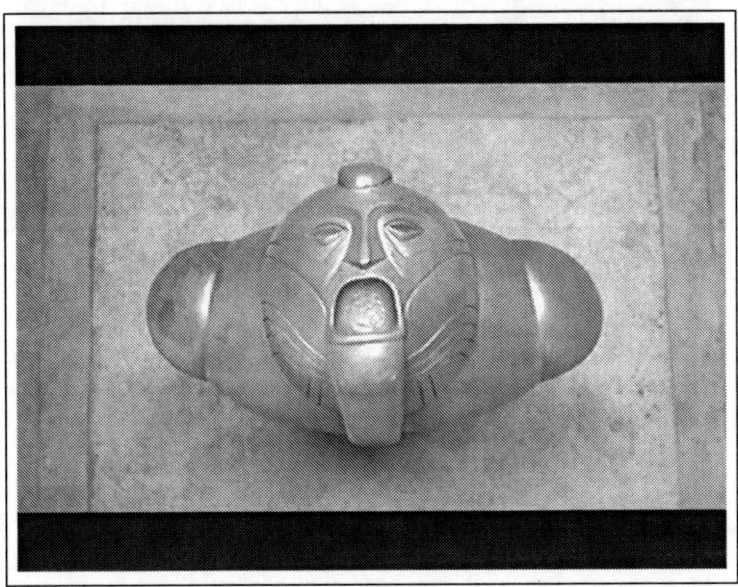

Figure 17. *'The Fifth Element', the perfect weapon for peace.*

Figure 18. *Leeloo (Milla Javovich), as the Fifth Element.*

Figure 19. *Korben (Bruce Willis) and others,*
making the elements (fire, here) work.

Her ultimate weapon—in Cornelius's words, 'what the ancients used to call "the light of all creation"'—is not of a spiritual nature in Besson's film.

Leeloo is meant to fight evil as the opposite of life, depicted by Besson as an immense dark planet with a fiery centre. If one were to re-consider the conflict between light and darkness in John's Prologue and the choice of 'to grasp' as a translation of καταλαμβάνω, one could paint a picture that presents darkness as a cosmic black hole, as death, to correspond to light as life. Due to its extremely intense gravity, a black hole is impossible to resist. The black hole holds everything, even light, firmly in its grasp. In our text, darkness wants to get hold of, to grasp, the light-and-life, although it does not understand, *not* the light, but what it is doing. Darkness perpetuates itself by virtue of its own gravitational pull. The singularity, which used to be a colossal star, attracts others into its own death zone naturally. Yet, the evil that Leeloo is meant to combat has consciousness, and it is an active evil. When this approaches Earth, the planet is covered in a frightening shadow, a heavy darkness.

However, although there is some speculation that Leeloo's weapon, the 'light of all creation', is truly love (for Leeloo releases it only after Korben initiates her into the matters of the heart through a kiss), I am not convinced. According to Besson's story, the Fifth Element is used every five thousand years, and this is implied to have happened prior to the time of our story, year 2257; and because the world still exists, one could therefore safely presume that the Fifth Element has been successful before. Yet Leeloo cries, 'Love? I don't know love. I was built to protect, not to love.' To remember Irigaray for a moment here, Leeloo's 'proper' use/place is as the ultimate guarantor of flesh and keeper of bodies. Her passion is without place and without propriety. It is not part of her vocabulary. Her grammar has been constructed for her within the volume or contours of the Name of the Father. As she has not known love before, it follows that Leeloo's power does not reside in love. Korben's kiss is important, however, because without it Leeloo is not certain that life should be saved. Leeloo's reluctance to save life develops upon her reading of the 'War' chapter in her encyclopaedia (she was 'Learning our history! The last five thousand years that she missed! She's been asleep for quite a while, you know', Cornelius explains). Perhaps Leeloo's disapproving and disappointed reaction to war, or what Irigaray calls 'the conflicts of men', is akin to Clytemnestra's. Leeloo may not be angry like the Greek character, but there is a similar depth to her feelings of depression (as the original script has it). Leeloo is a woman, after all. In fact, her feminine feelings impede her from being the warrior that she was created to be (Figs. 20 and 21). Korben's love, therefore, is not sufficiently scrupulous to be divine; it has invested interests. He uses Leeloo. And everyone is happy that she is used, or put back into use (Fig. 22). The audience loves a happy ending, where good defeats evil and the two heroes fall in love and live happily ever after.

Is Leeloo truly heard, however? I am not sure that she is. Her discourse is meant to be material, corporeal—contoured by the four stones, the four elements—and for the purpose of war (yes, she is on the good—read 'same', 'familiar'—side, but she is built for war, nevertheless). She is allowed only that, the language of the Father.

Figure 20. *Korben as Leeloo's saviour in their flight from the police.*

Figure 21. *Leeloo cannot perform her saving task without the help of Korben.*

Figure 22. *Released from Leeloo's mouth,*
the Light of all Creation destroys evil and saves planet Earth.

Whenever Leeloo wants to engage in a different type of discourse, a different type of grammar, she opens her mouth, but only dry, choked sounds come out. Her proper location is within the perimeter of the conflicts of men and, of course, in Korben's arms. Quite fitting for Besson's creation, the coming together of Leeloo and Korben at the end of the film sees the Oedipal drama fulfilled: Korben returns to the womb, which now belongs to men. It is the same container that had been used by the male scientists to recreate or give a second birth to Leeloo that now opens up for Korben and *his* perfect woman. All the while, Korben's own mother is bodily absent, represented only by the irritating—and thus rejected—voice at the other end of the phone.

To return to Irigaray's philosophy of the *non-existence* of the feminine, of the woman, it is worth noting that she explains the ownership of women by men as the function of the male imaginary, which needs to fantasize the female body as man's property. She insists,

> That from which women suffer comes also from the fact that men cannot conceive that they [women] do not exist. It is essential for men that they [women] exist. For men to have the possibility of thinking themselves or imagining themselves *causa sui* (self-caused), they have to think that the container 'belongs' to them. (Especially since the 'end of God' or the 'death of God' ...) For this ownership—without the guarantee of God—those who provide the container must necessarily exist. Therefore the maternal-female necessarily *exists* as cause of the *causa sui* of man. But not for herself. She exists necessarily but as *a priori* condition (as Kant would put it) of the space-time of the male subject. A cause never revealed under the threat that his identity would be torn apart, would plunge into the abyss. She does not necessarily exist as a woman because, insofar as she is a woman, his container is always open [*entrouverte*] ...[60]

This ownership is predicated on the prohibition of the woman/mother's voice and the reduction of woman/mother to the corporeal container that is owned, controlled by man. The mother of Christ and Leeloo are merely vehicles for the construction of the male identity. As in Freud's *fort–da* game, man never lets go entirely of the mother/woman; though out of sight/touch/hearing, she is always, as Whitford would have it, 'on the end of a piece of string'.[61] In our case, this ownership is written on the reduction of the mother of Christ and Leeloo to their used insides. On the end of a piece of string, the flesh containers open up and give man his *causa sui*. His salvation.

'One' or 'I'?

So, no, one cannot truly hear either the mother of Christ in John or Leeloo in *The Fifth Element*. Although they open different *lips*—thus forming not a crossroads but a plus sign, the semiotics of addition not subtraction—their discourse is performed in the Name of the Father, and their own, individual voices are sabotaged, if not silenced altogether.

But, of course, when one reads texts, it is one's own psyche and the play of the Imaginary that influence the reading. In this case, a woman's psyche and a feminine imaginary. According to Irigaray, 'the woman

60. Irigaray, *Ethique de la difference sexuelle*, cited in Whitford, *Luce Irigaray*, pp. 159-60 [*entrouverte* is more correctly 'half-open'].
61. Whitford, *Luce Irigaray*, p. 161.

always speaks with the mother, the man speaks in her absence'.[62] Perhaps the question should not, therefore, be 'Does *one* hear?', but 'Do I—the same I that Irigaray claims has yet to belong to a woman—Do I, as a woman, hear?' Paradoxically, the answer to that question would have to be 'yes' (in contrast to the definite 'no' I have just given). When I read John, my flesh gets caught between the lines.[63] I hear the mother because I read her there though I miss her there. Her being encircled by the language and grammar of the Father, her being covered by this wished invisibility cloak, marks, through the very efforts of removing her and keeping her out, her muted presence. When I read/watch *The Fifth Element*, I hear Leeloo for the same reasons. What does this mean? Do I hear the two women because we share the same flesh, the same sex, the same syntax? Do I, therefore, presume that they are not heard by the other sex and thus endeavour to give them a voice that will be heard? But do I speak within the grammar of the Father? Am I heard? Is my discourse 'shut up inside the spurious Phallocentric Performing Theatre'?[64] I wonder.

A New Script?
Perhaps we should engage in a rethinking, a refiguring of language and bodies.[65] Is it truly impossible to escape the dualities of mind/body, male/female?

If our present language cannot accommodate concepts that transgress such dualities, discourses that are not subjected to polarizations, perhaps we should consciously endeavour to develop, not a new language, but new ways of *seeing*, new ways of understanding. Notions like the ones Elizabeth Grosz suggests—'embodied subjectivity' or 'psychical corporeality' meant to express refusal of reductionism, resistance to dualism and suspicion over the holism and unity implied by monism[66]—may not be that difficult to grasp, although they may present merely new frontiers as new *borders* and thus limiting.

---

62.   Luce Irigaray, 'The Gesture in Psychoanalysis', cited in Whitford, *Luce Irigaray*, p. 161.

63.   Cf. Derrida, 'Plato's Pharmacy', p. 63: 'There is always a surprise in store for the anatomy or physiology of any criticism that might think it had mastered the game, surveyed all the threads at once, deluding itself, too, in wanting to look at the text without touching it, without laying a hand on the "object", without risking—which is the only chance of entering into the game, by getting a few fingers caught—the addition of some new thread ... [H]e who through "methodological prudence", "norms of objectivity", or "safeguards of knowledge" would refrain from committing of himself, would not read at all.'

64.   Cixous, 'The Newly Born Woman', p. 41.

65.   See Grosz's chapter on 'Refiguring Bodies', in *idem*, *Volatile Bodies*, pp. 3-24.

66.   Grosz, 'Refiguring Bodies', p. 22.

Perhaps it is also possible to consider corporeality no longer as directly linked to the female body. 'The body' has already been proven as an inadequate theoretical concept, replaced by 'bodies', a term that incorporates plurality of being and subjectivity. Bodies, like identities, are not singular, they are not united, and they are not fixed. As such, corporeality should no longer be perceived as belonging to one sex, as 'sex' itself is no longer monolithic, phallomorphic.

Furthermore, singular models of representation—the type or the norm—are no longer relevant. Although the use of such signifying categories still continues, an increasingly large number of qualifying statements are required for the painting of a full picture. One can no longer say 'a young white woman' and expect to be understood; it is more likely that one would have to say, 'possibly a woman, between thirtyfive and thirtyseven years of age, chestnut brown hair, curly at the top and rather spiky and blond at the bottom, possibly Caucasian (though her eyes may have been east Asiatic), with a large tattoo of a red budding rose on her left arm and another one only smaller just above her right ankle and so on, and so on.'[67] New means of representation should allow for an interactive discourse in which the outside and inside of the body and the biological and psychological no longer exist within the signification of the mind/body duality. From this, perhaps other binary oppositions predicated on the body, or on the mind/body distinction should be reconsidered. Thus, private/public, self/other, natural/cultural, psychical/social, instinctive/learned and so on may also undergo a refiguring (not a turn around—as this would only sustain the hierarchical modes of knowledge). As Grosz suggest, perhaps 'new terms and different conceptual frameworks must also be devised to be able to talk of the body outside or in excess of binary terms'.[68]

While I would readily subscribe to such *trans-formative* gestures, I am also weary of aiding the addition of yet another script to the list of plays of the actor human. Sometimes theories are themselves inadequate, appealing to elitist (as informed) academics. Unless truly understood and adhered to, political correctness is rather a charade that only limits one's freedom of speech. It becomes the adoption of an artificial, prescribed, voice. Then again, a conscious realization of that may also lead to an understanding of the subject's subjection, which may itself lead to transformation. Whether that is a revolution in language is another matter.

67. An admission of the limited nature of representation language may also lead to a transformation in cultural representations of beauty and desire, which form the topic of a different study.
68. Grosz, 'Refiguring Bodies', p. 24.

6

AUTOBIOGRAPHY? THE SOCIO-POLITICAL LOCATION OF THE SELF AND *THE MATRIX*

The Self in Context and Criticism

Jacqueline Rose has argued that the concept of identity, particularly the means by which it is constituted and maintained, constitutes the axis upon which psychoanalysis meets with the political field. Rose claims that *identity formation*—and the process of *identification* in particular—is

> one reason why Lacanian psychoanalysis came into English intellectual life, via Althusser's concept of ideology, through the two paths of feminism and the analysis of film (a fact often used to discredit all three). Feminism, because the issue of how individuals recognize themselves as male or female, the demand that they do so, seems to stand in such fundamental relation to the forms of inequality and subordination which it is feminism's objective to change. Film because its power as an ideological apparatus rests on the mechanisms of identification and sexual fantasy which we all seem to participate in, but which—outside cinema—are for the most part only ever admitted on the couch. If ideology is effective, it is because it works as the most rudimentary levels of psychic identity and the drives.[1]

To this, Stuart Hall adds the level of discursive formation and practices that comprise the social field as another reason for the effectiveness of ideology.[2] Identity therefore arises at the point of intersection between socio-cultural discourses and the human psyche and drives. As the play of the unconscious is beyond our grasp, however, the concept of identity is, in fact, 'the site of a perpetual postponement or deferral of equivalence',[3] and, though rather complex, it cannot be neglected for that very reason.

1. Rose, *Sexuality in the Field of Vision*, p. 5.
2. Hall, 'Who Needs Identity?', p. 7.
3. Stuart Hall, 'Fantasy, Identity, Politics', in E. Carter, J. Donald and J. Squites (eds.), *Cultural Remix: Theories of Politics and the Popular* (London: Lawrence & Wishart, 1995).

Rose makes reference to Althusser's well known 1971 essay, 'Ideological State Apparatuses', which introduced the concept of interpellation (at which we have looked already) and the idea of a speculary structure to ideology. What Althusser intended to achieve was, as Hall points out, the circumvention of the economism and reductionism that characterized classic Marxist theory of ideology, and the convergence of both the materialist role of ideology within the discourse of social production (compare Marx) and the symbolic role of ideology in the production of subjects (à propos Lacan).[4] However, Althusser's move has not convinced everybody, and Michelle Barrett has argued convincingly and comprehensively that Althusser's argument was 'profoundly divided and contradictory'.[5] While trying to develop Althusser's perspective, Michel Pêcheux also recognized the separating gap between the two sides of that argument in identifying the 'heavy absence of a conceptual articulation elaborated between ideology and unconscious'.[6] Pêcheux's argument, as Stephen Heath understands it, builds around the idea that

> [i]ndividuals are constituted as subjects through the discursive formation, a process of subjection in which the individual is identified as subject to the discursive formation in a structure or misrecognition (the subject thus presented as the source of meanings of which it is an effect). Interpellation names the mechanism of this structure of misrecognition, effectively the term of the subject in the discursive and the ideological, the point of their correspondence.[7]

It is this correspondence that was never quite resolved and instead attracted Hirst's criticisms of interpellation. In Hirst's view, this correspondence could only be predicated on the presupposition that the subject would be able to perform before she or he had been constituted through language as a subject. In other words, 'this something which is not a subject must already have the faculties necessary to support the recognition that will constitute it as a subject'.[8]

Though very influential, Hirst's critique may have brought a premature dismissal of Althusser's theory of interpellation. As Hall points out, Hirst seems to have assumed 'Althusser's Lacan' (Barrett's expression) in condensing Lacan's mirror stage to a moment. Thus, all that the mirror stage represents, Hirst perceives as supposed to happen as a

4. Hall, 'Who Needs Identity?', pp. 6-7.
5. Michele Barrett, *The Politics of Truth* (Cambridge: Polity Press, 1991), p. 96.
6. Michel Pêcheux, cited in Heath, *Questions of Cinema*, p. 106.
7. Heath, *Questions of Cinema*, pp. 101-102.
8. P. Hirst, *On Law and Ideology* (Basingstoke: Macmillan, 1979), p. 65.

simultaneous process; the entry into language, the consolidation of sexual difference, and the submission to the Law of the Father happen instantaneously. Hirst misses out on the finer points of Lacan's theories, particularly the concept of the subject as never fixed, never centred, namely the *sujet en procès*, which although Kristevan in expression does represent Lacanian thought. By focusing on the child as a 'small animal' and not a 'philosophical subject', Hirst himself misrecognizes the pre-symbolic faculties of the infant. As Lacan and Kristeva show, the infant does have the ability to recognize an element of separation from the mother through the *fort–da* game (Lacan) and the perception of the abject (Kristeva). The mirror stage, therefore, is not the *beginning* of something, but rather the *interruption* (or loss, lack, separation) that initiates the process of subject-formation. It would be an exaggerated reading of Lacan to suggest that the infant is a completely blank screen, a *tabula rasa*, before the mirror stage and the Oedipal crisis are resolved.[9] The problem that Althusser's argument has created, that of the correspondence between the individual and the subject, remains, however. How do we *choose* our subject position and what is it that *summons* us to those positions?

In the work of Michel Foucault one finds, among many other things,[10] a strong rebuttal of 'the great myth of interiority' when considering the notion of subject formation. In his opinion, the subject is constructed as an effect of, through and within, discourse and has no transcendental continuity or identity, no existence from one subject position to another.[11] Thus, the subject is associated with an actor who is erased by history 'like a face drawn in sand at the edge of the sea'.[12] If in his 'archaeological' works (*Madness and Civilization*, *The Birth of the Asylum*, *The Order of Things*, *The Archaeology of Knowledge*), one cannot find an explanation for the mystery behind the subject's choice of certain subject positions as opposed to others, as Foucault seems to take together the 'subject positions of a statement with individual capacities to fill them',[13] then this takes us back to Althusser's impasse.

---

9. As Hall observes; 'Who Needs Identity?', p. 9.

10. For the purpose of this study, I shall be looking only at elements relevant to the issues of identity.

11. Hall, 'Who Needs Identity?', p. 10.

12. Michel Foucault, *The Order of Things: An Archaeology of Human Sciences* (New York: Vintage Books, 1973), p. 387.

13. B. Brown and M. Cousins, 'The Linguistic Fault', *Economy and Society* 9.3 (1980), p. 272, cited in L. McNay, *Foucault: A Critical Introduction* (Cambridge: Polity Press, 1994), pp. 76-77.

However, the change in Foucault's approach, from archaeological to genealogical, allows for a double-sided character of *assujettissement*, or subjection/subjectification. Discourse is seen as both creative and created, and the entry into it as determined by, and comprising, the power relations within the social realm. It is through this understanding of the discourse of power that Foucault follows a thorough deconstruction of the body, perceived as the hiding place of 'man' and an attempt to reconstruct it within discursive practices. One of these, genealogy, is seen by Foucault as meant to 'expose the body totally imprinted by history and the processes of history's destruction of the body'.[14] Foucault makes a radical statement when suggesting that 'Nothing in man—not even his body—is sufficiently stable to serve as a basis for self-recognition of for understanding other men',[15] as discussed earlier.

As I have already mentioned, Foucault himself reaches the conclusion that the body is not as malleable, as docile, as all that, and he recognizes that it is not sufficient for the Law to summon, produce and regulate subjects, as this Law is dependent on the subjects' response to it. If in *assujettissement* Foucault saw the 'correlation between fields of knowledge, types of normativity and forms of subjectivity in particular cultures', he later realized these practices as

> [t]he practices by which individuals were led to focus attention on themselves, to decipher, recognize and acknowledge themselves as subjects of desire, bringing into play between themselves and themselves a certain relationship that allows them to discover, in desire, the truth of their being, be it natural or fallen. In short, with this genealogy, the idea was to investigate how individuals were led to practice, on themselves and others, a hermeneutics of desire.[16]

This practice indicates what Foucault himself described as 'a third shift, in order to analyse what is termed "the subject". It seemed appropriate to look to the forms and modalities of the relation to self by which the individual constitutes and recognizes himself *qua* subject.'[17] What seems to come forth is the theory that subjectification cannot be produced without the production of self as object in the world, the practices of self-formation, reflection and recognition as well as the rapport with the summoning Law. This rapport allows, however, for an interior dimension of the self. Furthermore, in Foucault's works one can follow

---

14. Foucault, 'Nietzsche, Genealogy, History', p. 63.
15. Foucault, 'Nietzsche, Genealogy, History', p. 63.
16. Michel Foucault, *The Use of Pleasure* (Harmondsworth: Penguin, 1987), p. 5.
17. Foucault, *The Use of Pleasure*, p. 5.

the thread of an aesthetics of existence, which is understood as a conscious stylization of the subject's life-style—a departure from prescribed identities characterized by the technologies used in the practices of self-production, a kind of performativity. Perhaps Stuart Hall is right in observing that Foucault's work moves towards a recognition that

> [s]ince the decentring of the subject is not the destruction of the subject, and since the 'centring' of discursive practice cannot work without the constitution of subjects, the theoretical work cannot be fully accomplished without complementing the account of discursive and disciplinary regulation with an account of the practices of subjective self-constitution. It has never been enough—in Marx, in Althusser, in Foucault—to elaborate a theory of how individuals are summoned into place in the discursive structures. It has always, also, required an account of how subjects are constituted.[18]

So, we go back to the concept of subject formation as the mysterious interplay between an exteriority—the summoning Law of society and culture—and an interiority—our 'aesthetics of existence', a sense of self different from and similar to others. In other words, we return to the concept of identity as formed on the line of suture, the intersection where meaning is found as the relational discourse between flesh and word, between self and context.

In this light, John's Prologue adds its own take on subject formation, as we have seen earlier. The children of God come into their subjectivity through the process of receiving the Word and believing in his name (Jn 1.12-13). Having sent forth his summoning Law through Moses, God now sends the means of identification through the visible Word-become-flesh. As Christ is perceived as fulfilling the Law (so Mt. 5.17), he becomes the 'intersection' where the summoning Law and human identities meet, confront and influence one another. The Prologue seemingly allows for an element of choice in identity formation: 'He came to his own, and his own did not receive him. But to all who received him, who believed in his name, he gave the authority to become children of God' (Jn 1.11-12). Thus some may choose to reject him and the summoning of God, while others may choose to follow. However, as v. 13 continues, the children of God 'were born not of blood nor of the will of the flesh nor of the will of man, but of God'. Therefore, the element of choice is shown to be deceptive, as it is the seemingly free subjection (à propos Althusser) that is at play. Some may look upon the visible Word—indeed, the visible God (see

18. Hall, 'Who Needs Identity?', p. 13.

Col. 1.5)—and desire to be like him, in his image (again the roles of image and mirroring, hence the unconscious, are very strong). Yet, it is still a mystery how the subject is formed within those grounds, where the will of the flesh and the will of a man[19] (where 'flesh' can be read in opposition to 'man', as in female flesh and male man, or body and mind) are both rendered impotent. It is instead the will of God that *subjects*, or attains the subjects' subjection and their subject formation, although the potential children of God are also involved at some level.

Perhaps is it all about changing subject positions (as Foucault would see it), a traversal from whatever to children of God, from darkness to light, from ignorance to knowledge, from death to life. This is, of course, the reading most associated with the application of John's Prologue for confessional purposes, which manages to defend the concept of human free will. This reading offers those who wish to be known as children of God the gift of agency and sufficient amounts of dignity to salvage the process of willing subjection and move beyond the Master–slave dialectic.[20] The subjects, here the children of God, work by themselves (as Althusser would have it) or seemingly freely at their Master's formation as Subject. They willingly subject themselves as mirrors, as reflections of the Subject, God in our case, as guarantors of the Subject's existence.

Autobiography?

> Thinking about my own sense of identity, I realize that it has always depended on the fact of being a migrant, on the difference from the rest of you ... Now that, in the postmodern age, you all feel so dispersed, I become centred. What I've thought of as dispersed and fragmented comes ... to be the representative postmodern experience! Welcome to migranthood.
>
> —*Stuart Hall*[21]

For the purpose of this study, it is the intersection between biblical text and self that interests me, and I see that as providing the locus for *homo religiosus*. Of course, by that I mean not merely the self-confessed believer, but all with an inclination and desire for the ultimate Other (whatever or whoever that may be). As Erich Auerbach has

---

19. Here is it alas, not ἄνθρωπος but ἀνήρ (Jn 1.13).

20. Although within the Hegelian Master–slave dialectic it is the Master, God here, who would be the limited figure, dependent entirely on the recognition acquired from the slave.

21. Stuart Hall, 'Minimal Selves', in Stuart Hall, *The Real Me: Postmodernism and the Question of Identity* (London: ICA, 1987), p. 44.

persuasively argued, the Bible appears to be indeed the narrative text upon which the self-definition of Western culture and its perception of the world are built.[22] It seems logical, therefore, to allow the Bible at least a place on the summoning Law bench.

Interestingly, some have argued, like Foucault, that identity is something that comes entirely from outside, not inside; that it is something we put on, not something we discover and reveal.[23] What becomes problematic, therefore, is the process of selection. How does the king choose his robes? And why do they fit? As Jonathan Ree observes,

> The problem with personal identity, one may say, arises from play-acting and the adoption of artificial voices; the origins of distinct personalities, in acts of personation and impersonation ... [Personal identity is] the accomplishment of a storyteller, rather than the attributes of a character.[24]

Again, Foucault's actor-subject moving from one subject-position to another as from one part to the next. Yet, while Jean Paul Sartre and Paul Ricoeur—whom Ree calls to his aid in sustaining his theory— argued that 'the unity of a life' is narrative, they also allowed for the existence of a recurring *belief* in personal coherence, which was renewed in the telling of tales; thus an interiority that was both expressed and reinforced by external narrative. Yet, Ree interprets it differently:

> The concept of narrative, in other words, is not so much a justification of the idea of personal identity, as an elucidation of its structure as an inescapable piece of make-believe.[25]

If Ree means by this that our identities are not fixed and united in a monolithic 'I', this appeals to me. If the cultural is the personal and vice versa, as Mark Slobin argues, then make-believe may be the means of expression as liberation. 'We all grow up with *something*, but we can choose just about *anything* by way of expressive culture', Slobin suggests.[26]

The issue of choice remains. Do we have a choice? Or are we the docile bodies of Foucault? Is choice perhaps illusory, part of the

22. Auerbach, *Mimesis*.

23. Simon Firth, 'Music and Identity', in Hall and du Gay (eds.), *Questions of Cultural Identity*, pp. 108-27 (122).

24. Jonathan Ree, 'Funny Voices: Stories, "Punctuation" and Personal Identity', *New Literary History* 21 (1990), pp. 1049-59 (1055).

25. Ree, 'Funny Voices', p. 1058.

26. Mark Slobin, *Subculture Sounds: Micromusic of the West* (London: Wesleyan University Press, 1993), p. 41.

Imaginary? Kwame Anthony Appiah problematizes the flow of the issue by claiming,

> Invented histories, invented biologies, invented cultural affinities come with every identity; each is a kind of role that has to be scripted, structured by conventions of narrative to which the world never quite manages to conform.[27]

By 'the world', I think Appiah means 'people', individuals. Thus, although we imagine that we express ourselves, it is only an expression of selves that have already been scripted for us by society, by the summoning Law. Choice is illusory, though we like to believe it true. Much of our invented or expressed selves would be beyond our conscious creation, anyway. One cannot grasp the unconscious, which plays a large part in subject formation.

What of autobiography, therefore? Within literary circles the newly emerged reading trope—the use of the personal voice—emerges out of New Historicism and the idea that there is no such thing as history but merely interpretations of events. Autobiographical critics, therefore, insist that they are simply open and honest about their involvement in their discipline. In his own fragmented autobiography, Roland Barthes points out that the subject used to be the victim

> of the old couple, the old paradigm: subjectivity/objectivity. Yet today the subject apprehends himself elsewhere, and subjectivity can return at another place on the spiral: deconstructed, taken apart, shifted, without anchorage: why should I not speak of 'myself' since this 'my' is no longer 'the self'?[28]

What Barthes offers, however, is a collection of reflections on his experience of writing and the duplicities of language (as such he writes in the third person, because, as he writes, 'it should all be considered as if spoken by a character in a novel').[29]

In the arena of biblical critical discourse, autobiographical readings are still perceived with much suspicion and cynicism, the necessary treatment, it seems, for all new critical methods. Explicit *autobiographical biblical criticism* has emerged only recently primarily through the work of Jeff Staley (*Reading with a Passion: Rhetoric*),[30] and Ingrid Rosa

---

27. Kwame Anthony Appiah, *In my Father's House* (London: Methuen, 1992), p. 232.

28. Roland Barthes, *Roland Barthes by Roland Barthes* (trans. Richard Howard; London: Macmillan, 1977), p. 168.

29. Barthes, *Roland Barthes by Roland Barthes*, p. 178.

30. J.L. Staley, *Reading with a Passion: Rhetoric, Autobiography, and the American West in the Gospel of John* (New York: Continuum, 1995).

Kitzberger, whose edited volumes *The Personal Voice in Biblical Inter-pretation* and *Autobiographical Biblical Criticism*[31] expose as false the supposed neutrality of the critical voice. Kitzberger argues,

> Although muted and suppressed, the personal voice of the critic has always been present in biblical criticism and has influenced the interpretative pro-cess even within the historical-critical paradigm. 'Objective' and 'neutral' criticism has never existed and never will. To be sure, the hidden personal voices of interpreters have exercised *over*-powering effects on the readers.[32]

Consciously or not, both ordinary readers and professional critics experience the Bible *through* their own unique voices and life stories, which in reverse act in shaping and transforming their readings and interpretations.

> The autobiographical turn in biblical criticism reveals (un-veils) the inter-preter's 'I' and reclaims it as an essential, necessary critical category. Thus, it challenges and dis-eases traditional, 'objective' criticism, demanding of practitioners and their critics to learn their ABCs anew.[33]

Kitzberger sees this un-veiling, this irruption of the I, as an empowering exercise, by which the reader takes, without shyness but with humility, his or her place in the formative relationship with the biblical text; it allows for a convergence of text and self and the creation of both in the process.

The products of these autobiographical interpretations cannot be easily categorized, however. Readers of these readerly texts are con-fused. Having approached biblical interpretation from a scientific, empirical angle, some scholars of the Bible (particularly those who find a comfortable home within the historical-critical *language*) find it very difficult to become interested in the personal voice—of them-selves and of others. Having disavowed their own self in their scholarly pursuits, some critics find very little critical material in autobiographi-cal criticism. They express their opinion somewhat like this: 'Why should I care how Staley felt when he became a father, or that Staley's son wrote a paper about him?'[34] 'Do I *really* need to hear about a critic's

---

31. Ingrid Rosa Kitzberger (ed.), *The Personal Voice in Biblical Interpretation* (London: Routledge, 1999); *idem, Autobiographical Biblical Criticism: Between Text and Self* (Leiden: Deo Publishing, 2003).

32. Kitzberger, *The Personal Voice in Biblical Interpretation*, p. 2.

33. Kitzberger, *Autobiographical Biblical Criticism*, p. ii. The reference to ABC is a veiled reference to the title of this volume.

34. À propos J.L. Staley's 'Fathers and Sons: Fragments from an Autobiographi-cal Midrash on John's Gospel', in Kitzberger (ed.), *The Personal Voice*, pp. 65-85.

weak bladder?' 'Is this *really* the place for "personal anecdotes"?'[35] 'I would never have imagined! Did you know that he was in a mental institution for a while? And that he had a homosexual affair? *Really!?!*'[36]

Such reactions to autobiographical criticism reveal a simultaneous dismissal of, and attraction to, the personal voice and life-story. The relationship between conscious and unconscious desires—namely between scholarly interest and voyeurism—play out through somewhat aggressive responses. Fuelled by a sense of 'this is not meant to happen', these reactions show just how successful willing subjection can be. Within the scripted procedures of scholarly approaches to the Bible it can be accepted that the Bible was written for flesh-and-blood readers, but it is not acceptable that the Bible is open to flesh-and-blood critics. The irruption of the 'I' becomes the irruption of the unconscious, the disturbing and disrupting function of the *chora*, bringing about the uncanny. Thus, a sense of migranthood can be experienced among those who have always felt that they belonged.

When I consider undergoing an autobiographical critical exercise, the sentiment that I experience first is fear. I do not have extroverted inclinations generally, and I choose my confidants carefully. Why should I expose myself to unknown eyes? (Indeed, why do others do it? Is it out of an exhibitionistic impulse?) Does the naked march truly achieve its purpose? Though illusory, 'One' is so much more anonymous than 'I'. It takes a considerable amount of *guts*—the flesh-and-blood, again—to own the many 'I's.

My own sense of identity is coloured by a taste of perpetual migranthood, thus difference. In choosing John's Prologue for this study I have betrayed my own fascination concerning the concept of identity in general and the identities of divinity and humanity and the relationships between them in particular. As the Prologue bears witness to the paradox of the Incarnation, I see in this text the birth of blurred boundaries and hierarchies, where the god becomes a man, the logos becomes flesh, in a gesture that unites and separates—in a relationship of interdependence—the above and the below, divinity and humanity, mind and matter, light and darkness, life and death. John's Prologue is the perfect test case for deconstruction and poststructuralism.

35. See Fernando F. Segovia, 'My Personal Voice: The Making of a Postcolonial Critic', in Kitzberger (ed.), *The Personal Voice*, pp. 25-37.

36. À propos Stephen D. Moore's 'Revolting Revelations', in Kitzberger (ed.), *The Personal Voice*, pp. 183-200.

Furthermore, it also manages to blur the concept of identity formation and subject positioning by insisting on the inadequacies of human mind and body in the process.

Red Herrings in Bullet-Time:
The Matrix, *the Bible, and the Postcommunist I*

> This machinery transforms individual bodies into a social body. It brings to bear in these bodies the *text* of a law. Another machinery doubles itself, parallel to the first ... It uses an individual, and no longer collective thera-peutics. The body that it treats is distinguished from the group. Only after having been a 'member'—arm, leg or hand of the social unit, or a meeting place of forces or cosmic 'spirits'—it gradually stood out as a totality with its diseases, its stabilities, its deviations and its own abnormalities. A long history has been necessary ... for it to become the basic unit of a society ... in which it appeared as a miniaturization of the political and celestial order—a 'microcosm'.
>
> —*de Certeau*[37]

Focusing in particular on the question of choice within the process of identity formation and adopting a reductionist approach, I argue here that, contrary to popular belief, there are no substantial parallels between the film *The Matrix* and Christian allegory. Instead, only red herrings. Rather than the Bible, Jean Baudrillard's book *Simulacres et Simulation*, itself featured in the film, seems to be the inspiration behind the script. *The Matrix* does rejuvenate certain myths, in mutant form, yet its aim is to introduce a new myth: that of the Matrix, or total, cybernetic control. Baudrillard's theory of neo-capitalist opera-tional simulation finds thus a stage well attended. This understanding of *The Matrix*, however, does expose my own Romanian Postcommunist hues. Autobiography is thus an integral part of this chapter's matrix.

***

In the beginning there are words. I hold my breath in the deep darkness of the cinema theatre. A black screen. Two voices interact in a whispered, inti-mate yet professional dialogue over what sounds like a telephone line. The conversation is cut short, and there is fear in her voice. What they do is illegal; I know it, and my loyalties are still with me. She is in a hotel room, an old place, abandoned, on course for demolition perhaps. Like the old yet beautiful buildings in Bucharest, vestiges of a more glorious past, torn down by the Communist government precisely for that reason. Policemen burst in.

---

37. De Certeau, 'Des outils pour écrire le corps', p. 118.

Uniforms do look the same everywhere, don't they? She is trapped. I am at the edge of my seat. Why do I choose her side? Am I still afraid of authority figures? She looks cool, calm, and composed; strong, stylish, and dignified. Her allure is powerful. She is not a 'little girl', as the policemen had so arrogantly labelled her. She is called Trinity. I wish I could have fought as she does. Jumped across rooftops as she does? Impossible! She's just flown across two buildings and in through a window! She falls skilfully down a flight of stairs, shows a trace of fear. I want her to win even more. The Securitate agents are after her. She runs but is crushed in the public phone booth. Defeated. I ache. The door to her tomb is removed, and her body is nowhere to be found. Instead, just the smashed phone. She's gone. Disappeared. How? I'm relieved and surprised; confused yet hooked. This promises to be interesting.

***

From real bullets to bullet-time photography, from one bloody and televised revolution to a less violent and fictional, cinematic representation of another, I find myself enjoying *The Matrix*. Produced by Joel Silver (known for his many other productions, like *Lethal Weapon*, *Conspiracy Theory*, *Demolition Man*, and *Die Hard*—to name only a few), *The Matrix* is a film in which Andy and Larry Wachowski, who wrote and directed it, appear to have created their manifesto. Audiences across the world have responded enthusiastically to this film, and heated discussions about its subtexts have become irresistible. Many believe the Bible to have been the principal source of inspiration for the Wachowski brothers. Thus, Neo is perceived as playing the role of Christ, Morpheus that of John the Baptist, and Cypher that of Judas Iscariot. From within a Christian location, one would, of course, welcome such familiar echoes. Yet, there are no substantial parallels between *The Matrix* and Christian allegory. While this film rejuvenates certain myths, *The Matrix* breathes an air in which the axes of linear time—and indeed of time and space—have collapsed. Past, present, and future, fact and fiction, and the identities inscribed in them are fluid in this film, and it is within this context that a new myth is born.

The Wachowskis' myth is not that of a new Messiah, however, but that of the Matrix, the embodiment of Jean Baudrillard's theory of neo-capitalist operational simulation; it presents the potential of a cybernetic order aiming at total control. Baudrillard's *Simulacres et Simulation* is the operative subtext of this film. As I said above, my reading of *The Matrix* is influenced by my own Romanian Postcommunist experience. I see it all through the prism of she who is I.

Recalling Fiction

The Matrix produces the image of an era in which technology has become alive and life-depending (Fig. 23). The time is close to 2199— although nobody really knows for sure—and represents an equally post- and pre-apocalyptic phase in human history. Post-apocalyptic in the culturally understood sense, in as much as it defines a time after the end of human civilization as we know it, and pre-apocalyptic in the Johannine sense of the term, in as much as it becomes the dawn of revelatory salvation of humankind. Both phases, however, are unknown to most people, who think it is still 1999 and enjoy life as they have always known it. The scenario is thus quite compelling: the entire human race is in bondage (it lives in a prison for the mind), and, of course, it needs saving. All people need to be disconnected from the Matrix (a computer generated dream world) and introduced to a new dimension, the true real. The process is rather delicate, and what is presupposed is a great deal of faith. In his training, Neo, the principal character, is taught how to free his mind by 'letting go of it all: fear, doubt, and disbelief'. A handful of people have managed that already and formed the Resistance. From it, we meet the crew of one ship, a hovercraft called Nebuchadnezzar. Morpheus, Trinity, and Cypher are some of its crew. Neo becomes the latest addition.

Figure 23. *The world of the Matrix,*
where human beings are grown as crop.

There is talk of the last human city, Zion, positioned close to the core of the earth, where it is still warm. There is talk of a precursor to Neo, a man *born* inside the Matrix (rather than *grown* by the machines), who had the 'ability to change whatever he wanted, to remake the Matrix as he saw fit'. After he died, 'the Oracle prophesied his return and that his coming should hail the destruction of the Matrix and the war, and bring freedom to the people'. Morpheus believes that Neo is indeed The One (Neo as an anagram for 'One'), who would achieve all that. In other words, Neo is the Saviour of humankind.

Quite obviously, the language of this film is pregnant with symbols, and the biblical echoes are strong. In his *Ultimate Matrix Concordance*, Jerry Glover declares that 'The Matrix is stacked with references. Which are verifiable and which are coincidental we may never know'.[38] What we do know, however, is that in a web conversation the Wachowskis declared that most of the religious symbolism is indeed intentional.[39] I would like to look at the textual weaving of this film, since I find it rather striking that much of the symbolism is veiled; its employment, covert. We are given encoded signifiers, which turn out to be red herrings.

Neo, a New Messiah?

As well as an anagram for the 'one', Neo can also mean 'new'. The new One? The new Messiah, perhaps? There are certainly quite a few people who would readily embrace this interpretation.[40] It has been reported, for instance, that a Lutheran pastor in Pembroke, MA 'preaches sermons based entirely on the film and shows it in youth confirmation classes', because he believes that *The Matrix* is based on the Passion narrative.[41] Let us investigate this theory.

Right from the start, Neo is thanked by Roy, one of his clients, with, 'You are my saviour, man; my own personal Jesus Christ'. Whether that is a veiled salutation and demarcation of the messianic figure or not is a different matter. For a Christian audience, however, the uncanny similarities between Christ and Neo seem easy to detect. Here are a few:

38. Glover, 'The Ultimate Matrix Concordance', p. 18.

39. Stephen Armstrong, 'The Gospel According to Keanu', *The Sunday Times* (13 February 2000), section 9, *Culture*, p. 22.

40. A lot has been written on *The Matrix* since its release. This piece was written before the sequels of *The Matrix* were released.

41. Armstrong, 'The Gospel According to Keanu', p. 22.

(1) The arrivals of both Christ and Neo appear to have been prophesied. The Gospel writers—particularly Matthew—make numerous references to Old Testament texts that seem to be fulfilled in the person of Jesus of Nazareth. These proclaim the future arrival of the Messiah, the Christ, the Anointed One. Jesus himself is represented as reading the scroll of Isaiah and declaring himself as the one on whom the Holy Spirit rested, the one 'anointed to preach the good news to the poor … proclaim release to the captives and recovering of sight to the blind, to set at liberty those who are oppressed' (Lk. 4.18, 19 // Isa. 61.1-2). Neo's arrival has been prophesied by the Oracle, Morpheus informs us, and his mission is to accomplish the destruction of the Matrix and bring freedom to the people and an end to the war.

(2) The births of both Christ and Neo seem to be perceived as incarnations. Christ is the pre-existent Word that becomes flesh (Jn 1.1, 14), and Neo becomes aware of his flesh for the first time having lived strictly at the cerebral level until he is unplugged from the Matrix.

(3) Both Christ and Neo are saviours, set to facilitate the traversal of humankind from one realm into another. Christ proclaims the kingdom of God and life eternal, while Neo is set to re-establish the reign of the human and the real over the cybernetic and the simulated. Zion as 'the city where the party would be' features in both scenarios; in *The Matrix*, Tank, the operator, day-dreams of it as the symbol of peace and liberation, while biblical texts mention it as the locus for celebrations, singing and everlasting joy, where, for example, 'the ransomed … will return; gladness and joy will overtake them, and sorrow and sighing will flee away' (Isa. 51.11).[42]

(4) Both Christ and Neo are announced. Jesus is heralded by John the Baptist, who declares that 'every valley shall be filled, every mountain and hill shall be brought low, the crooked shall be made straight, the rough ways shall be made smooth' (Lk. 3.46 // Isa. 40.3-5). Neo is introduced by Morpheus, who proclaims him to be 'the One', the unique individual with the 'ability to change whatever he wants, to remake the Matrix as he sees fit'. Similarly, both John the Baptist and Morpheus recognize the superiority of Christ and Neo respectively and are willing to sacrifice themselves for the others' advancement.

(5) Both Christ and Neo experience a type of water baptism, and they are both affirmed in their identities in the process. In the Synoptic Gospels, Jesus is reported to have been baptized in the river Jordan by John and acknowledged by God the Father as the 'beloved Son'.

42. See also Rev. 14.1-3.

Neo is unplugged from the Matrix and flushed down into the rivers of sewage, then picked up and acknowledged by Morpheus as the long awaited 'One'. It is interesting to notice that Morpheus himself is later acknowledged as 'our Father' by Tank, the operator.

(6) Both Christ and Neo follow a development process. Luke (2.52) reports that Jesus 'increase[s] in wisdom and stature', while Neo 'needs a lot of work'. First, his muscles had atrophied so they need 'rebuilding'. (It is surprising that, although Neo is uncomfortable with using his eyes for the first time, he can, nevertheless, speak fluently without any prior physical experience in verbal communication. But we will not go there. More fascinating is the fact that the image of Neo on the operating table unites the temporal axes of past and fictional present in powerfully evoking a post-mortem body of Christ at the dawn of Neo's true life. Christ's tomb is thus Neo's heaven, or vice versa.) Second, Neo also goes through a learning process—a painful one at that—leading to his increasing in wisdom (Morpheus does a very good job of helping Neo become acquainted with the 'true' history of humanity).

(7) Both Christ and Neo experience fear and doubt before climatic moments in their mission-impossible scenarios. Christ goes through the Gethsemane trial, in which he prays to the Father that the cup of his destiny would be removed (Mt. 26.36-46 // Mk 14.32-41 // Lk. 22.39-46), while Neo declares himself to be 'just another guy' and thus ill equipped for the destiny of a saviour.

(8) Both Christ and Neo are betrayed. Judas Iscariot delivers his master with a kiss and for a bag of silver (Mt. 26.14-16, 47-49), while Cypher betrays the Resistance over a 'juicy and delicious' yet simulated steak and for a place back in 'the power plant'; there he would be able to enjoy the virtual—yet, alas, not virtuous—life of a rich and important person: an actor (perhaps the best lifestyle for one who prefers the fantasy over the real). The betrayal itself is in both cases preceded by some close partaking of either food or drink.

(9) Having overcome their weakness, both Christ and Neo discover within themselves the strength to face their enemies and die. Christ is caught, tried, and crucified. Neo is fought, chased, and shot (Fig. 24). Both, however, are resurrected. To the astonishment of his disciples, Christ comes alive through the power of God the Father, and he returns to heaven having left the promise of his Holy Spirit on earth. Neo, on the other hand, is resurrected by the power of Trinity's love and faith, to the pleasant surprise of his friends and extreme annoyance of his enemies; after defeating Agent Smith, he returns to Reality. Both Christ and Neo are perceived as victorious.

Figure 24. *Neo fighting with the agents*.

Figure 25. *Trinity, fighting a police officer*.

(10) Furthermore, their victories are to be continued after their resurrection. Jesus ascends to God the Father in heaven, while Neo ascends to the sky, as a man who can fly.

So, here it is: Neo is Christ, Morpheus is John the Baptist, Cypher is Judas Iscariot—and Trinity? Well, she has been linked to the Mary Magdalene figure—just to prove that where there is a will there is a way. To quote a *Sunday Times* reporter, however, 'it's not terribly Mary Magdalene to wear tight black leather and kick the seven kinds of hell out of the bad guys, so the celestial jury is out on her' (Fig. 25).[43] I, on

43.   Armstrong, 'The Gospel According to Keanu', p. 22.

the other hand and just to play the game, would be tempted to suggest a different connection to Christian allegory altogether: Trinity is the Holy Spirit. Despite her not being very dove-like, she is the element that unites Neo (as the son) and Morpheus (as the father) in a tight trio right from the beginning. Her name is Trinity, so she is needed to complete the trinity. She contacts Neo for Morpheus; delivers Neo from the evil bug as a preparatory measure for Neo's first meeting with Morpheus; encourages and supports Neo throughout his travail and training while Morpheus bonds with him in a father-son fashion. She joins Neo in his mad rescue-Morpheus operation; then she loves Neo into living, and the trio is reunited. Again, not very orthodox; the trio of *The Matrix* could never be a trinity in the Christian sense.

I would like to argue that the celestial jury should indeed be out on them all. Leather or not leather, my opinion is not particularly linked to the characters' wardrobe—I do not want to be accused of a lack of imagination. To be fair and in response to the *Sunday Times* reporter, I would have to draw attention to the stark difference between the textile penury of the 'real' world—closer perhaps to our impression of the sense of fashion displayed by Christ and his followers—and the glossy resourcefulness of the Matrix; it is, after all, the residual self image projections of the characters that we are likely to remember first, for the simple reason that we are exposed to them for a lot longer during the film. So, I take a different stance.

If *The Matrix* is indeed intended to be Christian allegory (which I do not think to be the case), quite frankly, it fails to deliver. The very element of salvation has different connotations for Christ and Neo. Christ brings a freedom that pertains to the spiritual; he saves humans from spiritual ignorance and spiritual death; he refuses adamantly the political role that many Jews had associated with the messianic figure and does not participate overtly in his people's struggle against Roman control. Christ's message promotes meekness and forgiveness. Neo, on the other hand, takes a quasi-political identity. His fight is to free his people from a regime of total control, in which their minds, bodies, and resources are no longer theirs. Neo's salvation is pragmatic; his motivation quasi-Marxist, one could say, because consciousness and material context are intimately intertwined. His message is *To arms! We'll have a revolution!*[44]

44. The fact that the Wachowskis choose the Woman in Red as a distracting element for Neo still puzzles me a little. I can't make up my mind whether the deadly

Thus, although a saviour of sorts, Neo is not a convincing Messiah (and I mean it here in the Christian sense). His Superman qualities—his flying and fighting abilities, his tight attire and his long cloak-looking coat—are more evident. The Wachowskis themselves make no direct claims to the messianic status, although it could be argued that the absence of the biblical text in this film is much louder than its presence would have been. Furthermore, there are no direct propositions equating Neo with deity. Script and Scripture do not marry here.

Figure 26. *Neo manages to 'see the Matrix in code'.*

Indeed, Neo is 'just another guy' with an incredibly high IQ; as Mouse points out, his 'neuro-kinetics are way above normal'. I would like to suggest that his special qualities—the very ones that recommend him as a new Messiah to some—are entirely the results of acute intelligence. After all, Morpheus keeps encouraging Neo throughout his development to free his mind. Indeed, even the combat training—Jujitsu, Kung Fu, Drunken Boxing(?)—is all performed at cerebral level only. Neo's death and resurrection are located in the mind, too; they are not *real*. Neo is mortally wounded in the Matrix, but his brain

---

enemy masquerading as that charming package is supposed to be Communism—due to the colour of her dress—or bourgeois capitalism—due to the quality of her dress, her coiffure, and the tantalising demeanour of her healthy body (no rations there!). Is Neo a reincarnation of Roy Cohen or Lenin? I'm inclined to go with the latter.

is strong enough to survive it. Morpheus's statement that 'the body cannot live without the mind' is not entirely true, anyway, and so Neo finds the source of his simulated resurrection in a very fertile and focused mind. Furthermore, Neo develops the ability to see in code (Fig. 26), and thus manipulate and eventually defeat the program of the Matrix. If Neo is a god, he is only a god of the simulacrum. His super-hero intentions and abilities, however, I will not challenge.

Myth and The Matrix

Another element that I will not challenge is the fact that the Wachowskis use mythical language, an eclectic one at that. I have already pointed out the Saviour and the Superman myths. We are also presented with Morpheus, the Oracle, and the three-headed guardian program (evoking Cerberus), which find colourful echoes in Greek mythology.

Figure 27. *The Oracle.*

The information surrounding the Delphic Oracle is still rather cloudy. However, without going into too much detail, I will mention that the Oracle, or the Pythia, was reported to have been a prophet of the cult of Apollo. She was served by priests and has been depicted as purifying herself with fumigating laurel leaves and barley meal prior to delivering divine revelation, and sitting on a tripod throughout it. The enquirers were not admitted immediately into the temple, above which lay the inscription, 'Know Thyself'. They were also expected to offer a sacred cake on the main altar outside, as a charge for consulting the Oracle.[45] The Wachowskis' Oracle is a perceptive and charming middle-aged woman, who lives in a flat, smokes cigarettes, bakes cookies, and eventually sits on a kitchen stool (Fig. 27). Her voice and her wrinkles are soothing as those of a mother would be. After the expected *antechambre* yet performed slightly differently, Neo's consultation begins under the augury of Duke Ellington's 'I'm Beginning to See the Light', employs the 'Know Thyself' inscription, and finishes with Neo's biting into the cookie that the Oracle herself had baked. Very creative.

Morpheus was the god of dreams and the son of Father Sleep, mentioned by Ovid in his *Metamorphoses*. The god Morpheus 'excelled to imitate the human form ... the features, gait and speech of men, their wonted clothes and turn of phrase', as Ovid describes him (*Metamorphoses*, XI.616-754). This is not, however, the text of *The Matrix*, although the allusions to sleep and dreams may find themselves at home in it. Paradoxically, the character Morpheus is the one to wake Neo from his perpetual dreaming. The very fact that humanity is preserved in liquid-filled pods in *The Matrix* reminds one of the river Lethe, the river of oblivion in Hades, or the Underworld. The dead were said to traverse this river in order to induce forgetfulness of the real, or living world.

Figure 28. *Agent Smith (Cerberus?)*.

45. H.W. Parke and D.E.W. Warmell, *The Delphic Oracle*, I (Oxford: Basil Blackwell, 1956), pp. 17-45.

Speaking of Hades, the three agents of the Matrix, or the sentient programs, or indeed the prison wardens evoke Cerberus, the three-headed guard-dog of Hades. The role of Cerberus was to stop anyone from leaving the world of the shades and join the living, almost identical thus with the role of the sentient programs (Fig. 28). In all fairness, the agents are themselves stars in their own right. Embodied in this trio is the myth of the perfect AI machines, developed to the highest level, that of reproduction. Although they have the impeccable style of James Bond—indeed, Smith appears to think himself another 007 ('Smith, Agent Smith', he introduces himself to Morpheus)—the function of these omniscient programs is less glamorous; they are prison guards, as mentioned earlier. What I find to be the height of irony is that these gatekeepers are self-declared prisoners. When trying to extract Zion's mainframe computer codes from the tortured mind of Morpheus, it is Agent Smith who displays human weakness—the machines' greatest strength; he simply breaks down. 'I hate this place, this zoo, this prison', Smith declares. 'I must get out of here. I must get free, and in this mind is the key, my key'. And *he* is only a computer program.

Figure 29. *Morpheus is captured and tortured.*

On the other hand, the most interesting element of that scene is the striking resemblance between the tied and tortured Morpheus and the crucified Christ. One almost thinks of Jan Mostaert's *Man of Sorrows (Christ Crowned with Thorns)*. The helplessness, the heavy silence, the sweat and tears, and the crown of pain—thorns for Christ and electrodes for Morpheus—do seem to unite the film with the painting and Morpheus with Christ (Fig. 29). Again, the axes of fact and fiction, time and space, indeed the identities within them are fluid in *The Matrix*. The Wachowskis' creativity is not linear.

Having established that the mythological intertextuality is considerable, the question that surfaces is 'Why would a film such as *The Matrix* would employ mythological language at all?' I expected the film to shun metalanguage. The allusions to myths create connections to metanarrative, to history—at least in terms of cultural development. I wondered whether the Wachowskis were set on producing reassuring grounds for some great meaning to human existence (lost, apparently, within the postmodern). Should this be correct, Jungian critics would probably see in *The Matrix* a good case for the myth-as-compensation theory.

For Jung, mythology is, in its entirety, a projection for the collective unconscious, which is the common psychological foundation for all human life (similar to the *myth of origins* concept for Mircea Eliade). This is the image in which certain elements, 'the archetypes or dominants', Jung says, 'have crystallized out in the course of time. They are the ruling powers, the gods, the dominant laws and principles, and of typical, reoccurring events in the soul's cycle of experience.'[46] Myths are not spontaneous products of the individual psyche; they are culturally elaborated.[47] In the accumulated life of cultures, myths are said to 'compensate for the inadequacy and one-sidedness of the present … The artist seizes on [a compensatory] image, and in raising it from deepest consciousness he brings it into relation with conscious values, thereby transforming it until it can be accepted by the minds of his contemporaries according to their powers.'[48] In this light, even Ovid's *Metamorphoses* could indeed be perceived as compensatory, namely to

46. C.G. Jung, *Two Essays on Analytical Psychology* (trans. R.F.C. Hull; New York: Meridian Books, 1956), p. 105.

47. Steven F. Walker, *Jung and the Jungians on Myth: An Introduction* (London: Garland, 1995), pp. 3-23.

48. C.G. Jung, 'On the Relation of Analytical Psychology to Poetry', in *idem*, *The Spirit in Man, Art, and Literature* (Princeton, NJ: Princeton University Press, 1971), pp. 81-83.

the Augustan spirit of seriousness; its stories could easily be identified with a playful hedonistic spirit that was seen as subverting Augustan morality and the consolidation of imperial power.[49] It comes as no surprise that Ovid died in exile (on the shores of the Black Sea, in a Roman province which later became Romania, as it happens).

Steven Walker declares that Jung perceives myth as 'a potential compensation for the sense of meaninglessness that plagues modern culture, proud of its rationality but at the same time a prey to doubts and existential anguish'.[50] By extension, is this what *The Matrix* does? Employ myth and metalanguage as a compensatory method to bring cultural equilibrium to a now postmodern society with no clear parameters? Bronislaw Malinowski, who studied myth all his life, came to the conclusion that myth is indeed 'an indispensable ingredient of all cultures ... constantly regenerated; every historical change creates its mythology, which is, however, but indirectly related to historical fact. Myth is a constant product of faith, which is in need of miracles; of sociological status, which demands precedent; of moral value, which requires sanction.'[51] *The Matrix* does indeed rejuvenate certain myths, in mutant form; this is because the film breathes an air in which the horizons of linear time—and indeed of time and space—have col-lapsed.[52] Past, present, and future, fact and fiction, and the identities inscribed in them are fluid, not crystallized, in this film; it is in this context that a new myth is born. As Barthes would say, 'myth hides nothing and flaunts nothing: it distorts; myth is neither a lie nor a confession: it is an inflexion'.[53]

Contrary to popular belief, the Wachowskis' myth is not that of a new Messiah, but that of the Matrix. It is the myth of the world beyond the mirror of *Alice through the Looking Glass* and Dorothy's fantastic journey to Oz (both alluded to in the film). The new myth is that of operational simulation, indeed *simulacrum of the third order*— and I shall explain what I mean by that in a moment. The myth is that of the virtual, which happens to be more colourful than reality, if indeed distinguishable from it; that of the prison for the mind, which

49. Walker, *Jung and the Jungians on Myth*, p. 20.

50. Walker, *Jung and the Jungians on Myth*, pp. 22-23.

51. Bronislaw Malinowski, *Myth in Primitive Psychology* (London: Kegan Paul, Trench, Trubner, 1926), p. 21.

52. For a more detailed approach to the theory of collapsed linear time, see Keith Tester, *The Life and Times of Post-modernity* (London: Routledge, 1993), p. 131.

53. Roland Barthes, 'Myth Today', in Roland Barthes, *Mythologies* (trans. Annette Lavers; Paris: Vintage, 1993), pp. 109-59 (129).

is beyond human sensory perception. It is one in which all human axes of experience are subjugated by the code. Thus, perhaps the question should be not 'What is the Matrix?' (à propos the web site of the film), but 'What is the matrix of *The Matrix*?'[54]

The Matrix of The Matrix

At the beginning of their film, the Wachowski brothers offer the audience a sign, which in the myth becomes a signifier.[55] Neo takes a book from a shelf, opens it, and takes out a zip disc from its carved-out interior. The image of the hollow book reminds one of other films in which the Bible suffers the same treatment, that of cinematic prop. Neo's book, however, is Jean Baudrillard's *Simulacres et simulation*.[56] This and not the Bible I believe to be the matrix of *The Matrix*, the inspiration behind the script.

The myth of the simulated is not new to cinema. Other films like *The Truman Show* and *Ed TV* have dealt with similar issues, in which the medium becomes the message, the fabricated replaces the natural, the script replaces the real, and vice versa. However, Baudrillard goes further in his assessment; 'we must think of the media as if they were in outer orbit', he declares, 'a sort of genetic code which controls the mutation of the real into the hyperreal'.[57] The Wachowskis seem to have clothed Baudrillard's theory with the story of the Matrix. Baudrillard describes a world in which metaphysics goes with the simulation:

> No more mirror of being and appearance, of the real and its concept ... rather, genetic miniaturization ... The real is produced from miniaturized units, from matrices, memory banks and command models—and with these it can be reproduced an indefinite number of times ... It is hyperreal, the product of an irradiating synthesis of combinatory models in a hyperspace without atmosphere ... The age of simulation thus begins with a liquidation of all referentials—worse: by their artificial resurrection in a system of signs, a more ductile material than meaning, in that it lends itself to all systems of equivalence, all binary oppositions and all combinatory algebra.

54. I refer to the film itself when using *The Matrix*, to the computer-generated dream world featured in the film when using 'the Matrix', and to the dictionary meaning of the term when using 'the matrix'.

55. For further exploration of the transformation of signs into signifiers in myth, see Barthes, *Mythologies*, p. 115.

56. Although the original French title is *Simulacres et simulation* (Paris: Galilée, 1981), the book has been translated as *Simulations* in the Semiotext(e) Foreign Agents Series, in 1983.

57. Jean Baudrillard, *Simulations* (trans. P. Foss, P. Patton and P. Beitchman; Semiotext[e] Foreign Agents Series; New York: Semiotext[e], 1983), p. 55.

It is no longer a question of imitation, nor of reduplication, nor even of parody. It is rather a question of substituting signs of the real for the real itself, that is, an operation to deter every real process by its operational double, a metastable, programmatic, perfect descriptive machine which provides all signs of the real and short-circuits all its vicissitudes. Never again will the real have to be produced—this is the vital function of the model in a system of death, or rather of anticipated resurrection which no longer leaves any chance even in the event of death.[58]

Thus, moving beyond his first two orders of simulacra, one: *counterfeit*, as the dominant scheme of the classical period, from the Renaissance to the Industrial Revolution, and two: *production*, as the dominant scheme of the industrial era, Baudrillard envisages the simulacrum of the third order, or the *simulation*, as 'the reigning scheme of the current phase that is controlled by the code ... The great simulacra constructed by man, which pass from a universe of natural laws to a universe of force and tensions of force, to a universe of structures and binary oppositions. After the metaphysics of being and appearance, after that of energy and determination, comes that of indeterminacy and the code', Baudrillard postulates.[59]

What does Baudrillard mean? Inspired by McLuhan and his very high regard for the mathematical genius of Leibniz, who saw in 'the mystic elegance of the binary system that counts only the zero and the one the very image of creation', Baudrillard declares the genetic code as the most accomplished form of the *genesis of simulacra*. He describes the industrial simulacra—the new *operational* configuration (like the cybernetic control of *The Matrix*)—and declares 'digitality [as] its metaphysical principle (the God of Leibniz), and DNA, its prophet'. Baudrillard envisages a radical mutation with

Signals of the code, illegible, with no gloss possible, buried like program-matic matrices light-years away in the depths of the 'biological' body— black boxes where all the commandments, all the answers ferment! ... Such is the genetic code: an erased record, unchangeable, of which we are no more than cells-for-reading. All aura of sign, of significance itself is resolved in this determination; all is resolved in the inscription and decoding.[60]

The Wachowskis' Matrix seems to be just that. The binary oppositions create even the essence of the myth: the one and the zero (Neo and Cypher).[61] Thus, the transcendent finalities of humanity are reduced

58. Baudrillard, *Simulations*, pp. 3-4.
59. Baudrillard, *Simulations*, pp. 83-103.
60. Baudrillard, *Simulations*, pp. 103-105.
61. 'Cypher', or 'cipher' is the arithmetical symbol 0, from Arabic *sifr*, zero.

to a dashboard full of instruments. Human beings are grown as crop. The genetic code, now manipulated by the machines, controls all life.[62]

Through the 'I's

The Matrix engages me more than I had anticipated, and in a surprising fashion, too. I find myself wearing shoes that fit. Its echoes ring of some of my own experiences. Perhaps *The Matrix* and one of my previous locations have more in common than immediately apparent. The mighty co-operative, the Borg-like system, in which people's minds, bodies, and resources are centrally controlled and managed seems to be the means of both the Matrix and Marxist Communism. Even the classic concept of ideology as false consciousness presupposes a certain degree of social naivete, if not ignorance. After all, Marx's well-known attitude to ideology, as expressed in his *Capital*, is *sie wissen das nicht, aber sie tun es*, translated as 'they do not know it, but they are doing it'.[63]

Subtly manufactured in *The Matrix* and ideologically created and maintained in communism, culture as the medium of control is another shared element. Ironically, one of the most prominently argued points in the Marxist critique of capitalism is the idea that culture—and literature in particular—is a powerful political tool in the hands of the ruling class. Here, both the neo-capitalist scenario (the Matrix) and the Marxist product (communism) appropriate this tool rather skilfully.

After he scornfully dismissed philosophical pursuits in his eleventh thesis on Feuerbach by saying, 'philosophers have only interpreted the world, in various ways; the point, however, is to change it',[64] Marx later acknowledged that 'philosophy cannot realize itself without the transcendence of the proletariat, and the proletariat cannot realize itself without the realization of philosophy'.[65] This action-orientated ideology, or emancipatory knowledge—later known in Romania as

---

62. Baudrillard calls Jacques Monod 'the strict theologian of this molecular transcendence', and Edgar Morin 'the rapt disciple' who developed the AND anagram of DNA, to be read 'Adonai' (Baudrillard, *Simulations*, p. 109).

63. Karl Marx, *Capital: A Critical Analysis of Capitalist Production*, I (ed. Frederick Engels; trans. Samuel Moore and Edward Aveling; London: Swan Sonnenschein, Lowery, 1887), p. 45.

64. Karl Marx, 'Theses on Feuerbach', in L.S. Feuer (ed.), *Marx and Engels: Basic Writings on Politics and Philosophy* (London: Fontana, 1969), pp. 268-302 (286).

65. Karl Marx, *Early Writings* (trans. R. Livingstone, G. Benton. Harmondsworth: Penguin Books, 1975), p. 257.

'multilateral development', or 'higher degree of consciousness'—
plagued me as I grew up. In its anti-philosophical, anti-idealist, and
anti-utopian orientation, Marxism birthed a new kind of philosophy, a
new level of idealism, and a new image of utopia: communism. Marx
preached freedom, and instead his theory gave birth in the East to a
labyrinth of iron prisons (similar to the human power plant of the
Matrix) in which entire nations rotted; he preached progress, and
instead communism achieved not stagnation but regress (maintained
through the denial of individuality and its creative force and through
the promotion of blissful ignorance, imposed by means of closing all
borders, fabricating all news, and starving and tiring the masses to
exhaustion). Now I can say, echoing Guy Hocquengham in his critique
of the French system, that the Romanian Communist Party (PCR)
'played the role of a kind of bourgeois superego: it stood for the moral
principles which it accused the ruling class of respecting in theory,
only to betray them in practice'.[66]

The social workings of communism in Romania were not very different from the capitalist system, despite the fact that the latter was
supposed to be characterized by perpetual class struggles, according to
Marx. As noticed by Baudrillard, Marx only managed to hold up a
mirror to capitalism, since he appropriated its categories (like 'production', for example). Marx managed to subject the lives of his unfortu-
nate disciples to the capitalist-rationalist ideals of deferred gratification
and purely pragmatic usefulness.[67] I was taught that we had to make
costly sacrifices for the advancement of society; that I did not matter
as an individual but only as part of The People (even in the Matrix,
where all experience is manufactured, the corporate scenario of
Mr Rhineheart's software company, where 'every single employee
understands that they are part of a whole' exists). The few degrees of
separation between the two social systems resided within the defining
elements of class: although a non-class system in theory, Romanian
commonism promoted and maintained a very solid class system
in practice. Thus, the superhuman party leadership, the poor-yet-
honourable intelligentsia, the strong-and-proud proletariat, and the
humble-yet-honest peasantry were clearly demarcated. The pyramid
structure of this system, with the party leadership as its pinnacle, made

66. Guy Hocquengham, *Homosexual Desire* (trans. D. Dangoor; London: Allison
and Busby, 1978), p. 37.
67. Jean Baudrillard, *The Mirror of Production* (trans. M. Poster; St Louis, MI:
Telos, 1975), p. 26.

centralization of all power, knowledge, and resources an easy game. The bodies became indeed the social body upon which the text of communist law was inscribed.

Yet, total control can be imperceptible only up to a point, the point where a revolution is simply inevitable.

> Hence there is a major role for students, youth who are disqualified in advance, voluntarily or not, as well as all types of social groups … because, by the process of the centralization and technocratic pyramidization of the system, they fall into marginality, into the periphery, into the zone of dis-affection and irresponsibility. Excluded from the game, their revolt hence-forth aims at the rules of the game … This is what gives the new left or hippie movement its meaning. Not the open revolt of a few, but the immense, latent defection, the endemic, masked resistance of a silent majority, but one nostalgic for the spoken word and for violence. Some-thing in all men profoundly rejoices in seeing a car burn.[68]

Although Baudrillard's view focuses on the Western milieu, it can also describe (as well as any theory can encapsulate *histoire vivante*) the inceptive winds of December 1989, in Romania.

My own revolt manifested itself first through apathy and cynicism vis-à-vis the system (universal signs of a true teenager, perhaps). Then, it appropriated a more active existence in the element of personal Faith, or the shunned, ridiculed yet feared alternative. Indoctrinated in the communist ideology from kinder garden and essentially an atheist for half of my life, I was allowed to have my childhood and early teen-age years flavoured by Greek mythology, existentialism, theatre, and film. As windows into the beyond, these allowed my mind to rest now and again in its perpetual oscillations between dreams of demi-gods and my clearly understood yet angst-ridden mortality, between the world through the looking screen and the hard seats of the cinema theatre and between the fantastically fabricated attacks on my senses and the penury of my communist context. The illusions of another world, or the world of illusions masquerading as the answer fed me. Then, just like Neo, I realized that the question drove me further and further. What is the m/Matrix? Control. I have no clear recollection as to how the answer finally came; it just did. One day it was simply there, staring at me. And I knew it.

Having treated Christianity as yet another set of myths, my journey to believing in its God was even more taxing than Neo's own *via fidei* in *The Matrix*. When I eventually did manage to 'let go of it all: fear,

68. Baudrillard, *The Mirror of Production*, p. 67.

doubt, and disbelief',[69] I found in Christianity not a means to abhor Marxism; it had stopped being about giving communism the finger. I encountered and embraced answers, the euphoria that accompanied them, and, of course, an identity beyond one's social, political, and economic grounds, a world in which individuality and corporate identity could co-exist happily. Ironically, it was within these Christian circles that I became aware for the first time of my supposed subordinate status to men, my inferiority as a woman. Before that, I had always had the impression of equality with men. However, I readily inhaled the opiate, which was not at all of the masses. I stumbled first—like a newborn that I was—then stood upright, alone with a handful of like-spirited people. I refused membership in the Communist Youth and thus wore my visible new clothes, sewn on them, the star-eyed stigma of a *mad* outsider. A miracle-believing pariah.

I could not fly like Neo, however, and it was not my doing, but the miracle happened: the Romanian masses came to their senses. Riding on our gathered strength, we accomplished at the end of the 1980s a spontaneous revolution, or ideological regress (since the natural evolution of social systems saw, of course, this progression: capitalism was followed, through socialism, by communism; as much as the Stone Age was followed, through the Bronze, by the Iron). Yet, a revolution was the only available means not of progress but survival. The oligarchic power system was overthrown because we simply wanted our minds, souls, bodies, and resources back. At the end of it, the illusion was complete: we were finally and totally free. We had been unplugged from our Matrix. The memory of it continues to appear like a dream. My current context is genetically different, and I have to remind myself: I lived through a revolution, and our revolution was televised (sorry to prove you wrong, Gil Scott-Heron).

On closer inspection, I would find it difficult to articulate precisely whether it was pure freedom or a euphoric cocktail of freedom and anarchy which we tasted and tasted and drank and drank and lived and lived and became. (Who can *know* the unconscious?) Paradoxically, in order to join the masses, I forgot about individuality and difference—the very objects and objectives of my own struggle—and allowed myself to be dissolved within the larger identity of The People once again. One could say that, for a few days, I was essentially Marxist. In fighting against the rule of communism, I adopted a communist technique: the loss of individuality and the creation of the united

69. As Morpheus encourages Neo in *The Matrix*.

collective. *We* stood up, *we* marched, *we* held hands, *we* sang, *we* defied the authorities, the police, the army, the Securitate, and their bullets. Foucault's *madness*,[70] or the *sauvage* social movement of Baudrillard, where each and every person profoundly rejoices in seeing signs burn?[71] Perhaps that is why I enjoyed watching *The Matrix*, despite its being rather violent a film.

Death is always suffocatingly painful to watch in reality. Particularly, for me, the death of young people, mostly students—young, beautiful, bright, courageous human beings with a taste for freedom (an idealized image, of course). It is partly in their memory that I value my life and fight for my liberty. December 1989 was my second new birth; from blood and bullets, I emerged deciding that my earthly existence was going to matter, since its brevity was painted all over me in true red. Now, years later, I safeguard my uniqueness to the point of pain (mine and, alas, of those around me, sometimes). In resisting assimilation, my own revolution continues. It colours my decisions in life and my readings of texts, even my choice to watch and my desire to interpret *The Matrix*. As de Certeau observed, the limits of representation and the intertextuation of bodies:

> This discursive image must inform an unknown 'real', formerly designated as 'flesh'. From the fiction to the unknown that will embody it, the relay is effected by instruments multiplying and diversifying the unforeseeable resistances of the body to (con)formation. Between the tool and the flesh, there is ... a play which is translated on the one hand by a change in the fiction ... and on the other, by a cry, an inarticulate, unthought suffering of corporeal difference.[72]

There is more to the body than the raw flesh, the inscribable matter. The body is not simply a sign to read, a symptom to be deciphered, but also 'a force to be reckoned with'.[73]

My reading of *The Matrix* is that it upholds Baudrillard in his warning concerning the potential move of society towards the establishment of a neo-capitalist, cybernetic order that aims at total control. 'The Matrix is control', Morpheus declares, and I react by clenching my fists. Quite surprisingly, I do not object to the violence in the film,

---

70. See Michel Foucault, *Madness and Civilisation: A History of Insanity in the Age of Reason* [*Folie et déraison: histoire de la folie à l'âge classique*, 1961] (trans. R. Howard. London: Routledge, 1995).

71. See Baudrillard, *The Mirror of Production* and Jean Baudrillard, *For a Critique of the Political Economy of the Sign* (trans. C. Levin; St Louis, MI: Telos, 1981).

72. De Certeau, 'Des outils pour écrire le corps', p. 8.

73. Grosz, *Volatile Bodies*, p. 120.

because the heroes fight under my colours, and they win. If we are to believe Baudrillard,[74] the social mutation animated in *The Matrix* is not accidental. He describes it as 'the end of a history in which, successively, God, Man, Progress, and History itself die to profit immanence, the latter corresponding to a much more advanced phase in the vertiginous manipulation of social rapport'.[75] The Wachowski brothers appear to desire, like all storytellers, the role of the Muses. Their creation seems to wish to inspire fear of the Simulated and faith in the Real, at least. 'The Matrix cannot tell you who you are', so the viewing subjects may wish to change their positions.

Playing the Game
All this is on the *pellicule*, on the silver screen. It is in the film that the Matrix represents ultimate cybernetic control, and in the film that it is contrasted with the 'desert of the real'. Yet, reality is also fabricated. It is only the reality of the script, the reality of fiction. Baudrillard would declare,

> Here comes the great Culture of tactile communication under the sign of the technico-luminous cinematic space of total spatio-dynamic theatre … the completely imaginary contact-world of sensorial mimetics and tactile mysticism; essentially an entire ecology grafted on this universe of operational simulation, multisimulation and multiresponse.[76]

Here comes control through the means of popular culture, in other, fewer, words.

Then again, maybe *The Matrix* is *only* a film, whose entertaining qualities create its commercial value. After all, the special effects are indeed revolutionary: the bullet-time photography manages to leave many mouths open. After the release of *The Matrix*, martial arts clubs have reported an enormous influx of new recruits, all aspiring to a Keanu, or demi-god status (proving perhaps that people do not always need personal faith or ideology. Culture is sometimes sufficient). Certain mobile phones and the web search engines, among other things,

74. Baudrillard has been accused of 'talking nonsense' by some of his critics, after all. I, on the other hand, side with Chris Rojek and admire Baudrillard for his desire to provoke. According to Rojek, 'he *wants* to be accused of talking nonsense in order to compel critics to confront the nonsense which lies behind their own assumptions and proposals' (See Chris Rojek, 'Baudrillard and Politics', in Chris Rojek and Brian S. Turner [eds.], *Forget Baudrillard?* [London: Routledge, 1993], pp. 107-23 [111]. Italics in original.)
75. Baudrillard, *Simulations*, p. 111.
76. Baudrillard, *Simulations*, pp. 139-40.

are advertised in the film; an entire generation of *The Matrix* memora-
bilia is available in shops and on the net. There were three million
videos and one million DVDs sold worldwide by April 2000; *The
Matrix* is indeed the best-selling DVD in Britain.[77] Quite lucrative,
and quite capitalist; it reminds me of Marx's idea of the *fetishism of
commodities*.[78]

In conclusion, *The Matrix* is a fabulous motion picture. Yes, it introduces a new myth. It is not, however, the myth of a new Messiah. The
references pointing that way can indeed be inspiring (attracting audiences and a profit, therefore), but are just a source of red herrings.
There are some similarities, but no substantial parallels between *The
Matrix* and biblical allegory, for the simple reason that there are no
straight lines in this film; everything is circular, indeed spiral, layer
after layer, viewed in supra-fashion, in which there are no perceivable
originals; instead, only hybrids. At the dawn of the twenty-first century, the new myth is that of the Matrix, or total cybernetic control
beyond human sensory perception. Baudrillard's theory of *operational
simulation* seems to be the matrix of *The Matrix*. The code of the
apparently encoded film.

That said, however, we are still left with a paradox. The film introduces the myth? That means that the fantasy exposes the simulation.
The audience is warned against the virtual by the virtual. Perhaps that
is immaterial. Perhaps we should indeed remember that *The Matrix* is
only entertainment, an element of pop-culture and not necessarily a
controlling tool. That we 'don't believe in all that crap', as the Oracle
says. That we are in control of our own destiny. We should take stock
of the fact that our lives are indeed ours and they are indeed real. Or
are they?

Perhaps the motion picture is, as the Disneyland machine for
Baudrillard, 'a deterrence set up in order to rejuvenate in reverse the
fiction of the real', to conceal the fact that the real is no longer real,
and thus save the reality principle.[79] In other words, perhaps the dream
on the silver screen is there to help us accept and not challenge the
dream in which our lives are real, or really free, in which they are all
they can be.

Then again, these are only the visions of a post-communist eye/I.
Without a red pill and with only the cinematic expression of the

77. Armstrong, 'The Gospel According to Keanu', p. 22.
78. Marx, *Capital*, pp. 41-65.
79. Baudrillard, *Simulations*, p. 25.

Matrix and the televised reports of the communist system, the Western world would indeed perceive the spiritual elements in this film more readily; hence the frequent connections to biblical elements. The political allusions are perhaps far more open to those whose lives have been taken through the iron fist of control, and for whom overthrowing such a system has a precedent. Locations are intrinsic to interpretation. Always.

7

Not Quite a Conclusion

At the end of this journey through texts and selves, I experience a sense of non-ending, unsurprisingly.

It seems that the Bible remains, through its afterlives, the collection of narrative texts upon which Western culture and its perception of the world find different self-definitions. In focusing on the Prologue to John's Gospel as the text accommodating what has been perceived as the pre-existent, transcendent Logos/Word, commonly identified with Christ, I have addressed the postmodernist move away from *logocentrism* and produced new readings of John's Prologue that were meant to explore the contours of identity as a decentred, fragmented work of the subject, many times *this* subject, through identification with elements of visual, legible texts.

Investigating the subject-of-language in particular, I have engaged with various theories that perceive identities as constructs of the reiterative power of various discourses, the power to create that which they both name and order; identities as determined in and through difference and thus inherently dislocated—dependent upon an 'outside' that both denies them and provides the premise of their prospect; and subjects as interpellated by, or sutured to, the subject positions made available in discourse through the function of the unconscious. Because the Bible continues its influence on society and the formation of subject positions, I pursued the fragmented afterlives of John's Prologue and their different discursive effects on subject formation (with a particular focus on *homo religiosus* and feminine 'I's) through a choice of postmodern films. In my pursuit, I called to my aid contemporary theoretical currents.

Thus, as a postmodern exercise, I have produced in this work *intertextual* readings of John's Prologue and *The Pillow Book*, *The Fifth Element* and *The Matrix*, while investigating the Incarnation of the Word and the inscription of the flesh, women's discourses, the veiling and un-veiling of 'I's, and bodies and the ideologies of power. Theoretically,

I engaged with Derridian deconstruction and poststructuralism, Lacanian psychoanalysis and post-Lacanian feminisms, suture and autobiography. A pastiche of cuts and stitches of texts and selves.

In reading the biblical text through the play of *différance*, text and reader, word and flesh, can come together in a co-habitation with tones of *jouissance*. Reading with our eyes and 'I's becomes the territory of reciprocity, which is but a *hymen/veil* uniting and separating the human and the divine, the immanent and the transcendent, flesh and word, this world and the other, the audience and the book, desire and its fulfilment. If the subject and object of our desire is the Word, who in the Biblia writes on the Biblia, then we develop *hope* of orgasmic heaven, clothe ourselves with our own Pillow Book, allow our flesh to be inscribed through fugitive foreplay, and *dream* of becoming one with the Word while we read of the Word becoming one with us.

If one, however, does not accept yet another veil, the veil of *human*, which, if not resisted, subtly becomes the veil of flesh and corporeality when given to women, then one should highlight sexual difference and through it identities that are plural and *inter*-dependent, not merely monist and phallomorphic. In reading John's Prologue, women can, therefore, identify with the creative Father, who speaks the world into being and writes himself through a body. The Logos of John's Prologue could provide, through the play of *différance*, the link between the Bible and *écriture féminine*, or *parler-femme*, through which women also find identities of their own—their houses in language.

Should the phallus remain the 'kingpin in the bowling alley of signification', the work of many psychoanalytical feminists seems to argue for a choice between the Father and the Mother, system and silence, rigid structure and anarchy.[1] Thus many theorists finds themselves located within awkward grounds, seduced by psychoanalysis (the Father) and forced to address questions of sexuality, while psycho-analysis itself may have been seduced by feminism and forced to face is delusions of mastery.[2]

Elizabeth Grosz suggests the cultivation of critical *ambivalence*, a simultaneous love and distance, a paradoxical inhabiting yet living outside its precepts.[3] It may be a transitional stage in between love and indifference. Lacan asserts that the phallus is *never* a matter of indifference for women:

1. Sarup, *Jacques Lacan*, p. 144.
2. Jane Gallop, *Feminism and Psychoanalysis: The Daughter's Seduction* (London: Macmillan, 1982), p. 155.
3. Grosz, *Jacques Lacan*, pp. 190-91.

> Ever since Rabelais we have known that the phallus, her man as she calls it, is not a matter of indifference for her. Only, and this is the whole issue, she has various ways of taking it on, this phallus, and of keeping it for herself.[4]

'But what if she *is* indifferent?' Grosz wonders and then envisages,

> This indifference itself may be the mark of her (sexual) difference, the trace of her location elsewhere. From her *indifference to*, and thus her distance from, the phallus, and from psychoanalysis itself, her autonomy as a desiring subject may be theorized.[5]

Could this be possible? Maybe. The problem that arises is that even the frame of sexual differences is largely normative, envisaged as heterosexual, male and female (if the 'second' sex is allowed, eventually). Thus, it seems almost an impossible task to highlight sexual difference only to realize that the process of reaching new frontiers loses its liberating power almost immediately and becomes the process of establishing new but limiting borders.

That is why the fluidity of identities, even *sexuate* identities, and the polymorphous and multiple character of the 'I's are so important. The discursive relationships between the summoning Law and the will of the subjects are still rather mysterious, since they are influenced dramatically by the unconscious.

Cinematic narratives can either help or hinder the process of identity formation of subject positioning, as they can either reinforce the phallocratic Law of the Father (thus, women as image, men as viewers), or help create a certain resistance to the system by offering inspiration. Postmodern cinematic experiences are multiple, multidimensional and polysemic, and they encourage, through the role of the Imaginary, identifications with an apparent *choice* of subject-positions. These 'phantasmatic efforts of alignment, loyalty, ambiguous and cross-corporeal cohabitations', as Judith Butler would say,[6] disrupt the 'I', and so identifications are ephemeral, challenged by new ideas, images and subject positions. The 'I' is perpetually remodelled, reconstructed. The disruption of the 'I' is, therefore, part of the process of *becoming* subjects; it is after all the life of the *sujet en procès*. Never fixed, always moving, flowing, becoming anew. Lived selves and lived bodies.

This perpetual movement can, however, be rather unsettling for some who need the illusion of unity and stability—a seemingly

---

4. Rose and Mitchell (eds.), *Feminine Sexuality*, p. 145.
5. Grosz, *Jacques Lacan*, p. 192.
6. Butler, *Bodies that Matter*, p. 105.

complete identity—in order to know *who* they are (essentially), rather than *where* they are (now). This discomfort only shows that subjects are the products of the discursive powers of language and society. As symptomatic of this, cinematic experiences form an interesting study. In a postmodern, multi-screen, image-driven culture, identity formation is influenced heavily by the media texts that our cultural context produces. These texts frequently fashion new role and gender models together with new behavioural patterns, subtly sold as preferable to those gone before. The problem is not change, but rather the speed with which change is achieved, which may not afford understanding and thus may be responsible for some of the flatness connected with the postmodern, as I mentioned earlier.

By following the infinite Logos and reading the Word as creative force, I have attempted in this work to show, even illustrate, that there is never just one, fixed, stable, defined meaning, sense, word, flesh, sex, 'I'. Whether we want it or not.

BIBLIOGRAPHY

Althusser, Louis, 'Ideology and Ideological State Apparatuses', in *idem*, *Lenin and Philosophy and Other Essays* (London: New Left Books, 1971), pp. 170-86.

Appiah, Kwame Anthony, *In my Father's House* (London: Methuen, 1992).

Armstrong, Stephen, 'The Gospel according to Keanu', *The Sunday Times* (13 February 2000), Section 9, *Culture*, p. 22.

Ashton, John, *Studying John: Approaches to the Fourth Gospel* (Oxford: Clarendon Press, 1994).

Auerbach, Erich, *Mimesis: The Representation of Reality in Western Literature* (trans. Willard Trask; Princeton, NJ: Princeton University Press, 1953).

Augustine, *Confessions* (trans. R. Pine-Coffin; New York: Penguin Books, 1961).

Barrett, C.K., *The Gospel According to John: An Introduction with Commentary and Notes on the Greek Text* (London: SPCK, 1955).

—*The Gospel of John and Judaism* (London: SPCK, 1975).

Barrett, Michele, *The Politics of Truth* (Cambridge: Polity Press, 1991).

Barthes, Roland, *Image, Music, Text* (trans. Stephen Heath; London: Fontana Press, 1987).

—'Myth Today', in *idem*, *Mythologies* (trans. Annette Lavers; Paris: Vintage, 1993), pp. 109-59.

—*The Pleasure of the Text* (trans. Richard Miller; Thetford: Lowe & Brydone, 1976).

—*Roland Barthes by Roland Barthes* (trans. Richard Howard; London: Macmillan, 1977).

Baruch, Elaine Hoffman, and Lucienne J. Serrano, *Women Analyze Women in France, England, and the United States* (London: Harvester Wheatsheaf, 1988).

Bataille, Georges, *Eroticism* (London: Marion Boyars, 1987).

Baudrillard, Jean, 'The Ecstasy of Communication', in Foster (ed.), *The Anti-Aesthetic*, pp. 126-34.

—*For a Critique of the Political Economy of the Sign* (trans. C. Levin; St Louis, MI: Telos, 1981).

—*The Mirror of Production* (trans. M. Poster; St Louis, MI: Telos, 1975).

—*Simulations* (trans. P. Foss, P. Patton and P. Beitchman; Semiotext[e] Foreign Agents Series; New York: Semiotext[e], 1983).

Beasley-Murray, G.R., *John* (WBC, 36; Dallas: Word Books, 1987).

Benvenuto, Bice, and Roger Kennedy, *The Works of Jacques Lacan: An Introduction* (London: Free Associations Books, 1986).

Bible and Culture Collective, The, *The Postmodern Bible* (London: Yale University Press, 1995).

Brown, B., and M. Cousins, 'The Linguistic Fault', *Economy and Society* 9.3 (1980), p. 272.

Brown, Raymond E., *The Gospel According to John* (Anchor Bible, 29, 29A; New York: Doubleday, 1966).

Bultmann, Rudolf, *The Gospel of John* (Oxford: Basil Blackwell, 1971).

—'The History of Religions Background of the Prologue to the Gospel of John', in John Ashton (ed.), *The Interpretation of John* (London: SPCK, 1986), pp. 27-46.

Burch, Noel, *Theory of Film Practice* (trans. R. Lane; New York: Praeger, 1973).

Buren, John van, *The Young Heidegger: Rumor of the Hidden King* (Bloomington: Indiana University Press, 1994).

Burke, Sean, *The Death and Return of the Author: Criticism and Subjectivity in Barthes, Foucault and Derrida* (Edinburgh: Edinburgh University Press, 1992).

Burkett, D., *The Son of the Man in the Gospel of John* (JSNTSup, 56; Sheffield: JSOT Press, 1991).

Butler, Judith, *Bodies That Matter* (London: Routledge, 1993).

—'Bodies That Matter', in Carolyn Burke, Naomi Schor and Margaret Whitford (eds.), *Engaging with Irigaray* (Feminist Philosophy and Modern European Thought; New York: Columbia University Press, 1994), pp. 141-74.

—*Gender Trouble: Feminism and the Subversion of Identity* (New York: Routledge, 1990).

Caputo, John D., *The Prayers and Tears of Jacques Derrida: Religion without Religion* (Bloomington: Indiana University Press, 1997).

Caputo, John D., and Michael J. Scanlon (eds.), *God, the Gift, and Postmodernism* (Bloomington: Indiana University Press, 1999).

Carson, D.A., *The Gospel According to John* (Grand Rapids: Eerdmans, 1991).

Céline, L.-F., *Death on the Instalment Plan* (trans. Ralph Manheim; New York: New Directions, 1966).

Certeau, Michel de, 'Des outils pour écrire le corps', *Traverses* 14–15 (1979), pp. 3-14.

Charlesworth, J.H., 'The Odes of Solomon—Not Gnostic', *CBQ* 31 (1969), pp. 357-69.

Charlesworth, J.H., and R.A. Culpepper, 'The Odes of Solomon and the Gospel of John', *CBQ* 35 (1973), pp. 298-322.

Cixous, Hélène, *'Coming to Writing' and Other Essays* (Cambridge, MA: Harvard University Press, 1991).

—'De la scène de l'Inconscient à la scène de l'Histoire: Chemin d'une écriture', in Françoise van Rossum-Guyon and Myriam Diaz-Diocaretz (eds.), *Hélène Cixous, chemins d'une écriture* (Saint-Denis: Presses Universitaires de Vincennes, 1990), pp. 18-23.

—*The Newly Born Woman* (trans. Betsy Wing; Minneapolis: Minnesota University Press, 1986).

—'The Newly Born Woman', in Sellers (ed.) *The Hélène Cixous Reader*, pp. 36-55.

—'Preface', in Sellers (ed.) *The Hélène Cixous Reader*, pp. xv-xxiii.

—'Savoir', in Cixous and Derrida, *Veils*, pp. 1-16.

—'(With) Ou l'art de l'innocence', in Sellers (ed.) *The Hélène Cixous Reader*, pp. 95-104.

Cixous, Hélène, and Mireille Calle-Gruber, *Hélène Cixous, Rootprints: Memory and Life Writing* (trans. Eric Prenowitz; London: Routledge, 1994).

Cixous, Hélène, and Jacques Derrida, *Veils* (trans. Geoffrey Bennington; Stanford: Stanford University Press, 2001).

Clément, Catherine, *The Lives and Legends of Jacques Lacan* (New York: Columbia University Press, 1983).

Colpe, C., 'Heidnische, jüdische und christliche Überlieferung in den Schriften aus Nag Hammadi. III', *JAC* 17 (1974), pp. 109-25.

Coward, Rosalind, and John Ellis, *Language and Materialism* (London: Routledge & Kegan Paul, 1977).

Culler, Jonathan, *On Deconstruction: Theory and Criticism after Structuralism* (London: Routledge, 1993).

Cunningham, Valentine, *In the Reading Gaol: Postmodernity, Texts, and History* (Oxford: Basil Blackwell, 1994).

—'Word and World', in idem, *In the Reading Gaol*, pp. 4-61.

Curti, Lidia, *Female Stories, Female Bodies: Narrative, Identity and Representation* (London: Macmillan, 1998).

Davies, Margaret, *Rhetoric and Reference in the Fourth Gospel* (JSNTSup, 69; Sheffield: JSOT Press, 1992).

Dayan, Daniel, 'The Tutor Code of Classical Cinema', in Bill Nichols (ed.), *Movies and Method* (Berkley, CA: University of California Press), pp. 438-50.

Derrida, Jacques, 'The Almost Nothing of the Unpresentable', in idem, *Points ... Interviews, 1974–1994*, pp. 78-88.

—*Dissemination* (trans. Barbara Johnson; London: Athlone Press, 1981).

—'The Double Session', in idem, *Dissemination*, pp. 172-286.

—'Edmond Jabès and the Question of the Book', in idem, *Writing and Difference*, pp. 64-78.

—'Ellipsis', in idem, *Writing and Difference*, pp. 294-300.

—'Force and Signification', in idem, *Writing and Difference*, pp. 3-30.

—*Glas* (trans. J.P. Leavey, Jr and R. Rand; Lincoln: University of Nebraska Press, 1986).

—*Of Grammatology* (trans. Gayatri Chakravorty Spivak; Baltimore: The Johns Hopkins University Press, corr. edn, 1997).

—*On the Name* (ed. Thomas Dutoit; Stanford: Stanford University Press, 1995).

—'Plato's Pharmacy', in idem, *Dissemination*, pp. 61-172.

—*Points ... Interviews, 1974–1994* (ed. Elisabeth Weber; trans. Peggy Kamuf et al; Meridian: Crossing Aesthetics Series; Stanford: Stanford University Press, 1995).

—*Positions* (trans. Alan Bass; London: Athlone Press, 1987).

—'Semiology and Grammatology: Interview with Julia Kristeva', in *Positions* (first published in *Information sur les sciences sociales* 7, 3 June 1968; trans. Alan Bass; London: Athlone Press, 1972), pp. 15-36.

—'A Silkworm of One's Own', in Cixous and Derrida, *Veils*, pp. 17-92.

—'Structure, Sign, and Play in the Discourse of the Human Sciences', in idem, *Writing and Difference*, pp. 278-93.

—'Structure, Sign, and Play in the Discourse of the Humanities', in R. Macksey and E. Donato (eds.), *The Languages of Criticism and the Sciences of Man: The Structuralist Controversy* (Baltimore: The Johns Hopkins University Press, 1970), pp. 247-65.

—'Violence and Metaphysics', in idem, *Writing and Difference*, pp. 79-153.

—*Writing and Difference* (trans. Alan Bass; London: Routledge & Kegan Paul, 1978).

Doane, Mary Anne, *The Desire to Desire: The Woman's Film of the 1940s* (Bloomington: Indiana University Press, 1987).

Dodd, C.H., *The Interpretation of the Fourth Gospel* (Cambridge: Cambridge University Press, 1992).

Douglas, Mary, *Purity and Danger* (London: Routledge & Kegan Paul, 1979).

Duncan, R.L., 'The Logos: From Sophocles to the Gospel of John', *Christian Scholar's Review* 9 (1979), pp. 121-30.

Ellis, John M. *Against Deconstruction* (Princeton, NJ: Princeton University Press, 1989).

Ellis, Peter F. *The Genius of John: A Composition-Critical Commentary on the Fourth Gospel* (Collegeville, MN: The Liturgical Press, 1984).

Ellman, Maud, 'Introduction', in *idem* (ed.), *Psychoanalytic Literary Criticism*, pp. 1-35.

Ellman, Maud (ed.), *Psychoanalytic Literary Criticism* (London: Longman, 1994).

Evans, Craig A., *Word and Glory: On the Exegetical and Theological Background of John's Prologue* (JSNTSup, 89; Sheffield: JSOT Press, 1993).

Firth, Simon, 'Music and Identity', in Hall and du Gay (eds.), *Questions of Cultural Identity*, pp. 108-27.

Flaubert, Gustave, *Préface à la vie d'écrivain* (Paris: Seuil, 1963).

Foster, Hal (ed.), *The Anti-Aesthetic: Essays on Postmodern Culture* (Seattle: Bay Press, 1983).

Foucault, Michel, *Madness and Civilisation: A History of Insanity in the Age of Reason* [*Folie et déraison: histoire de la folie à l'âge classique*, 1961] (trans. R. Howard; London: Routledge, 1995).

—'Nietzsche, Genealogy, History', in P. Rabinow, P. (ed.), *The Foucault Reader* (Harmondsworth: Penguin Books, 1984), p. 63.

—*The Order of Things: An Archaeology of Human Sciences* (New York: Vintage Books, 1973).

—*The Use of Pleasure* (Harmondsworth: Penguin Books, 1987).

Freud, Sigmund, *New Introductory Lectures on Psycho-Analysis* (London: Penguin Books, 1973).

—*On Metapsychology: The Theory of Psychoanalysis* (London: Penguin Books, 1984).

—'The Uncanny', in Rivkin and Ryan (eds.), *Literary Theory*, pp. 154-67.

Freidberg, Anne, 'Identification and the Star: A Refusal of Difference', in Christine Gledhill (ed.), *Star Signs* (London: BFI Publishing, 1982).

Gallop, Jane, *Around 1981* (London: Routledge, 1992).

—*Feminism and Psychoanalysis: The Daughter's Seduction* (London: Macmillan, 1982).

—*Men by Women: Women and Literature* (New York: Holmes & Meier, 1981).

—'Nurse Freud: Class Struggle in the Family', *Hecate* 3.1 (1982), pp. 35-36.

—*Reading Lacan* (Ithaca, NY: Cornell University Press, 1985).

—*Thinking through the Body* (New York: Columbia University Press, 1988).

Gay, Paul du, Jessica Evans and Peter Redman, 'General Introduction', in *idem* (eds.), *Identity: A Reader* (London: Sage, 2000), pp. 1-5.

Gellner, Ernest, *Postmodernism, Reason and Religion* (London: Routledge, 1992).

Gieve, Katherine (ed.), *Balancing Acts: On Being a Mother* (London: Virago, 1989).

Glover, Jerry, 'The Ultimate Matrix Concordance', in Simon Goodman (ed.), *Inside Film* 7 (1999), pp. 18-20.

Greenaway, Peter, *The Pillow Book* (Kasander & Wigman Productions IBV/Alpha s.a.r. Woodine Films Ltd., Film Four Distributors, 1995).

Greenlee, D., *Peirce's Concept of Sign* (The Hague: Mouton, 1973).

Grosz, Elizabeth, *Jacques Lacan: A Feminist Introduction* (London: Routledge, 1990).

—'Philosophy, Subjectivity and the Body: Kristeva and Irigaray', in Carole Pateman and Elizabeth Grosz (eds.), *Feminist Challenges: Social and Political Theory* (Sydney: Allen & Unwin, 1986).

— Refiguring Bodies', in *idem*, *Volatile Bodies*, pp. 3-24.

—*Sexual Subversions: Three French Feminists* (Sydney: Allen & Unwin, 1989).

—*Volatile Bodies: Toward a Corporeal Feminism* (Bloomington: Indiana University Press, 1994).

Haenchen, E., *John 1: A Commentary on the Gospel of John: Chapters 1–6* (Hermeneia; Philadelphia: Fortress Press, 1984).

Hall, Stuart, 'Fantasy, Identity, Politics', in E. Carter, J. Donald and J. Squites (eds.), *Cultural Remix: Theories of Politics and the Popular* (London: Lawrence & Wishart, 1995).

—'Introduction: Who Needs Identity?', in Hall and du Gay (eds.), *Questions of Cultural Identity*, pp. 1-17.

—*The Real Me: Postmodernism and the Question of Identity* (London: ICA, 1987).

Hall, Stuart, and Paul du Gay (eds.), *Questions of Cultural Identity* (London: Sage, 1996).

Heath, Stephen, 'Notes on Suture', *Screen* 18.2 (1977–78), pp. 65-66.

—*Questions of Cinema* (Basingstoke: Macmillan, 1981).

Hicks, Peter, *Evangelicals and Truth: A Creative Proposal for a Postmodern Age* (Leicester: Apollos, 1998).

—*Truth: Could It Be True?* (Carlisle: Solway, 1996).

Hirst, P., *On Law and Ideology* (Basingstoke: Macmillan, 1979).

Hocquengham, Guy, *Homosexual Desire* (trans. D. Dangoor; London: Allison & Busby, 1978).

Hoskyns, E.C., *The Fourth Gospel* (ed. F.N. Davey; London: Faber & Faber, 2nd edn, 1947).

Howard, Richard, 'Note on the Text', in Barthes, *The Pleasure of the Text*.

Hurtado, L., *One God, One Lord: Early Christian Devotion and Ancient Jewish Monotheism* (Philadelphia: Fortress Press, 1988).

Irigaray, Luce, *An Ethics of Sexual Difference* (trans. Carolyn Burke and Gillian C. Gill; London: Athlone Press, 1993).

—'The Bodily Encounter with the Mother' ('Le corps-à-corps avec la mère'), in Whitford (ed), *The Irigaray Reader*, pp. 34-46.

—*Ethique de la difference sexuelle* (Paris: Minuit, 1984).

—'Interview', *Ideology and Consciousness* 1 (1977), pp. 64-65.

—*Sexes et parentés* (Paris: Minuit, 1987).

—'Sexual Difference', in Whitford (ed.) *The Irigaray Reader*, pp. 165-77.

—*Speculum: Of the Other Woman* (trans. Gillian C. Gill; Ithaca, NY: Cornell University Press, 1985).

—*This Sex Which Is Not One* (trans. Catherine Porter and Carolyn Burke; Ithaca, NY: Cornell University Press, 1985).

—'When our Lips Speak Together' (trans. C. Burke), *Signs* 6 (1980), pp. 69-79.

—'Women-Mothers, the Silent Substratum of the Social Order', in Whitford (ed.), *The Irigaray Reader*, pp. 47-52.

Jabès, Edmond, *Livre de questions* (Paris: Gallimard, 1936).

Jakobson, R., and M. Halle, *Fundamentals of Language* (The Hague: Mouton, 1959).

Jameson, Fredric, 'Postmodernism and Consumer Society', in Foster (ed.), *The Anti-Aesthetic*, pp. 111-25.

—*Postmodernism, or the Cultural Logic of Late Capitalism* (Durham: Duke University Press, 1991).

—'Postmodernism, or the Cultural Logic of Late Capitalism', *New Left Review* 146 (1984), pp. 53-93.

Jasper, Alison, *The Shining Garment of the Text: Gendered Readings of John's Prologue* (JSNTSup, 165; Gender, Culture, Theory, 6; Sheffield: Sheffield Academic Press, 1998).

Jung, C.G., 'On the Relation of Analytical Psychology to Poetry', in idem, *The Spirit in Man, Art, and Literature* (Princeton, NJ: Princeton University Press, 1971), pp. 81-83.

—*Two Essays on Analytical Psychology* (trans. R.F.C. Hull; New York: Meridian Books, 1956).

Johnson, Barbara, 'The Frame of Reference', *Yale French Studies* 55–56 (1977), pp. 457-505.

Kamuf, Peggy (ed.) *A Derrida Reader: Between the Blinds* (New York: Harvester Wheatsheaf, 1991).

Kearney, Richard, 'Desire of God', in Caputo and Scanlon (eds.), *God, the Gift, and Postmodernism*, pp. 112-45.

—*The Wake of Imagination* (London: Routledge, 1994).

Kellner, Douglas, *Media Culture: Cultural Studies, Identity and Politics between the Modern and the Postmodern* (London: Routledge, 1995).

Kilpatrick, G.D., 'The Religious Background of the Fourth Gospel', in F.L. Cross (ed.), *Studies in the Fourth Gospel* (London: Mowbrays, 1957), pp. 36-44.

Kitzberger, Ingrid Rosa (ed.), *Autobiographical Biblical Criticism: Between Text and Self* (Leiden: Deo Publishing, 2003).

—*The Personal Voice in Biblical Interpretation* (London: Routledge, 1999).

Kofman, Sarah, *Lectures de Derrida* (Paris: Editions Galilée, 1984).

Kristeva, Julia, 'A New Type of Intellectual: The Dissident', in Moi (ed.), *The Kristeva Reader*, pp. 292-300.

—*Au commencement était l'amour: psychanalyse et foi* (Paris: Hachette, 1985); ET: *In the Beginning Was Love: Psychoanalysis and Faith* (trans. Arthur Goldhammer; New York: Columbia University Press, 1987).

—*Histoires d'amour* (Paris: Denoel, 1983); ET: *Tales of Love* (trans. Leon S. Roudiez; New York: Columbia University Press, 1987).

—'Interview—1974', *m/f* 5–6 (1974), pp. 158-72.

—'Oscillation between Power and Denial', in Elaine Marks and Isabelle de Courtivron (eds.), *New French Feminism* (Brighton: Harvester Press, 1985), pp. 165-68.

—*Pouvoirs de l'horreur. Essai sur l'abjection* (Paris: Seuil, 1980).

—*Powers of Horror: An Essay on Abjection* (trans. Leon S. Roudiez; New York: Columbia University Press, 1982).

—*The Revolution in Poetic Language* (New York: Columbia University Press, 1984).

—'Signifying Practice and Mode of Production', *Edinburgh Review* 1 (1976), pp. 65-78.

—'Stabat Mater', in Moi (ed.), *The Kristeva Reader*, pp. 160-86.

—'Women's Time', in Moi (ed.), *The Kristeva Reader*, pp. 188-213.

Kroker, Arthur, and David Cook, *The Postmodern Scene* (New York: Saint Martin's Press, 1986).

Kysar, Robert, *John* (Augsburg Commentary on the New Testament; Minneapolis: Augsburg, 1986).
—*John, the Maverick Gospel* (Atlanta: John Knox Press, 1976).
Lacan, Jacques, *Ecrits: A Selection* (trans. Alan Sheridan; London: Tavistock, 1977).
—'God and the Jouissance of Woman', in Mitchell and Rose (eds.), *Feminine Sexuality*, pp. 137-48.
—'The Instance of the Letter in the Unconscious or Reason since Freud', in Rivkin and Ryan (eds.), *Literary Theory*, pp. 190-205 (191).
—'The Meaning of the Phallus', in Mitchell and Rose (eds.), *Feminine Sexuality*, pp. 74-85.
—'The Mirror Stage as Formative of the Function of the I as Revealed in Psycho-analytic Experience', Paper delivered at the sixteenth International Congress of Psychoanalysis, Zürich, 17 July 1949, in Robert Con Davis and Ronald Schleifer (eds.), *Contemporary Literary Criticism: Literary and Cultural Studies* (trans. Alan Sheridan; New York: Longman, 3rd edn, 1994), pp. 382-86.
—Opening Address to Caracas Conference, July 1980, in *L'âne* 1 (1980), pp. 30-31.
—*The Seminar. Book II: The Ego in Freud's Theory and in the Technique of Psychoanalysis* (trans. Sylvana Tomaselli; Cambridge: Cambridge University Press, 1988).
—'The Signification of the Phallus', in *idem*, *Ecrits*, pp. 271-80.
—'The Subversion of the Subject and the Dialectic of Desire in the Freudian Uncon-scious', in *Ecrits*, pp. 294-324.
—'The Symbolic Order', in Rivkin and Ryan (eds.), *Literary Theory*, pp. 184-89.
Lauretis, Teresa de, *Alice Doesn't: Feminism, Semiotics, Cinema* (London: Macmillan, 1984).
—*Technologies of Gender: Essays on Theory, Film and Fiction* (Bloomington: Indiana University Press, 1987)
Lauretis, Teresa de (ed.), *Feminist Studies/Critical Studies* (Bloomington: Indiana University Press, 1986).
Lecercle, Jean-Jacques, *Philosophy through the Looking Glass: Language, Nonsense, Desire* (London: Hutchinson, 1985).
Lechte, John, *Julia Kristeva* (London: Routledge, 1990).
Leitch, Vincent B., *Deconstructive Criticism: An Advanced Introduction* (London: Hutchinson, 1983).
Levinas, Emmanuel, *Totality and Infinity* (trans. A. Lingis; Pittsburgh: Duquesne University Press, 1969).
Lévi-Strauss, Claude, *The Elementary Structures of Kinship* (trans. James Harle Bell, John Richard von Sturmer and Rodney Needham; Boston: Beacon Press, 1969).
—*The Savage Mind* (Chicago: University of Chicago Press, 1986).
Locke, John, *An Essay Concerning Human Understanding* (London: J.M. Dent, 1947).
Lindars, B., *The Gospel of John* (NCB; London: Marshall, Morgan & Scott, 1972).
Lyotard, J., *The Postmodern Condition: A Report on Knowledge* (trans. G. Bennington and B. Massumi; Manchester: Manchester University Press, 1984).
Malinowski, Bronislaw, *Myth in Primitive Psychology* (London: Kegan Paul, Trench, Trubner, 1926).
Madonna, 'Nothing Really Matters', in *Ray of Light* (Maverick Recording, Warner Bros., 1998).
—'The Power of Good-bye', in *Ray of Light* (Maverick Recording, Warner Bros., 1998).

Marty, Joseph, 'Toward a Theological Interpretation and Reading of Film: Incarnation of the Word of God—Relation, Image, Word', in John, R. May (ed.), *New Images of Religious Film* (trans. Robert G. Robinson; Communication, Culture and Theology; Kansas City: Sheed & Ward, 1997), pp. 131-50.

Marx, Karl, *Capital: A Critical Analysis of Capitalist Production*, I (ed. Frederick Engels; trans. Samuel Moore and Edward Aveling; London: Swan Sonnenschein, Lowery, 1887).

—*Early Writings* (trans. R. Livingstone and G. Benton; Harmondsworth: Penguin Books, 1975).

—'Theses on Feuerbach', in L.S. Feuer (ed.), *Marx and Engels: Basic Writings on Politics and Philosophy* (London: Fontana, 1969), pp. 268-302.

Metz, Christian, *Psychoanalysis and the Cinema: The Imaginary Signifier* (London: Macmillan, 1982).

McKnight, Edgar V., *Postmodern Use of the Bible: The Emergence of Reader-Orientated Criticism* (Nashville: Abingdon Press, 1988).

McNay, L., *Foucault: A Critical Introduction* (Cambridge: Polity Press, 1994).

Mercer, K., 'Welcome to the Jungle: Identity and Diversity in Postmodern Politics', in J. Rutherford (ed.), *Identity: Community, Culture, Difference* (London: Lawrence and Wishart, 1990), pp. 43-72.

Miller, Jacques-Alain, 'Suture: Elements of the Logic of the Signifier', *Screen* 18.4 (1977–78), pp. 25-26.

Minh-ha, Trinh T., *Woman Native Other: Writing Postcoloniality and Feminism* (Bloomington: Indiana University Pres, 1989).

Mitchell, Juliet, and Jacqueline Rose (eds.), *Feminine Sexuality: Jacques Lacan and the Ecole Freudienne* (London: Macmillan, 1982).

Moi, Toril, *Sexual/Textual Politics: Feminist Literary Theory* (London: Methuen, 1985).

Moi, Toril (ed.), *The Kristeva Reader* (Oxford: Basil Blackwell, 1986).

Montefiore, Jan, *Feminism and Poetry* (London: Pandora, 1987).

Moore, Stephen D., *God's Beauty Parlor: And Other Queer Spaces in and around the Bible* (Contraversions: Jews and Other Differences; Stanford: Stanford University Press, 2001).

—*Literary Criticism and the Gospels: The Theoretical Challenge* (New Haven and London: Yale University Press, 1989).

—*Mark and Luke in Poststructuralist Perspectives: Jesus Begins to Write* (New Haven: Yale University Press. 1992).

—*Poststructuralism and the New Testament: Derrida and Foucault at the Foot of the Cross* (Minneapolis: Fortress Press, 1994).

—'Revolting Revelations', in Kitzberger (ed.), *The Personal Voice*, pp. 183-200.

Morris, Ivan (ed.), *The Pillow Book of Sei Shonagon* (trans. Ivan Morris; Harmondsworth: Penguin Books, 1967).

Muller, John P., and William J. Richardson, *Lacan and Language: A Reader's Guide to Ecrits* (New York: International Universities Press, 1982).

Mulvey, Laura, 'Visual Pleasure and Narrative Cinema', *Screen* 16.3 (1975), pp. 6-18.

Nietzsche, Friedrich, *The Will to Power* (trans. Walter Kaufmann; New York: Vintage Books, 1968).

Norris, Christopher, *Deconstruction: Theory and Practice* (New York: Routledge, rev. edn, 1991).

—*The Truth about Postmodernism* (Oxford: Basil Blackwell, 1993).

—*Truth and the Ethics of Criticism* (Manchester: Manchester University Press, 1994).

Parke, H.W., and D.E.W. Warmell, *The Delphic Oracle*, I (Oxford: Basil Blackwell, 1956).

Peirce, Charles Sanders, *The Writings of Charles Sanders Peirce*. II. *Collected Papers* (ed. C. Hartshorne, P. Weiss and A.W. Burks; Cambridge, MA: Harvard University Press, 1931–58), pp. 125-44.

Pinker, Steven, *The Language Instinct* (London: Penguin Books, 1994).

Potterie, I. de la, 'Structure du prologue de Saint Jean', *NTS* 30 (1984), pp. 354-81.

Ree, Jonathan, 'Funny Voices: Stories, "Punctuation" and Personal Identity', *New Literary History* 21 (1990), pp. 1049-59.

Reitzenstein, R., *Das iranische Erlösungsmysterium* (Bonn: Marcus & Weber, 1921).

Ridderbos, Herman, *The Gospel of John: A Theological Commentary* (trans. John Vriend; Grand Rapids: Eerdmans, 1997).

—'The Structure and Scope of the Prologue to the Gospel of John', *NovT* 8 (1966), pp. 180-201.

Rivkin, Julie, and Michael Ryan, 'Strangers to Ourselves: Psychoanalysis', in *idem* (eds.), *Literary Theory*, pp. 119-27.

Rivkin, Julie, and Michael Ryan (eds.), *Literary Theory: An Anthology* (Oxford: Basil Blackwell, 1998).

Rojek, Chris, 'Baudrillard and Politics', in Chris Rojek and Brian S. Turner (eds.), *Forget Baudrillard?* (London: Routledge, 1993), pp. 107-23.

Rorty, Richard, 'Is Derrida a Transcendental Philosopher?', in David Wood (ed.), *Derrida: A Critical Reader* (Oxford: Basil Blackwell, 1992), pp. 235-46.

Rose, Jacqueline, and Juliet Mitchell (eds.), *Feminine Sexuality: Jacques Lacan and the Ecole Freudienne* (New York: Norton, 1982).

Rose, Jacqueline, *Sexuality in the Field of Vision* (London: Verso, 1986).

Sanders, J.T., 'Nag Hammadi, Odes of Solomon, and New Testament Christological Hymns', in J.E. Goehring *et al.* (eds.), *Gnosticism and the Early Christian World: In Honour of James M. Robinson* (Sonoma, CA: Polebridge Press, 1990), pp. 51-66.

Sarup, Madan, *Jacques Lacan* (London: Harvester Wheatsheaf, 1992).

Saussure, Ferdinand de, *Course in General Linguistics* (trans. Wade Baskin; New York: Philosophical Library, 1959).

Schnackenburg, R., *The Gospel According to St John*, I (New York: Crossroad, 1987).

—'Logos-Hymnus und johanneischen Prolog', *BZ* 1 (1957), pp. 69-109.

Segovia, Fernando F., 'My Personal Voice: The Making of a Postcolonial Critic', in Kitzberger (ed.), *The Personal Voice*, pp. 25-37.

Sellers, Susan, 'Introduction', in *idem* (ed.), *The Hélène Cixous Reader*, pp. xxvi-xxxi.

Sellers, Susan (ed.), *The Hélène Cixous Reader* (London: Routledge, 1994).

Silverman, Hugh J. (ed.), *Derrida and Deconstruction* (Continental Philosophy, 2; London: Routledge, 1989).

Silverman, Kaja, *The Subject of Semiotics* (Oxford: Oxford University Press, 1983).

—'Suture: The Cinematic Model', in *idem*, *Subject of Semiotics*, pp. 199-215.

Slobin, Mark, *Subculture Sounds: Micromusic of the West* (London: Wesleyan University Press, 1993).

Sloyan, Gerard S., *John* (Interpretation; Atlanta: John Knox Press, 1988).

Smalley, Stephen S., *John: Evangelist and Interpreter* (Exeter: Paternoster Press, 1978).

Smith, Anne-Marie, *Julia Kristeva: Speaking the Unspeakable* (Modern European Thinkers; London: Pluto Press, 1998).

Spelman, Elizabeth, 'Woman as Body: Ancient and Contemporary Views', *Feminist Studies* 8 (1982), pp. 109-31.

Spivak, Gayatri Chakravorty, 'French Feminism in an International Frame', *Yale French Studies* 62 (1981), pp. 157-79.

—*In Other Worlds: Essays in Cultural Politics* (London: Methuen, 1987).

Stacey, Jackie, 'Feminine Fascinations: Forms of Identification in Star-Audience Relations', in Christine Gledhill (ed.), *Stardom: Industry of Desire* (London: Routledge, 1991), pp. 141-63.

Staley, J.L., 'Fathers and Sons: Fragments from an Autobiographical Midrash on John's Gospel', in Kitzberger (ed.), *The Personal Voice*, pp. 65-85.

—*Reading with a Passion: Rhetoric, Autobiography, and the American West in the Gospel of John* (New York: Continuum, 1995).

Storr, Anthony, *Music and the Mind* (London: HarperCollins, 1992).

Tester, Keith, *The Life and Times of Post-modernity* (London: Routledge, 1993).

Thiselton, Anthony C., *New Horizons in Hermeneutics: The Theory and Practice of Transforming Biblical Reading* (Grand Rapids: Zondervan, 1992).

Tobin, T.H., 'The Prologue of John and Hellenistic Jewish Speculation', CBQ 52 (1990), pp. 252-69.

Tudor, Andrew, *Image and Influence: Studies in the Sociology of Film* (London: Allen & Unwin, 1974).

Tyson, Lois, *Critical Theory Today: A User-Friendly Guide* (New York: Garland, 1999).

Walker, Steven F. *Jung and the Jungians on Myth: An Introduction* (London: Garland, 1995).

Walkerdine, Valerie, 'One Day my Prince Will Come: Young Girls and Preparation for Adult Sexuality', in A. McRobbie and M. Nava (eds.), *Gender and Generation* (London: Macmillan, 1984), pp. 162-84.

—'Video Replay: Families, Films and Fantasy', in V. Burgin *et al.* (eds.), *Formations of Fantasy* (London: Routledge, 1986), pp. 167-99.

Warner, Marina, *Alone of All her Sex: The Myth and Cult of the Virgin Mary* (London: Picador, 1985).

—*Managing Monsters: Six Myths of our Time* (The Reith Lectures; London: Vintage Books, 1994).

Whitford, Margaret, *Luce Irigaray: Philosophy in the Feminine* (London: Routledge, 1991).

Whitford, Margaret (ed), *The Irigaray Reader* (Oxford: Basil Blackwell, 1991).

Winterson, Jeanette, *Written on the Body* (London: Jonathan Cape, 1992).

INDEXES

INDEX OF REFERENCES

OLD TESTAMENT/ HEBREW BIBLE

Genesis
1–2   107
1.1-3   16

Exodus
25.21   108
26.33   108

Psalms
74.9   16

Proverbs
4.18-19   21
8.27-30   21
8.35   21

Ecclesiastes
2.13   21

Isaiah
40.3-5   160
51.11   160
55.11   16
61.1-2   160

APOCRYPHAL/DEUTERO-CANONICAL WORKS

Wisdom of Solomon
7.29-30   105
13.1   15

Baruch
4.1   21

1 Maccabees
4.41-50   16
14.41   16

NEW TESTAMENT

Matthew
5.17   150
14.32-41   161
26.14-16   161
26.36-46   161
26.47-49   161

Luke
2.52   161
3.46   160
4.18   160
4.19   160
22.39-46   161

John
1.1-18   128
1.1-2   32, 34
1.1   32, 44, 107, 160
1.1b   46
1.3   107
1.4-5   105
1.5   106
1.9-13   105
1.9   105
1.10   105, 107
1.11-12   150
1.12-13   150
1.13   150

1.14   32, 34, 44, 47, 160
1.14b   52
1.17   119
1.18   105-107, 113, 119, 128
1.18a   107
2.3-5   137
2.4   136
8.12   106
9.5   106
11.25   20
12   106
12.45-46   106
12.45   106
12.46   106
12.49   106
14.6   20
19.25-27   137

Romans
1.19-20   15
11.36   15

1 Corinthians
8.6   15

2 Corinthians
1.22   52

Colossians
1.5   150
1.16   15

Revelation
14.1-3   160

PSEUDEPIGRAPHA
Odes
xviii.6   105

Testament of Benjamin
9.2   16

PHILO
De cherubim
35 §127   107

Conf. Ling.
14 §§62-63   107
28 §§146-47   107
28 §146   107

De fuga et inventione
18 §97   107
19 §101   107

De opificio mundi
5 §20   107
6 §24   107

De posteritate Caini
48 §169   107

Quaestiones in Exodum
2.68   107, 108
2.94   108

De somniis
1.39 §§228-30   107
1.39 §230   107

CLASSICAL WORKS
Athanasius
*De incarnatione Verbi
Dei*
2.8   48
3.16   47
8.54   47, 51

Ovid
Metamorphoses
XI.616-754   161

Plato
Philebus
38e-39e   26

INDEX OF AUTHORS

Althusser, L. 109
Appiah, K.A. 153
Armstrong, S. 159, 162, 178
Auerbach, E. 5, 152

Barrett, C.K. 106, 147
Barthes, R. 22, 34, 35, 47, 48, 153, 169, 170
Baruch, E.H. 127
Bataille, G. 116
Baudrillard, J. 28, 170-74, 176-78
Beasley-Murray, G.R. 107
Benvenuto, B. 116
Brown, B. 148
Brown, R.E. 14-18, 20, 21, 107
Bultmann, R. 106
Burch, N. 68
Buren, J. van 51
Burkett, D. 107
Butler, J. 124, 125, 129, 182

Caputo, J.D. 50
Carson, D.A. 107
Céline, L.-F. 102
Certeau, M. de 124, 159, 174
Charlesworth, J.H. 106
Cixous, H. 85-88, 91-94, 97, 100, 101, 110, 119, 120, 130, 144
Clément, C. 63
Colpe, C. 106
Cook, D. 28
Cousins, M. 148
Coward, R. 28
Culler, J. 24
Culpepper, R.A. 106
Cunningham, V. 33, 34, 49, 50, 52
Curti, L. 91, 95, 103, 113, 121, 122

Davies, M. 120
Dayan, D. 69
Derrida, J. 1, 10, 12-15, 17, 19, 24-28, 32-34, 40, 42, 44-47, 50, 87-91, 93, 103, 108, 120, 144
Doane, M.A. 72
Dodd, C.H. 106, 107
Douglas, M. 112
Duncan, R.L. 107

Ellis, J. 28
Ellman, M. 131, 132
Evans, C.A. 107, 108
Evans, J. 6

Firth, S. 152
Flaubert, G. 1
Foucault, M. 123, 124, 148, 149, 176
Freidberg, A. 72
Freud, S. 53, 62

Gallop, J. 60, 86, 100, 103, 130-32, 181
Gay, P. du 6
Gieve, K. 136
Glover, J. 159
Greenaway, P. 9, 102
Greenlee, D. 22
Grosz, E. 75, 77-79, 81, 86, 118, 122-24, 126, 129, 144, 145, 176, 181, 182

Haenchen, E. 107
Hall, S. 71, 124, 125, 146-48, 150, 151
Halle, M. 65
Heath, S. 69, 71, 147
Hirst, P. 147
Hocquenghem, G. 173
Hoskyns, E.C. 107

Howard, R. 34
Hurtado, L. 107

Irigaray, L. 82-84, 95, 117-19, 127, 130,
    132-34, 136, 138, 143, 144

Jabès, E. 45
Jakobson, R. 65
Jameson, F. 28, 29
Jasper, A. 110, 113, 114
Johnson, B. 56
Jung, C.G. 168

Kearney, R. 50, 51
Kellner, D. 28-30
Kennedy, R. 116
Kilpatrick, G.D. 107
Kitzberger, I.R. 154
Kristeva, J. 78-81, 102, 111-15, 117,
    121
Kroker, A. 28

Lacan, J. 52, 55-62, 73-75, 109, 116,
    130
Lauretis, T. de 73, 134
Lévi-Strauss, C. 75
Lecercle, J.-J. 57
Lechte, J. 79, 80, 111, 116, 117
Leitch, V.B. 22, 23
Levinas, E. 19
Lindars, B. 107
Locke, J. 23

Madonna 13, 20
Malinowski, B. 169
Marty, J. 22, 30, 31, 64, 66
Marx, K. 172, 178
McNay, L. 148
Mercer, K. 87
Metz, C. 64, 66
Miller, J.-A. 67
Minh-ha, T.T. 95
Mitchell, J. 182
Moi, T. 81
Montefiore, J. 132
Moore, S.D. 13, 126, 155
Morris, I. 36

Muller, J.P. 74
Mulvey, L. 71, 96

Nietzsche, F. 28

Parke, H.W. 166
Peirce, C.S. 22
Potterie, I. de la 106
Redman, P. 6

Ree, J. 152
Reitzenstein, R. 106
Richardson, W.J. 74
Ridderbos, H. 106
Rivkin, J. 53, 59, 60, 96
Rojek, C. 177
Rorty, R. 11
Rose, J. 5, 72, 77, 96, 146, 182
Ryan, M. 53, 59, 60, 96

Sanders, J.T. 106, 107
Sarup, M. 58, 62, 63, 66, 75, 181
Saussure, F. de 22, 25, 26
Schnackenburg, R. 106, 107
Segovia, F.F. 155
Sellers, S. 86, 101
Serrano, L.J. 127
Silverman, K. 67, 68, 70, 71
Slobin, M. 152
Spelman, E. 129
Spivak, G.C. 79, 122
Stacey, J. 72
Staley, J.L. 153, 154
Storr, A. 1, 27

Tester, K. 169
Tobin, T.H. 107
Tudor, A. 72
Tyson, L. 11

Walker, S.F. 168, 169
Walkerdine, V. 71, 72, 77, 96
Warmell, D.E.W. 166
Warner, M. 116, 135, 136
Whitford, M. 119, 137, 138, 143
Winterson, J. 103

INDEX OF SUBJECTS

abject/ed/ion 102, 110-13, 119, 125, 128, 148

ambiguity 74

authorial intention 17

autobiographical criticism 153-55

Barthes, Roland 22, 34-36, 47-49, 153, 169

Baudrillard, Jean 156, 157, 170, 171, 173, 174, 176-78

Beauvoir, Simone de 54, 122

binary opposition 26, 49, 84, 85, 113, 129, 145, 170, 171

Butler, Judith 123-25, 182

capitalism 164, 172, 173, 175

Cixous, Hélène 54, 76, 82, 84-89, 91-97, 99-101, 103, 110, 114, 123, 130, 134

consumerism 28

Culler, Jonathan 24

Cultural criticism 1-3, 28, 72, 124

decentred 6, 21, 28, 33, 78, 86, 89, 119, 180,

decentring 150

deconstruction 4, 7, 21, 22, 26, 32, 86, 121, 149, 155, 181

deconstructive 1, 5, 7, 26, 45

deferral 4, 12, 24, 50, 146

Derrida, Jacques 4, 7-28, 32-34, 40, 45-47, 49, 50, 52, 84, 86-91, 93, 94, 102, 108, 120, 130, 132, 134

différance 4, 8-10, 12, 14, 24, 48, 50, 132, 181

discourse 2, 4, 6, 23, 25, 27, 29, 32, 53, 58, 67, 68, 70-72, 77-79, 82, 83, 114, 117, 119-21, 123-25, 127, 129, 130, 133, 134, 137, 138, 141-50, 153, 180

dissemination 1, 4, 29, 34, 42, 90, 103

écriture féminine 81, 82, 84, 85, 95, 100, 103, 114, 119, 181

ego 53, 55, 57-59, 61-65, 72, 94, 109, 111

eros 51

evil drive 50

feminine 6, 15, 71, 77-120, 122, 123, 125, 129-34, 141, 143, 180

Foucault, Michel 123-25, 148, 149, 151, 152, 176

French feminism 100

Freud, Sigmund 7, 53-55, 57, 62, 67, 75, 76, 80, 82, 86, 93, 127

Gallop, Jane 60, 75, 76, 86, 100, 123, 131

gender 5, 71, 72, 85, 91, 121, 123-27, 139, 183

Grosz, Elizabeth 76, 78, 79, 86, 112, 123, 126, 129, 144, 145

Hall, Stuart 71, 124, 146-48, 150

hybridity 17, 103

id 53, 55, 61, 63, 64

identity 2, 4-6, 20, 25, 27-29, 31, 36, 54, 55, 58-60, 62, 66, 72, 77, 83, 84, 86, 87, 90, 91, 94-96, 99, 100-103, 105, 108-10, 112, 114, 118-22, 124-26, 132, 134, 136, 137, 139, 143, 146, 148, 150-53, 155, 156, 163, 175, 180, 182, 183

ideology 5, 49, 93, 108, 109, 123, 146,
    147, 172, 174, 177
image 1, 2, 5, 26-28, 30, 32, 34, 35, 50,
    60-64, 69, 82, 95, 96, 100, 107-
    109, 130, 151, 158, 161, 163,
    168, 170, 171, 173, 176, 182, 183
indeterminacy 4, 171
Irigaray, Luce 76, 78, 82-86, 94-96, 114,
    117-19, 123, 127-34, 136-41,
    143, 144
Jung, Carl 168, 169

Kristeva, Julia 33, 76, 78-82, 86, 96,
    110-12, 114-17, 123, 148

Lacan, Jacques 55-65, 67, 73-77, 81, 82,
    86, 87, 97, 109, 116, 118, 124,
    127, 130, 147, 181
langue 23-25, 83, 134
Lévi-Strauss, Claude 75
literary criticism 3, 23, 55
logocentrism 11, 22, 25, 44, 130, 180
logos 5, 8, 11, 15-19, 27, 32, 42, 44-48,
    84, 92, 105, 107, 113, 128, 155,
    180, 181, 183

Marx, Karl 147, 150, 172, 173

Oedipal 54, 73, 75, 78, 80, 83, 97, 99,
    142, 148
Oedipus complex 54, 55, 75, 128
Other 8, 11, 13, 57-59, 61, 63, 66, 69-
    71, 73, 74, 82, 93, 109, 110, 112,
    113, 115, 122, 151

parler femme 82-84, 94, 119, 120, 181
parole 15, 23-25
patriarchy 72, 84, 122, 128
penis envy 54, 55
performativity 124, 125, 150
phallic 86, 100, 103, 114, 118, 132
phallic/ization 86
phallogocentrism 113, 130
Plato 10, 11, 26, 27, 33, 129
poststructuralism 1, 3, 26, 32, 155, 181

rhetorical 78, 132

semiotics 4, 5, 22, 23, 34, 35, 81, 143
sexuality 52-55, 77, 85, 100, 103, 116,
    124, 181
speech 8-10, 13-15, 23-27, 32, 40, 45-
    49, 58, 60, 67, 69, 70, 82, 132,
    134, 138, 145, 166
structuralism 3, 23, 24, 56
subjectivity 29, 60, 62, 66, 67, 73, 75,
    77, 78, 83, 85, 91, 94, 108, 114,
    117, 119, 121, 144, 145, 149, 153
superego 53, 55, 63, 65, 173

woman 36, 39, 60, 71, 72, 81-84, 87,
    91-96, 98-101, 103, 110, 113-15,
    117, 119, 121, 125, 126, 129,
    130, 132-38, 141-45, 163, 166,
    175

Lightning Source UK Ltd.
Milton Keynes UK
21 March 2010

151638UK00002BA/113/A

9 781905 048250